The Knowledge Advantage

THE
KNOWLEDGE
ADVANTAGE

*14 Visionaries Define Marketplace Success
in the New Economy*

Edited by

Rudy Ruggles

and

Dan Holtshouse

Foreword by
John Seely Brown

CAPSTONE

The right of Ernst & Young LLP to be identified as the author of this work has been asserted in accordance with the Copyright, Designs and Patents Act 1988

First published 1999 by
Capstone US
Business Books Network
163 Central Avenue
Suite 2
Hopkins Professional Building
Dover
NH 03820
USA

Capstone Publishing Limited
Oxford Centre for Innovation
Mill Street
Oxford OX2 0JX
United Kingdom
http://www.capstone.co.uk

CIP catalogue records for this book are available from the British Library and the US Library of Congress

ISBN 1-84112-067-7

Typeset in 11/14 pt Goudy Old Style by
Sparks Computer Solutions Ltd, Oxford
http://www.sparks.co.uk
Printed and bound in the United States of America by
Bookcrafters

This book is printed on acid-free paper

Substantial discounts on bulk quantities of Capstone books are available to corporations, professional associations and other organizations. If you are in the USA or Canada, phone the LPC Group for details on (1-800-626-4330) or fax (1-800-243-0138). Everywhere else, phone Capstone Publishing on (+44-1865-798623) or fax (+44-1865-240941).

Contents

Foreword   ix
John Seely Brown, Xerox PARC

1   Gaining the Knowledge Advantage   1
    Rudy Ruggles, The Ernst & Young Center for
    Business Innovation
    Dan Holtshouse, Xerox Corporation

Part I   Knowledge and the Individual   21

2   Consilience: A Unity of Knowledge   25
    Edward O. Wilson, Harvard University

3   Knowledge is Power! Welcome Democracy!   41
     Alan Webber, *Fast Company*

4   Managing Knowledge Workers in a Changing World 51
     Peter Drucker, Claremont Graduate School of Business

Part II   Knowledge and the Organization   59

5   The Dynamics of Knowledge Creation   63
     Ikujiro Nonaka, University of California at Berkeley

6   Turning Knowledge into Innovation   89
     Dr Bob Bauer, Xerox PARC

7   The Knowledge-Based Organization:
     A Managerial Revolution   103
     Christopher A. Bartlett, Harvard Business School

8   Maximizing Innovation Using Intellect, Science
     and Technology   123
     James Brian Quinn, Amos Tuck School of Business,
     Dartmouth College

Part III   Knowledge and Strategy   141

9   The Knowledge Perspective: A New Strategic Vision   143
     Stephen Denning, The World Bank

10   Building Knowledge into Products   163
     Stan Davis

11   Designing Business Strategy in the Knowledge Era   177
     Professor Karl-Erik Sveiby

Part IV   Knowledge and the Economy   **191**

12   New Economics for a Knowledge Economy:
      The Law of Increasing Returns   195
      W. Brian Arthur, The Santa Fe Institute

13   Brainpower and the Future of Capitalism   213
      Lester Thurow, Massachusetts Institute of Technology

14   The Role of Knowledge in the Connected Economy   245
      Stan Davis and Chris Meyer, The Ernst & Young
      Center for Business Innovation

      Afterword: Whither Knowledge Management?   *267*

      Appendix: Participants in The Knowledge Advantage   *271*

      Index   *275*

Foreword

John Seely Brown,

Xerox PARC

When I was a child, I became angry with my mother because she had urged me to read a novel. Full of adolescent certainty, I told her, "When that author understands his own ideas well enough to write an equation, then I'll read that novel. Because all I have to do is read an equation, and five minutes later I've got it."

I'm happy to say that such dogmatism has not stuck with me. As a scientist, I moved from equations and formulas to artificial intelligence, and from there to a growing appreciation of the power of the narrative – the power of realizing that generalities are different from abstraction. After all, what do we know now that we didn't know ten years ago? That learning and knowledge are the result of multiple, intertwining forces: content, context, and community.

In the knowledge economy, the real formula for success (which is, of course, less mechanistic than an equation) calls on the need to learn continuously. And to learn continuously, we must learn to see, and do, things differently.

We learn through conceptual frameworks, and we can continue to expand our knowledge incrementally within these existing frameworks. But if we are to create new frameworks and see new opportunities, our evolving world calls on us to challenge the assumptions on which our traditional intellectual constructs rest.

Furthermore, it is important to understand that learning is less about absorbing information than it is about becoming part of a community. Diversity of experience and practice, therefore, is paramount. For what better way is there to foster a different perspective than to see that perspective from another person's point of view?

Consider Silicon Valley, London's theater district, or New York's financial district. All are dominant locales in their respective fields, and communities of practice exist within each of these locales. Members of these communities are bound together by both a sense of purpose and the need to know what each other knows. They communicate with each other and share knowledge via a web of overlapping personal networks. These locales benefit from the porous relationships (which enable the flow of information) among their many communities. In an environment of complex symbiosis and social reciprocity, partners and competitors alike benefit from the movement of people and ideas.

But where the rubber hits the road is in negotiations between communities. Inside a community, ideas are validated by the shared practice or paradigm of that community. Taking an idea outside the community requires the testing not just of the idea but of the paradigm itself. Negotiations between communities, therefore, make knowledge more robust and force us to understand the barriers to knowledge sharing.

By being able to see differently and to create new perspectives through diversity, new knowledge is constructed. The key? Understanding the knowledge construction process and harnessing and leveraging the diversity found in such communities. What are the dynamics underlying the construction of wealth? The construction of the firm? The construction of self? How do those things come together, and how do firms come to understand and leverage these knowledge dynamics?

At Xerox PARC, there is a group of people we call "knowledge artists." The role of knowledge artist, someone who can describe or present what he sees differently, may become a new and important discipline in the knowledge workplace.

Artists are known for their ability to bring life to an idea or concept. Our knowledge artists at Xerox intermingle with the scientists, crafting visual performances that contribute to the construction, sharing, and leveraging of knowledge. By presenting a perspective from a different point of view, or by introducing a new perspective altogether, knowledge artists provide new frameworks, bring learning to life, and further enrich the diversity of knowledge and ideas within the organization.

Ideas, and knowledge, are usually constructed with the help of a document or book. A document does not contain knowledge; it contains information. But documents put into motion a dynamic of social reciprocity, in which knowledge is shared and social construction of understanding takes place.

Documents evoke reactions and creations in the knowledge construction process. What's more, documents are not independent. Every document is, in some way, related to another (as illustrated by footnotes, annotations, and textual references to previous works and other authors). But perhaps most important, shared documents often provide the basis for disagreement within communities – thereby representing not the ending, but the beginning of the process of negotiation, learning, and knowledge-sharing.

And as my mother attempted to teach me, storytelling too enriches the sharing of knowledge. A good story is emotionally engaging, and it has a degree of transportability. It provides a broader framework that enables us to understand the generalities, or looseness, of ideas. Stories can be embedded in a new context, and the nuggets of knowledge contained in these stories can be applied to a new range of settings.

Stories are transported and resuscitated through the process of listening, which goes hand in hand with storytelling. Because a story is interactive, the listening is as much an activity as the telling. We call this "deep listening." One of the things organizations must discover is how to construct a context, a space in the corporate world, that encourages deep listening.

Even a scientist (such as I) must admit that knowledge cannot be captured via a formula or equation. It calls for new intellectual constructs and the challenge of background assumptions. And it is enriched by events, objects, people, or situations – such as storytelling, documents, knowledge artists, and communities of practice – that provide us with different perspectives and lenses through which to view the world.

This compilation, in many respects, contains various lenses through which to view new knowledge landscapes. The richness of perspective, the diversity of frameworks, and the depth of insights these authors provide on the subject of knowledge and knowledge creation offer a wealth of information that is seldom found in one place, or within the covers of a single book.

It is our hope that these compiled articles, their contributors, and their multiple perspectives will help you to create new frameworks for constructing new knowledge and lay the foundation for future discussion, negotiation, and sharing. And that this wealth of information will make the transition in your organizations, from information to knowledge.

Chapter 1

Gaining the Knowledge

Advantage

Rudy Ruggles,

The Ernst & Young Center for Business Innovation

Dan Holtshouse,

Xerox Corporation

"The most valuable asset any company can possess is knowledge. The ability to create and share knowledge will be the #1 factor for success in the next century."

– Manager at a US automotive firm

What's left to say about knowledge management? Does the world really need another book on why and how a more active approach to managing the creation, acquisition, representation, transfer, incorporation, and application of knowledge can transform organizations? Peter Drucker's oft-repeated statement that "knowledge has become the key economic resource and the dominant – and perhaps even the only – source of competitive advantage" has succinctly declared the urgency of taking knowledge seriously since he first wrote it in 1995.

Today, the average manager is deluged with brochures, news clippings, and software "solutions" emblazoned with the bold banner "knowledge management." Surely, that's plenty.

This book was created precisely because of the situation described above. Certainly the world is not clamoring for more soundbites about the power of knowledge and learning. What people are clamoring for is the very element that this whole movement revolves around: knowledge. And more importantly, people want that knowledge put into the sort of context that only human judgment and experience can provide. People want meaning and wisdom. That, then, is the purpose of this book: to present the real meaning and wisdom about gaining a competitive advantage through knowledge.

Before getting to the wisdom, however, it is important to have some background and some perspective on this topic. This opening chapter, therefore, lays out our view of some of the history of knowledge management and reflects that history through the lens of the Knowledge Advantage colloquia, with its events which have played a key role in bringing together practitioners, academics, and other advisors to explore the main issues in leveraging knowledge. While the events were only a part of the ongoing dialog that the Knowledge Advantage effort engendered, they were important milestones in the evolution of the thinking, and practice, around knowledge management.

Throughout the five years that Knowledge Advantage has existed, we have had the great fortune to hear from many of the wisest men and women of our time on this subject. We have selected their timeless ideas and insights as the basis of this book and we will introduce them in this first chapter. Although readers can certainly benefit from the material no matter where they dive in, we hope that by giving this background, by setting the context, we can help people draw the pieces of this puzzle together so as to gain the greatest insight from these thoughts as a whole.

A brief history of knowledge management

There have been quite a few notable works in recent years focused on the topic of knowledge management, including Ikujiro Nonaka and Hirotaka Takeuchi's *The Knowledge-Creating Company*, Tom Stewart's cover stories in *Fortune* magazine about brainpower and intellectual capital, not to mention his book *Intellectual Capital*, and Peter Senge's *Fifth Discipline*, which helped to bring the term "learning organization" into general business conversation. Even so, the roots of this topic reach much farther back than that.

Some roots lie in artificial intelligence and expert systems, where computer and cognitive scientists worked diligently at making knowledge explicit, hoping to be able to embed it in thinking machines, or at least applications. In the late 1960s and early 1970s, people thought computers were going to do the knowledge work for us, and even though there have been some very interesting breakthroughs in that field, knowledge remains firmly stuck within humans (at least for the time being).

In the late 1980s, downsizing forced companies to think about different ways of moving information around. The stripping out of middle management had direct and indirect impacts on organizational knowledge. First, those "downsized" took with them a tremendous amount of tacit (deeply embedded) knowledge. But their departure had a significant secondary impact as well. Historically, middle management had the informal role of knowledge guides – knowing what information was around and where to find it – and when they disappeared this important function was left unfulfilled.

Simultaneously, business process re-engineering was trying to harness process-related knowledge, but some of the famous BPR failures highlighted what happens when only explicit knowledge is accounted for in process redesigns. Such efforts, combined with Total Quality Control (TQC) and ISO metrics systems, did a lot to force many organizations to be explicit about what they know and what they do. Documentation and learning became a fact of life.

Other notable recent influences include Leif Edvinsson, with his work at Scandia, producing an intellectual capital report supplement to the annual report, and Margaret Wheatley, whose work (including her book *Leadership and the New Sciences*) offers a complete break with the ideas of traditional leadership. What is more, the rise of the Internet into popular culture, fueled by the universal availability of browser software, allows everyone inside and outside organizations suddenly to have access to a tremendous amount of data and information.

But even before this current batch of business-based discussions, knowledge and learning were being studied by people such as Nobel Laureate Herbert Simon (e.g. *The Sciences of the Artificial*). In the 1930s, 1940s, and 1950s, there was a great deal of work done on how organizational learning curves improve routines over time. Michael Polanyi discussed the difference between tacit and explicit knowledge years and years ago. Our history is guided by the more recent publications, but they rest strongly on these foundations of knowledge research, clearly the predecessors of more modern ideas.

If such discussions have been going on at various levels and in various guises over so many years, why is there such a buzz today? Companies are facing bigger problems now, that are taking even larger numbers of people to address. Unfortunately, there are not enough highly skilled workers being produced by the current educational system to meet this growing demand. Also, with the demographics showing that many of the senior, most experienced people at organizations throughout the world are about to retire, companies are faced with the issue of trying to capture their knowledge before they leave. It's the downsizing problem all over again.

It goes even deeper than that though, since the people who are left must in fact work differently. The entire business model is changing. It used to be that decisions were made and people would just follow orders. Around the early 1980s, people started being put into work teams and told to decide for themselves how their work was to be done. To operate like that, people need complete information, and they want knowledge faster. The percent of people who are expected to learn, observe, draw conclusions, and share what they know while they work is increasing. There are also more customers now, increasing the complexity of the environment even further. There used to be more process control; each step was more predictable. Now it is unclear what to do with the processes and toolkits of old, since everything seems variable. There is an interesting cycle here: we have different work expectations, then technology is developed which supports different work styles, which has allowed our work expectations to grow even more. Before, our expectations were limited by the available technologies. Now, the technologies available have opened up whole new doors as to what it is possible for any given individual to know and apply. Knowledge is recognized as a tool for all to be able to use, and not just available to some special set of people. For example, in Africa in the 1960s, the solution was to give people grain, not teach them how to farm, but that has changed. People now want the knowledge, not just the by-products.

Recent developments

So why all of this talk about knowledge now? If knowledge-related activities and investigations have been going on for decades, what has happened in the last five years to create such attention to the topic? The active management of organizational knowledge is inextricably linked to the broader business world. In the last five years, there have been major changes in the general business environment which, in turn, have created an even greater need for active knowledge management than has ever existed before. We must be prepared to lift our heads out of the knowledge discussion for a minute to understand better the environment in which knowledge management is taking place.

Although not explicitly about knowledge management, Chris Meyer and Stan Davis's book *BLUR* lays out the implications of the combination of the steady increases in the speed of change, the value of intangibles, and inter-connectivity which have been observed over the past several decades. Mind-work is starting to outstrip muscle-work in the value it adds to the global economy, as reflected in the rise in value contributed by intangibles. As George Gilder puts it in his book *Microcosm*, "The central event of the twentieth century is the overthrow of matter. In technology, economics, and the politics of nations, wealth in the form of physical resources is steadily declining in value and significance. The powers of mind are everywhere ascendant over the brute force of things." Knowledge is applied to create value more effectively. Further, electronic connectivity allows us to link people together over long distances to create and share ideas, which is especially important for industries and companies in which intangibles matter more. (It's tough for teams to assemble a car over distance, but it can be quite efficient for teams to design a car on-line.) But even for traditional, tangible-based firms, things change so quickly that they have to learn new things constantly, from within and from the world around them.

So, knowledge management is a product of its environment. It is an organizational response to the major changes surrounding it. While the important resources worth managing effectively in the past were land, labor, and financial capital, now there's a need to manage that elusive, yet highly valuable asset: intellectual capital. That's where the value lies, these days more than ever.

The rise of knowledge management

Knowledge management itself hasn't stayed still either in the last five years. Certainly the buzz around the term and its associated tools and techniques has grown rapidly. We have already mentioned some of the history of the concepts, but as a topic in and of itself, knowledge management has garnered quite a following. Devotees come from academia, technology, consulting, organizational design, learning, human resources, competitive intelligence, process change, library science, and a host of other fields. In many cases, "knowledge management" was the banner which rallied and unified what had until then been related, although separate, conversations and perspectives. Of course, in other cases, "knowledge management" became the equivalent of the "new and improved" label slapped onto the same bill of goods, merely trying to capitalize on the market associated with a new buzz phrase.

As time has marched on over the last five years, the growing interest in the subject has been marked by many indicators. Conferences on knowledge management in the US and Europe have continued to proliferate with more recent activity in the Asia-Pacific region. Conferences are one of the tools of the knowledge economy for developing thought leadership (ideas, viewpoint/market coalescence) around a new subject, such as knowledge management. Conferences are also ways for disparate ideas to coalesce.

The early years of the knowledge management movement were without the benefit of market analysis and research support until DataQuest published one of the first market assessment reports for knowledge management in 1996. Now most all of the industry market research organizations have areas of focus around knowledge management.

In a similar sense to the DataQuest report, you could say that the beginning of the knowledge-related publication boom occurred in 1995, with the Nonaka/Takeuchi book *The Knowledge Creating Company* and Dorothy Leonard-Barton's book *Wellsprings of Knowledge*. Since then, there continue to be an increasing number of business books on knowledge along with a range of journals, reviews, and magazines devoted to knowledge management. All this signifies a deepening of the knowledge management roots taking hold in our society.

Lastly, the issue of market size and definition is still open to debate, although certain classes of software tools and dedicated professional services for knowledge management are now generally accepted as constituting the knowledge management market. As groupware, workflow, and document management vendors include knowledge management features in their offerings, the market boundaries continue to expand.

So the knowledge movement, while underway for four to five years, is still emergent in many respects but is gaining momentum as a top business trend and force in the industry. For example, a recent survey by the Foundation for the Baldridge award found knowledge management coming in surprisingly high on the CEOs' most important trends list (see Fig. 1.1). The 300 CEOs surveyed ranked knowledge

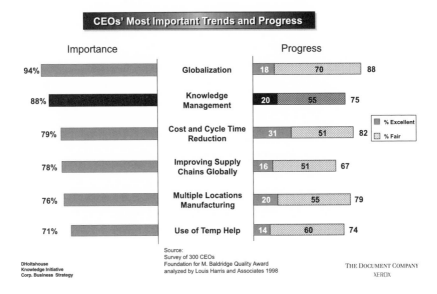

Figure 1.1: Knowledge management picked as a top business trend

management second in importance only to globalization trends. It was also notable that although most were not very far along in their efforts, 20% indicated excellent progress in implementing knowledge management programs in their organization. This is evidence that knowledge management, while still young and emergent, is being taken very seriously.

It is significant that the rise in knowledge management has not been all talk. Over the years, we have learned much about principles in action. For instance, it became quickly apparent that knowledge management is not all of one flavor, nor should it be. Depending upon the perspectives at the root of any given knowledge management effort, the priorities, tools, and approaches can be very different indeed. Further, the specific application of a given set of knowledge management ideas will also differ depending upon the intent of the effort. Plus, context is key. Sharing lessons learned in the context of a large pharmaceutical firm's new product development center will have some very different issues from sharing lessons learned while drilling oil on offshore rigs all over the world. Experience over the years has taught us a great many lessons about how knowledge management works in action, in a very wide variety of situations.

Furthermore, the general belief is that knowledge management is making a difference. In a survey conducted of all Knowledge Advantage participants over the years, we asked people to indicate on a Likert scale their level of agreement (strongly disagree = 1, strong agreement = 7) with the phrase "Knowledge Management has had a positive impact on business." Their answers are displayed in Fig. 1.2.

With 74% of the respondents answering 5 or more, it is apparent that those most involved in knowledge management activities believe that their efforts are not in vain. Another way to think about this question is the impact of *not* doing knowledge management. James Cox, president of Jcoxcorp, Inc., stated this well in saying that, "Knowledge management *can* have a positive impact. More properly, *lack* of KM will have a negative impact."

What has also changed over the years is the scale of the knowledge management activities. What started as just an attempt to better understand the role of knowledge in organizations in the hope

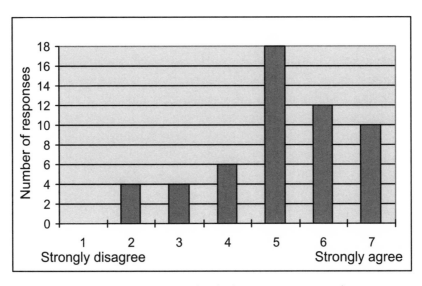

Figure 1.2: Knowledge Management has had a positive impact on business

that such insights would lead to a better understanding of the "real" workings of firms, has developed into a much more active approach to managing knowledge. Knowledge management has generally come to mean organizing infrastructure (e.g. technology, space), processes, intellectual capital (content), and internal structure (e.g. incentives, reporting/teaming configurations) to better create, capture, access, and apply knowledge. This is usually done with the intention of reducing rework/reinvention, reducing errors, or improving processes.

While these internally focused efforts are excellent applications of knowledge management ideas, an increasing number of companies are also taking an externally focused view when looking at how best to create value through knowledge. Firms like Microsoft and Teltech have set up intricate, knowledge-based relationship structures with other organizations, designed primarily for knowledge sharing and co-creation. Other firms have moved into new markets altogether by drawing upon their knowledge and packaging it up in new offerings. For instance, 3Com has the market-leading handheld personal information device, the Pilot, beating out Apple, HP, Sharp, and a host of other firms that normally specialize in such handheld devices. How did they do this? Among other things, they got the synchronization right, which makes sense given 3Com's primary competence: connectivity. They were able to see that the Pilot was more about being a connected information device than it was about being like a calculator, and they were able to capitalize on that knowledge.

In our vocabulary, knowledge-based businesses are ones that explicitly leverage knowledge throughout their business model, from infrastructure, to process, to products, to strategy. Such organizations align their resources to create the maximum value from what they know, not (for instance) what they own. An excellent example of an organization which is in the midst of a transition to this model is the World Bank. James D. Wolfensohn, president of the World Bank Group, has declared that they are to be a "knowledge bank," and not just a lending institution. Steve Denning relates the story of this transition in his chapter later in this book, but it is worth noting here that this type of thinking is by no means the domain of the software or consulting firms which tend to be the obvious examples of "knowledge-based" organizations. It is our belief that there are wonderful opportunities available to organizations which not only develop effective knowledge management practices, but which are willing to change their model to become truly knowledge-based, in thought and action.

So are we at the point where most businesses are re-conceptualizing their whole strategies around knowledge? Not quite. Most organizations are still trying to sort through knowledge management's vocabulary, technology advertisements, and theoretical frameworks to find the real value. Even among those who have gotten far enough to put ideas into practice, there is a feeling that there is still a way to go before the full value of actively leveraging knowledge will be realized. In the survey of Knowledge Advantage attendees, we presented people with the Gartner Group's maturity curve and asked people to mark where they feel knowledge management is today (see Fig. 1.3).

Although it is encouraging that about 30% of the respondents felt that knowledge management has come out of the "Trough of Disillusionment" and is making progress up the slope towards productivity, that also means that some 70% feel like there is still a considerable roller coaster ride ahead. However, it is important to keep in mind that as more people feel that the practice of knowl-

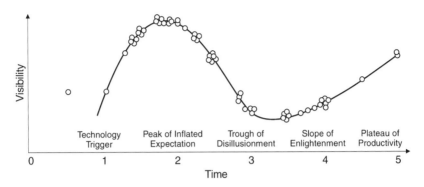

Figure 1.3: The Gartner Curve (each circle represents one response)

edge management is indeed producing results, the concept itself will be perceived by others as productive. In other words, not every organization which tackles KM will need to experience the same ups and downs, so this 30% can in fact be very influential in bringing others along quickly.

The Knowledge Advantage colloquia

So, as an issue, knowledge management is maturing and going through the trials and tribulations of growth and adoption. While there are those who are still not sure about the long-term viability of knowledge management as a practice, who don't see that it will ever really ascend the "Slope of Enlightenment" to the "Plateau of Productivity," we have seen many examples where this maturation is already happening. The five Knowledge Advantage colloquia have given us exposure not only to the snapshots of state of the art practices in knowledge management, but collectively allow us to look at how the state-of-the-art has progressed over time. In the early years, companies working on these issues tended to use specific, usually traditional, tools and approaches in very specific applications. Because "knowledge management" was not a widely used term, most of the initiatives which were in fact related to leveraging knowledge better did not use that vocabulary at all. Vince Barabba of

General Motors described how they used the Decision Dialog Process as a team-based strategy for using individual and organizational knowledge to make better decisions. Meanwhile, firms such as Skandia were looking at intellectual capital measurement, a much more quantitative approach. The initial power of these colloquia was to bring together these different approaches in a conversation about the similarities and differences, exploring their strengths and weaknesses in various contexts.

As the years progressed, the Knowledge Advantage events continued to bring practitioners together with academics and other thought leaders to explore this territory. The scale and scope of many knowledge management initiatives continued to grow from local to enterprise level. In 1995, Dick Armstrong described Bechtel's organizational efforts to create and implement a full knowledge management process, complete with new roles (e.g. Chief Knowledge Officer) and infrastructural elements (e.g. Knowledge Bank). Such large-scale efforts were also described by speakers from Hughes Space & Communications, Ford Motor Company, Monsanto, and Ernst & Young.

At later gatherings, more and more of the practitioners described knowledge management efforts which reached outside of their own corporate borders to embrace customers, suppliers, and other relationship partners. At Knowledge Advantage III, in 1996, Dennis Gaukel of Pioneer Hi-Bred and Lynn Brown of Wachovia each discussed how their firms were better using market knowledge to enhance their customer relationships. In other sessions, speakers from UPS, Intel, and Kyocera International explained how their organizations were setting up and managing knowledge-based relationships with strategic partners. This is right in line with Peter Drucker's admonition in his closing talk at that event that companies should not get caught only looking internally at how better to leverage knowledge. While certainly there are costs that can be cut and efficiencies to be gained in looking inside, the growth opportunities will all be found externally.

The 1997 Knowledge Advantage conference saw firms tying together a wide variety of enterprise-wide and local, quantitative and qualitative approaches to leveraging knowledge. This event really highlighted the "knowledge-based business" approach, where firms were working on leveraging knowledge at each, and in some cases all, of the following seven levels:

- *infrastructure* – creating the physical and technological support environments which allow knowledge sharing and representation
- *content* – representing, embedding, organizing, and supporting knowledge content and intellectual capital
- *processes* – actively bringing knowledge to bear in the context of specific processes (e.g. new product development)
- *organization* – consciously designing and structuring elements of the organization to support knowledge management and application (e.g. recognizing communities of practice, creating incentive systems which support knowledge sharing)
- *relationships* – establishing and maintaining knowledge-based relationships with customers, suppliers, and other strategic partners
- *products and services* – enhancing the organization's offers by embedding knowledge within them or in their interactions with their users (see Stan Davis' talk on knowledge-based products in Chapter 10)
- *strategy* – setting corporate strategy based upon the belief that knowledge is the key resource, realizing that the basic strategic question is "How can we create the most value from what we know as an organization?"

The efforts at most companies, even the state-of-the-art ones presenting at the Knowledge Advantage events, are still primarily concerned with getting the first three or four of the above areas working well. However, there are some, such as Capital One and the World Bank, which have quite explicitly focused on becoming knowledge-based businesses, per our definition. Looking at their initiatives and activities, one finds efforts in each of the seven domains listed above. Admittedly, the vocabulary here is ours, but the efforts are theirs.

The fifth Knowledge Advantage colloquium, held in 1998, was once again a snapshot of practical excellence. The event was filled with examples of how various organizations were creating greater value by applying a variety of tools and approaches to solve problems and open up opportunities throughout the seven levels of knowledge-based businesses. Having scoped out the territory in previous years, having heard about the possibilities, practitioners came to share results. As in the Gartner curve, eventually one gets to the "Plateau of Productivity." Given an understanding of the big picture – including the macro trends of increasing speed, connectivity, and intangible value – and of the potential strategic impact of knowledge-based business, which lies far beyond just knowledge management, companies are hard at work making ideas reality. As a result, what was a broad topic, was becoming more specific. Many conferences and events had sprung up already which focused on the application of knowledge management ideas to very specific segments (i.e. healthcare or supply chain management). The Knowledge Advantage event itself was broad, but it was important to help people with specific roles or tasks navigate its discussions, so for the first time there were three tracks: new product/service development, operations, and (customer) connections. While still broad, these three areas roughly describe the three areas where most practitioners tend to find the best footholds and starting points for their knowledge management activities. After all, coming up with new ideas (development), making them happen (operations), and then supporting and learning from them (customer connections) is important for any organization. This really drives home the fact that "knowledge-based business" is not just for some special-case companies. It is a new approach to taking all organizations to even higher levels of effectiveness and innovativeness.

This book

In the midst of such changes and transitions entailed by such activities within organizations, it is sometimes easy to lose sight of the essence of the effort. Whatever the starting place, whoever the owner, and whatever the vocabulary, the overall intention shared by such efforts is to leverage knowledge better to create extraordinary value. What this looks like and feels like in practice changes based on the tools at hand, the people involved, and the nature of the problems to be solved. However, as we mentioned in the beginning of this chapter, this book is about those guiding ideas and principles, which remain steady throughout. We know what it is like to take the roller coaster ride described by the Gartner curve. As people plummet down into the "Trough of Disillusionment" about knowledge management, a glance through the rich thinking contained in this volume should remind them about why they are on this ride in the first place.

We have arranged the chapters of this book into four sections, reflecting our belief that the knowledge advantage exists at various levels: individual, organizational, strategic, and economic. Although many of the chapters span several categories, we have tried to position them where we believe the thinking has been most influential, or where it adds the most new food for thought. Although we will introduce each section with some thoughts, we thought a quick overview would be in order here.

Individual

The order, individual to economic, represents our belief that knowledge is at its essence very personal. It is at its richest when in the heads (and hearts) of people and loses some of its life every time it is taken out of that environment. Edward O. Wilson's background uniquely qualifies him to speak about knowledge at this level. With a background in ethnobiology – a field he essentially founded – he has been deeply immersed in knowledge work of his own. However, it is his most recent work that brought him into the knowledge advantage discussion. Even though most agree that knowledge is richest at the individual level, it has long been believed that there are three great branches of knowledge, classified as the natural sciences, the social sciences, and the humanities. Professor Wilson's challenge to the world is to look for ways to make these three branches consilient, that is, coherent and interconnected by cause and effect explanation. No discussion of knowledge would be complete without this level of thinking about how people actually deal with knowledge structure and classification. Discussions of knowledge work and knowledge workers take on whole new levels of meaning when knowledge is understood as the rich, complex subject that it is.

Alan Webber believes that the terms "knowledge management" and "knowledge advantage" are misleading. He believes that what is really going on is a knowledge *revolution*! He reminds us that in knowledge-based businesses, in an economy based on intellectual capital, it is the people who hold the keys. Drawing us from Wilson's focus on knowledge itself and into the world of the knowledge workers, Webber shows us a glimpse of the battle lines of this revolution. At the level of the individual, there are choices to be made about what this new wave of thinking means to him or her. Being, or becoming, a knowledge worker in an organization that does not seem to value knowledge will not be easy. There will be new kinds of leaders who will take what has so much power at the individual level and find ways to use it to make a difference to the organization and to the world.

Peter Drucker is the father of the knowledge worker. As such, no book of timeless wisdom on the subject would be complete without his thoughts on the changing nature of management in a world of knowledge work. As Webber has expressed, there is indeed a revolution afoot. So what does one do about it? He believes that the greatest challenge facing managers these days is how to help all of these knowledge workers become productive! The problem is that the productivity tools of the past, brought to us by Frederick Taylor and the school of scientific management, do not work with today's knowledge workers. Not only do their tasks not lend themselves to this sort of optimization, but the workers must be managed less as 'employees' and more like volunteers. Drucker's comments segue nicely from Webber's first-person knowledge worker perspective to knowledge worker management, creating a wonderful lead-in to the discussion of the organizational impacts of more active knowledge management.

Organization

Unfortunately, although knowledge is richest at the individual level, it is least leveragable there. Overcoming the stickiness of knowledge so that it can produce large-scale value is the classic knowledge management problem. This movement of knowledge from individual/tacit (deeply embedded within a single person), through individual/explicit, shared/explicit, and into shared/tacit (embedded within a group) has been the focus of Ikujiro Nonaka's work for years. His *Harvard Business Review* article and book *The Knowledge-Creating Company*, with Hirotaka

Takeuchi, have become required reading on this subject. Organizations have not been effectively structured to take advantage of the new knowledge flows that are now possible using today's technology.

The key to successful technologies that support knowledge initiatives is to ensure that they support the complementary "structures" of organizational practice. Bob Bauer points out that the organization of the knowledge workscape can be characterized by both the *authorized* structure within which work is done (designed structure: the structure around the work of organizations) and the *emergent* structure within that work (generated structure: the structure within the work of organizations.) Three types of technologies support the richness of this duality in work practice: tools of the practice, enterprise libraries, and conversational tools. All of these must be present to individuals and communities of practice for the infrastructure to provide sustenance for successful knowledge ecologies.

Chris Bartlett's research on international organizational structures has been groundbreaking. It is no surprise then that he was talking about "knowledge-based organizations" way back in 1994. He had seen already some of the shortcomings of traditional organizational models in effectively leveraging and deploying knowledge, especially on a global basis. His views on the changes in managerial approaches highlight how to organize when people's intelligence indeed matters.

James Brian Quinn has been investigating what sorts of organizational forms can better create and leverage knowledge to create those leading companies which are creating, as per the title of Quinn's most recent book, an "innovation explosion." He has seen the significance of the impact of new ways of working and focuses on how to create and run organizations that capitalize on intellect. His previous book, *The Intelligent Enterprise*, winner of two awards for best business book of the year, was essentially the textbook on knowledge-based business. His chapter here is the perfect bridge between organizing for knowledge and capitalizing on it, strategically and economically.

Strategy

An organization managing knowledge well has the potential to create significant value, but only if it is linked to the overall strategy and strategic decisions. In fact, such an organization is most potent when it opens up new strategic opportunities altogether. Stephen Denning's story about the World Bank is one of transition. He tells how a large, bureaucratic organization took knowledge seriously and changed its whole strategy, literally almost overnight. This new strategy shift – going from a financial organization to a knowledge organization – is a wonderful example of the changes that are sweeping the world when a knowledge-based view takes hold. However, Denning's real story is about what such a change actually entails as it ripples through the organization.

The World Bank's new strategy is about changing from seeing its product as money to seeing its product as knowledge. At the strategic level, products (or services) can essentially be thought of as how an organization makes money, or creates value, from what it knows. If that is true, certainly there must be some interesting implications for an organization's products when viewed through the knowledge-based business lens. Stan Davis has thought about such ideas for years, painting a very interesting picture of what a world filled with products with explicit and embedded intelligence will be like, for individuals that use them and the organizations that deploy them.

Karl-Erik Sveiby has been researching, and participating in, knowledge-based organizations for over a decade. His contributions to the conversation have been immense, with seven books on the subject, for starters. In the context of this book, he draws together the previous elements and links them to the economic aspects through a discussion of the topic of measurement, and specifically the measurement of intangibles like intellectual capital. With that as a leaping-off point, it becomes even more interesting to look at the economic impacts of knowledge-based business.

Economy

As the world begins to fill with "knowledge" workers, creating and sharing knowledge in new ways within knowledge-based businesses, the economy looks different than it did just ten years ago. W. Brian Arthur's work on increasing returns shows the significant differences in the dynamics of an economy built upon intangibles. Although the idea of increasing returns has long existed in the world of economics, Arthur was one of the very first to realize that today's business world actually demonstrated that it was more than theory. In fact, these ideas, once considered peripheral, hold the key to understanding many of the competitive dynamics of the "new" economy. The science of economics just became much less dismal.

How do firms adjust to this new reality? What happens to those that can't? Lester Thurow, also an economist, has looked at these questions through the eyes of retailers, manufacturers, high-tech firms, health care firms, and a host of other industries. What he has seen is that in every case, the rules have either already changed or they are just about to do so. His explorations have led him into some intriguing waters, looking at the future of capitalism in a world turned on its head.

Chris Meyer and Stan Davis' discussion of the implications of increases in the value of intangibles, the speed of change, and interconnectedness of the economy provides substantial food for thought as to how interesting the world becomes when these changes begin to play out. They describe the implications of a greater knowledge-intensity in all aspects of the business model, from strategy, to products, to organization, processes, and infrastructure. They also address the basic question, what is the appropriate unit of business in a knowledge economy? Is it the organization, or is it the individual? With the rise of free agency as a feasible option for more and more people, the best answer may be the latter one. And so the connection is made back to the beginning, back to knowledge at the level of the individual. No one element of these four (economy, strategy, organization, individual) is dominant. They all drive each other, with knowledge being the primary coin of the realm.

We truly believe that the thoughts collected here represent some of the best thinking on how to gain the knowledge advantage. We are indebted to the contributors who shared their ideas, their time, and their attention with us. In the truest spirit of knowledge management, we are extremely delighted to share their wisdom with you. Of course, written words are never as dynamic as a conversation, but we have tried to capture in this book the timeless ideas of knowledge management and knowledge-based business, which will hopefully lead to richer, more fruitful conversations and activities in the years to come.

Part I

Knowledge and
the Individual

We will begin each section of the book with some thoughts on how a more active approach to leveraging and managing knowledge has had an impact in recent years at each of the levels discussed. We will also share the results of the survey we did of all past Knowledge Advantage participants. Certainly, given the self-selected nature of the population sampled the results do not represent the business world as a whole. Still, we believe that the answers are in fact more interesting *because* of the bias of this group. What do the "believers" think about the impact of this set of ideas and practices? Who better to comment than the lead users of this new set of tools and approaches?

Each of the survey questions asked respondents to rate the significance knowledge management has had at a given level. The options were arrayed on a seven-point Likert scale, from Insignificant (1) to Extremely Significant (7). When we asked this question about the impact of KM at the individual level, we gave examples such as knowledge sharing behaviors and cognition. Our goal was to determine whether people felt like knowledge management was actually making a difference to individuals, where knowledge really resides most richly and where the knowledge "work" gets done. The responses are graphed in Fig. I.1.

While certainly the most popular response was 5, indicating that KM was having a relatively significant impact, about half the respondents answered 2, 3, or 4. It is interesting that although the individual is where the intellectual rubber meets the road, knowledge management is not perceived as having a tremendous impact here. Knowledge worker productivity needs work. Tom Trimmer, president of grapeVINE Technologies, notes that "while significant awareness has been created, enabling systems and procedures are still in the early stages of implementation." Even those heavily involved in creating the tools to help know that there is still a long way to go.

Why is this? The chapters of this section hold many clues. As is apparent from Ed Wilson's piece, human cognition and the nature of knowledge are not easy topics to "manage." Science has been working for decades and, in fact, centuries to determine how and why

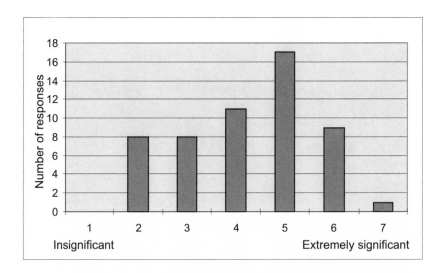

Figure I.1: The significance of knowledge management at the level of the individual

humans think and behave as they do. Although more is understood every day, the challenges are many. Furthermore, Alan Webber points out that switching over to a knowledge work mentality entails different roles and behaviors. So people are not only learning to think in new ways, they are learning to act and organize themselves in new ways.

Part of the problem is in trying to approach new practices with old mindsets. Peter Drucker's sentiments on this new world of management are right in-line with those of Rick Gerwe of Senco Products, Inc., who believes that "knowledge management has not had the impact it deserves because we have tried to 'manage' it in traditional ways. Knowledge resides in people's minds, not in files or computerized information systems." These sorts of transitions will take a long time to make, especially at the individual level. The impact of knowledge-based business approaches are just now starting to ripple through society, and not all of them are positive for all (stratification into "knows" and "know nots", for instance). However, we believe that Webber is right, this is a new revolution and the individual is the key.

Chapter 2

Consilience:
A Unity of Knowledge

Edward O. Wilson,

Harvard University

What does a biologist have to say to a business audience? A great deal, it turns out – especially given my belief that human knowledge is not well served by the divisions that have grown up between disciplines of study. As each discipline – whether pure science, physical science, social science, humanities, or the arts – has created its paradigms, its own jargon, it's become more and more difficult for knowledge to advance. What's needed now is consilience, or literally a 'jumping together' of the many branches of human knowledge.

Knowledge bridges and borderlands

What I'm going to talk about is what I consider to be a new frontier in science, and equally a new frontier in the social sciences and humanities. I hope to convince you that this is very relevant to the information initiative, and to the knowledge advantage. Essentially, what I am suggesting is that although it is widely assumed that there are many ways to account for the human condition, in fact there are only two ways to account for it.

The first one comes from the natural sciences, whose practitioners set out more than four centuries ago, and with considerable success, to understand how the world works. And they've promoted that particular enterprise.

The second way to account for the human condition is all the other ways. Since the 18th century, the great branches of learning have been classified into the natural sciences, the social sciences and the humanities.

Today we have a choice between, on the one hand, trying to make the great branches of learning consilient, that is, coherent and interconnected by cause and effect explanation; or on the other hand, not trying to make them consilient. Surely universal consilience is worth a serious try. After all, the brain, the mind and culture are composed of material entities and processes. They do not exist in an astral plane that floats beyond and above the tangible world.

The most useful term to capture the unity of knowledge is surely consilience. It means the interlocking of cause and effect explanations across different disciplines. As for example between physics and chemistry, between biology and chemistry and, more controversially now, between biology and the social sciences.

The word "consilience" was introduced in 1840 by William Whewell, the founder of the philosophy and history of science. Its meaning, as coherence or interconnectedness for the convergent theory of truth, has been preserved due to its scarcity of usage since then. Now it is the mother's milk of the natural sciences. It is material understanding of how the world works, and the technological spin-off is the foundation of modern science.

The time has come for those in social sciences and humanities to consider more seriously the relevance of this conception of how the world works. It's still a minority view even within the academy.

The best support for it comes from extrapolation of the consistent past success of the natural sciences. Its strongest appeal is in the prospect of intellectual adventure and, given even modest success, the value of understanding the human condition, which is what we're all concerned with here, with a higher degree of certainty.

But I also believe that it's a matter of practical urgency to focus on the unity of knowledge. Let me illustrate that claim with this example: think of the two intercepting lines forming a cross, picture the four quadrants thus created, and label them:

- ◆ environmental policy,
- ◆ ethics,
- ◆ biology, and
- ◆ social science.

Environmental policy is my special interest, but each of these subjects has its own experts and its own language. Each has rules of evidence, and its own criteria of validation. If we focus now on more specific topics – forest management is common to each of these quadrants – we see how general theory about knowledge translates into the analysis of practical problems. If we talk about national forest policy, the deforestation of tropical regions, the maximum use of land in timber production and extraction and so on, then we somehow have to learn how to travel clockwise from one subject to the next in a single discussion, maybe in a sentence or two in that discussion, and it's necessary to travel that entire circuit to cross all those fields.

Now move through concentric circles toward the intersection of the disciplines. As we approach the intersection, where most real world problems exist, all these subjects come together, the circuit becomes more difficult, and the process becomes more disorienting and contentious.

Now the nub of the problem, vexing a great deal of human thought, is the general belief that a fault line exists between the natural sciences on one side, and the social sciences and the humanities on the other side. Now I believe that this is not an epistemological division. It is not some kind of a Hadrian's wall, the kind that the Romans built across England to keep out the Scots. Many would have it that Hadrian's Wall is needed there, as a line between the great branches of learning, to protect high culture from the reductionist barbarians of sciences. What we are beginning to understand at last is that this line does not exist as a line at all. It is instead a broad domain of poorly understood material phenomena that awaits cooperative investigation from both sides.

During the past 20 years four borderland disciplines have grown dramatically in the natural sciences, or more precisely in the biological sciences, that have begun to bridge that intermediate domain.

1   *The cognitive neurosciences* – also known as the brain sciences – are making extraordinary advances. There is an acceleration in the mapping of brain activity during the different forms of perception and thought. There is an increasing fineness of resolution, a fineness of grain in doing the mapping, up to and including complex subjective thought.
2   *Human genetics*, including behavioral genetics is the borderland discipline next to the cognitive neurosciences. The genes that underline the self-assembly of the brain and the formation of the mind are being mapped. That is proceeding very rapidly, also at an accelerating rate, with complete mapping of the human genome by nucleotide pairs and genes in immediate prospect.
3   *Evolutionary biology* is an attempt to reconstruct the deep genetic history of humanity, especially as it pertains to the origins of human nature. This includes sociobiology, also known as evolutionary psychology, that has gained more and more acceptance in the past two decades.
4   *Environmental sciences* are presenting a clearer picture of the arena in which the human species originated. They question – with differing degrees of urgency – the reasons why we are intimately locked to this particular climate of environment, living and physical.

We can look at the social sciences in this area where the old lines between the great branches of learning are being replaced. We can see that cognitive psychology and biological anthropology are intertwining to an increasing degree, and some branches of social sciences and even the humanities are now beginning to become consilient with the four disciplines listed above. This, I would suggest, is the major intellectual event of our time. It is historic, it will occur only once, and it has enormous implications for development of technology. Furthermore, the connections are strengthening very rapidly, as exemplified by rates of DNA sequencing and gene mapping in the human genome, which are increasing exponentially, or even super-exponentially. The world effort for complete human DNA sequencing is now on target for completion by the year 2005.

Why is this conjunction among the great branches of learning important? Because it offers the prospect of characterizing human nature with the greater objectivity, precision, and exactitude that is key to human self-understanding. The intuitive grasp of human nature has been the substance of the creating arts. It's the underpinning of the social sciences, and it's a beckoning mystery to the natural sciences. To grasp human nature objectively, to explore its depths scientifically, and to grasp its ramifications, would be to approach, if not attain, the Grail of scholarship and to fulfill the dreams of the enlightenment of the 17th and 18th century. And I might add, it would have enormous import for the knowledge advance with which businesses are concerned, particularly the information revolution. In what directions is it going to be most profitable, most important, most beneficial to humanity to move, in the development of all of this marvelous technology?

Human nature and epigenetic rules

Rather than let the matter hang in the air rhetorically, I want to suggest a preliminary definition of human nature, and illustrate it for you with examples, to show you the nature of this new move into the borderland area between the great branches of learning. Human nature is not the genes. They prescribe it. Human nature is not the cultural universe like the incest taboo and rites of passage. They are the products of human nature. Rather, human nature is the epigenetic rules, the inherited regularities of mental development. These rules are the genetic biases in the way our senses perceive the world, the symbolic coding by which we represent the world, the options we open to ourselves, and the responses we find easiest and most rewarding to make, in ways that are beginning to come into focus at the physiological and in a few cases the genetic level.

The epigenetic rules alter the way we see and linguistically classify color. They cause us to evaluate the aesthetics of artistic design and the degree of complexity. They lead us differentially to acquire fears and phobias concerning dangers from the environment for specific objects and not others, innately, instinctively, as for snakes and heights. To communicate with certain facial expressions and forms of body language, the bond with infants, the conjugal bond, and so on across a wide range of categories in behavior and thought. This ensemble defines the very essence of humanity. Most of these epigenetic rules are evidently very ancient, dating back millions of years in mammalian ancestry, but others, like the sages of linguistic development, are uniquely human and probably only hundreds of thousands of years old.

Let me give a couple of examples. Imagine a color spectrum from left to right, and lower to higher intensity from bottom to top. When you raise or lower the intensity of light in a room with a dimmer switch, the optical cortex sees it or senses it, codes it, and the brain interprets it as a fluid transition from low to high brightness. But when you start with a monochromatic light, say at the lower (left) end of the wave length of visible light, and then you gradually increase the wave length of the monochromatic light you're showing, you don't see that as a continuum. Rather, the mind travels across blocks of primary color that you think you are seeing, and then it passes to another primary color, blue to green and green to yellow and yellow to red across zones in the visible wavelength spectrum, in which there is ambiguity and instability to be sure.

We understand a great deal of the basis of this visual interpretation right down to the level of the genes. We know how the sensitive color cones of the retina respond to different wavelengths, different cells respond to different pigments so that different signals come into the neurons behind the retina, the retinal inter-neurons. We know how this information is coded by bringing signals together in synthesizing neurons. That information is passed on back through the thalamus, the main relay center, and then passed on back to the back of the head, the occipital region, the optical visual cortex, and there put into coded form for integration with other forms of information.

Only within just the last few months, the more precise location of color information coding has been located down at the bottom of that visual cortex. We understand a lot of this. We know the genetics of color pigment variation, and we know the base pair genetic code underlying the pigment formation and the variations on it that cause color blindness.

Native language speakers encompassing a range of about 20 languages have been asked to position the color terms of their language intuitively on a color spectrum. It's been found, not surprisingly perhaps, that they locate those colors in the least ambiguous areas of the primary colors. When people from a tribe in New Guinea, with only two color terms, took part in voluntary tests, they were given artificial vocabularies to learn, which described a greater range of colors. Some words were placed in the least ambiguous areas, in the middle of the primary colors, and others were placed perversely between them in the ambiguous areas. The result was that those who had their terms in the least ambiguous areas learned them more quickly and retained the color terms longer. And when given a choice, these people then placed new terms that they were told to learn in the least ambiguous areas.

So this is an example of a solidly based physiological epigenetic rule, in that we see and name and develop vocabulary around color. But there's more. Studies have also shown that, like the variation in color vocabulary from one culture to another around the world, there is a variation from two color terms. Cultures have from two to eleven terms. There are 11 primary colors, or perhaps we should call them basic colors. This is the number of colors that can be mapped from one culture, from one language to another around the world; one on one or one on many or many on one. They are inter-mappable. Two to eleven is the variation.

It's been found that when there are only two words, generally speaking the two color terms are black and white. If there are three – black, white and red. If four – black, white, red, and yellow or green. If five – black, white, red, yellow and green and so on. In other words, there is a constraint in the way color vocabularies evolve. This is undoubtedly a biological constraint in cultural evolution. This is an important result.

The number of possible pathways in evolving from two to eleven terms in different combinations and numbers of terms is 2036. However, the number followed is primarily limited to about 22! We don't know yet the physiological basis of this, but this is a wide-open problem for future research.

As a second example of epigenetic rules, let me suggest to you the instinct to avoid incest. Its key element is the Westermarck effect, named after Edward Westermarck, the Finnish anthropologist who discovered it over a century ago. When two people live in close domestic proximity during the first 30 months in the life of either one of the two people, both are desensitized to later close sexual attraction and bonding. The Westermarck effect has been well documented in anthropological studies, although again the exact genetic prescription leading to it and the neurobiological mechanics mediating it remain to be studied.

What makes the human evidence the more convincing concerning the Westermarck effect is that all of the non-human primates – monkeys and apes – whose sexual behavior has been closely studied also display the Westermarck effect. Every organism, every species that's outbreeding, has its own personal and species-specific inbreeding avoidance mechanism. It can be different kinds of mating. It can be the requirement that a certain pheromone is present that avoids it and on and on and on.

In the case of the primate, humans included, the method is the Westermarck effect. That makes it more likely that we've inherited it, and therefore we need to turn to the Westermarck effect to understand exactly why we feel the way we do about incest fundamentally. And, of course, we know what the adaptive or Darwinian advantage of this is. People who inbreed at the level of brother/sister, mother/offspring, produce a significantly higher number of defective offspring or aborted offspring or have higher levels of infertility. It therefore seems likely that the trait of this particular form-proximate mechanism for avoiding incest prevailed in the human ancestral line millions of years before the origin of *Homo sapiens*, our present day species.

Consider another wholly different realm of human nature – that's what I'm talking about now, human nature, as it can be analyzed scientifically and understood through different levels of complexity – consider the basis of aesthetic judgement. Neurobiological monitoring, and particularly measurement of the damping of the alpha wave during presentations of abstract designs generated randomly by computer, have shown that the brain is most aroused by patterns in which there is about a 20 percent redundancy of elements. Or put very roughly, the amount of complexity found in a simple maze, or two turns of a logarithmic spiral, or an asymmetric cross.

It may be a coincidence that about the same property is shared by a great deal of the art in friezes, grillwork, colophons, logo graphs and flag designs. It crops up again in the glyphs of ancient Egypt and Meso-America as well as the pictographs of modern Asian languages. It is where Mondrian, for example, ended up in the evolution of art from literalism to the final abstractions of the height of his career. And, moreover, upon that level of complexity and design has been built art, in other words cultural evolution.

One form of calligraphy that has turned Japanese writing into high culture in the arts is called the Reisho style of Japanese calligraphy. It has a flourishing start and finish, with bold strokes to give a stern and commanding appearance. It was an impression of strength, and this is the style used in plaques and back covers and announcements. Thus I would suggest that art rises upon the compounding of epigenetic rules. In this case, maximum arousal and also possibly the visual releases, the triggers of assertiveness and dominance in style and gesture.

Certainly none of this is proof, but the universal nature and preponderance of the effect has to be considered very suggestive and awaits testing. I would suggest that the theory of the arts and the humanities, which seemed at first for centuries so remote from any contact with the natural sciences, awaits its Mendeleev. It awaits those who can formulate the basic organizing principles in the evolution of the arts.

I should also mention biophilia, the innate affiliation people seek with other organisms, and especially with the natural world. It's a concept I've worked on for a number of years. Studies have shown that, given complete freedom to choose a setting for their homes or offices, people gravitate toward an environment that combines three features. They want to:

- be on a height looking down,
- see open savannah-like terrain with scattered trees and copses, and
- be near a body of water, such as a river or a lake.

Landscape architects and real estate entrepreneurs intuitively understand these desires, and the three elements can be purely aesthetic, and not functional. People will pay enormous prices to have a view like this. Why?

People want a retreat in which to live, and a prospect of fruitful terrain in which to forage. And in the prospect they like distant, scattered large animals, and trees with low, nearly horizontal branches. Further, it appears they like these trees to have divided compound delicate leaves. Many of these elements are brought together in a formal Japanese garden, or for that matter, a formal English garden.

In short, people want to be in the environments in which our species evolved over millions of years, that is, hidden in a copse or against a rock wall, looking out over savannah and transitional woodland at acacias and other similar dominant trees of the African open environment. And why not? Is that such a strange idea?

Zoologists know that all mobile animal species have a powerful, often sophisticated inborn guide for something called habitat selection, and we know the physiological basis of much of it, and even some of the genetics of it in other animal species. Why not human beings?

Another aspect of biophilia worthy of mention is that you can further understand the basics of aesthetics as a response to nature. Charles Darwin, and many other field biologists also, understood that the tropical rain forest, the biologically richest of all environments on earth, is the ultimate form of this phenomenon. As a young man, Darwin saw an engraving made by Charles Fortier in 1822 from a painting entitled *Interior of a Virgin Forest in Brazil*. Darwin then went to the forest himself, found it accurate and, as he put it, "clever."

There is first beauty, the calming reflective examination of colors and shapes in the forest, for which we have a pleasant and quite likely innate resonance. Then there is sublimity, which Darwin in particular expressed so well. It is the absorbing attraction of the unknown, sufficiently deep and baffling, so as to elude, not just our senses, but even the reaches of our immediate imagination, that draws us on to unknown horizons. It is something that can also be appreciated in the recent paintings of Alex Rockman. First beauty, in Rockman's representations of the Guyana rain forest. Then sublimity, as in the mysterious and receding wilderness of the Guyana forest in mist. Anyone who has gone through wilderness, as you can still do in the great wilderness areas of the tropical rain forests, must know exactly what I'm talking about when I speak of the immense pull of the unknown as you enter these tangled and extremely rich environments.

Lastly, let us examine briefly the biologically important realm of erotic aesthetics, the basis of sexual attraction. There is the matter of preferred female facial beauty that has now come open to objective analysis. Reports on it can be found in journals such as *Nature*. There are similar studies going on with male beauty. The ideal, subjectively preferred female facial beauty is not the exact average, as once thought. It is the average of the subset considered most attractive and then blended by computer. The ideal has higher cheekbones than the average, a smaller chin, shorter upper lip and wider eyes, all relative to the face. The evolutionary biologist might surmise that these traits combined are the signs of juvenescence, that is, youthfulness and health, still in the faces of young women, hence relative youth, reproductive and reproductive potential.

How much do we know about the innate basis of such aesthetics? Not a lot, and certainly very little about the genetics and neurobiology, in particular the epigenetic rules. Not because they've been investigated and then found wanting, not because they are technically daunting, but simply because they haven't been studied. The right questions have not been asked. Only recently have researchers begun to ask the right questions within the borderland disciplines, between biology, the social sciences and the humanities, including the interpretation or theory of the creative arts.

Gene–culture co-evolution

I want to move a little farther into this subject, with a bit more speculation, to suggest the range of possibility for research in this area. In the arts I believe we convey emotion with what are sometimes called releasers. For example, careful studies – emerging in the borderland area around the political sciences – have shown the way political leaders convey leadership, the feel of leadership, by gestures and movements of ancient origin for mood and dominance.

Do you remember JFK's finger gesture, the forward movement of the hand, dominant and assured? This gesture reaches a peak in the triumphant gesture of the successful athlete. Dictators fold their hands. The royals fold their hands. In so doing – and often with the arms behind their backs – they show complete assurance. The hands are not needed for defense, others will take care of that. These are the interpretations that come out of that branch of political science, and they are a good deal more solidly based and less theatrical than they may at first appear.

Genetic evolution and cultural evolution are closely interwoven, and we are only beginning to obtain a glimmer of the nature of this process. This is the open frontier into which the natural sciences are moving, and this is the lower level of organization, self-assembly and complexity which the social sciences and the humanities are slowly beginning to explore.

We know that cultural evolution is shaped substantially by biology. We know that biological evolution of the brain, especially the neo-cortex, has occurred in a social context. So they interact. They are interwoven with each other, but the principles and the details of gene–culture co-evolution are the great challenge in the emerging borderland disciplines to which I have referred.

In my opinion gene–culture co-evolution is the central problem of the social sciences. Nature, and how it has determined or affected the cultural evolution of our institutions and our social mores, is the central problem. It's also a central problem of much of the humanities, and it's one of the great remaining problems of the natural sciences.

The natural sciences have not come to an end. They have simply moved to a new frontier, the most challenging and in some ways the most important frontier of all. Solving this problem of gene–culture co-evolution is the obvious means by which the branches of learning can be foundationally united.

Critics have said, and will continue to say, that whether the concept is correct or not, the program is impossible. I hear this from the traditional academy, from the professorati, and from the mainline academic intellectuals, but mostly I hear it from philosophers for reasons that are perfectly obvious; namely, this is pre-empting their domain. But I believe that they have fiddled around too long. They have not kept up with neurobiology and genetics and evolutionary biology. They have not seen where science has taken us in the possible new comprehension of the subjects that are considered central to philosophy, the nature of mind, the nature and significance of existence, and of humanity. Naturally they are irritated by a suggestion that this has now taken on a whole new life, and is being pursued by combinations of scientists and other scholars in the humanities and social sciences outside the realm of philosophy.

Still, I have hope. I was wondering, with a colleague, about how *Consilience* was going to be taken in *The New York Review of Books*, and other strongholds of traditional academia. My colleague, Charles Lumsden – a biophysicist and mathematician with whom I've done a fair amount of work in the past – said, "Forget about it. Your people are the *Wired* crowd." And sure enough, I got very nice profiles in *Wired* and *Forbes* magazines. I believe that maybe a new generation has come along that is interested in solving these problems and may see that this is technologically the kind of interesting subject into which the best of science and technology might profitably penetrate.

Knowledge is growing concerning some of the circuitry of complex behavior, including social behavior in human beings – something that was declared by the critics, quite a few of them philosophers or paleontologists, to be impossible to grasp 10 or 20 years ago. There exists, for example, the circuit running from the basal ganglia, which are ancient sub-cortical centers of the brain concerned with repetitive movements to the thalamus, a central relay station. Remember, it's in the thalamus, for example, that visual information is passing out to the prefrontal cortex, the controlling center of thought and decision and culture, and then back again to the basal ganglia. You'll have here a center for very elementary instinctive or patterning process, in hard-wired *basal nuclei*. You have travel in the circuit through one of the main relay stations of the brain, where information can be synergized and coordinated or transferred out to other centers.

And then you have this patterning, moving forward to the prefrontal cortex where our conscious thought is located, that can then affect reasoning, decision making, and even the evolution of culture. This circuit is where much of the activity occurs that controls repetitive behavior, as part of many of the cultural universals; rituals, formulaic prayers, ceremonies, incantations, purification rites, movements, stock phrases to ward off harm and so on. The same thing is repeated rhythmically over and over again with powerful, sometimes jackhammer emotional force.

Tipped too far, that circuit turns into the pathological condition of OCD or obsessive compulsive disorder. This is how it was discovered, by tendencies in individuals to OCD as a disorder. When regulated, that circuit is a key element of human behavior that appears to underlie a great deal of cultural evolution.

To summarize, in this description of human nature and the scientific probes moving into it from many directions, biologists, social scientists and humanity scholars by meeting within the borderland disciplines, as noted here, they have begun to discover increasing numbers of epigenetic rules. I've illustrated some, and frankly speculated on others. Many more rules and their biological processes, I'm confident, will come to light as scholars shift their focus to search for these phenomena explicitly.

I'm very aware that the conception of a biological foundation of complex social and cultural structures runs against the grain for many of the scholars, particularly the academic scholars. They object that too few such inherited traits have been found. Plus, they believe that higher mental processes and cultural evolution are still too complex, in spite of the fact that we seem to be getting up to the borders of some of it.

In the history of the natural sciences, however, a common sequence has predictably unfolded as follows: an entry point to a complex system is found by analytic probing. At first one and then more such paradigmatic predictions are accomplished. Examples are multiplied as a whole system opens up, and the foundational architecture is laid bare. Finally, when the mystery is at last partly solved, the cause and effect explanations seem in retrospect to have been obvious and even inevitable.

You can stay above, beyond or in front of the curve of understanding of human nature, which is fundamental to the direction of new forms of technology and industrial or post-industrial innovation. You will stay ahead of this curve if you continue to pay attention to research on human nature, its relation to biomedical research and abnormal conditions, its explanations of addiction, of preference and so on. This is not a nightmare scenario. We are not moving toward complete determinism of our understanding or control of the mind, or anything of this sort. We are moving toward self-understanding and in fact the kind of knowledge we need to produce a more lasting and productive and satisfying form of human society.

The value of this consilience program, which is, shall we say, a late 20th century renewal of the enlightenment agenda, is that at long last we appear to have acquired the means either to establish the fundamental truth of the unity of knowledge or to discard the idea. I think we're going to establish it, with many consequences for education, for innovation, for science, and for technology.

Chapter 3

Knowledge Is Power!

Welcome Democracy!

Alan M. Webber,

Fast Company

A new economy is emerging built on knowledge and innovation. At its center are knowledge workers, whose mission is not only to create a world of new products and services, but also to rethink the larger purposes and day-to-day practices of the world of business. That is a revolution. That is our dream.

It's not a movement, it's a revolution

I have a quibble with the title of this book. *The Knowledge Advantage* is a misnomer because it suggests that knowledge creation and management are just the latest terms in the management style handbook – listed right after *competitive advantage*. But knowledge is not a fad, nor a movement, nor the next business era to be written off as just another out-of-date and off-the-mark strategy. The way in which knowledge has become critical to the way that we do business is nothing short of a revolution

Knowledge Advantage is also too bloodless a phrase. It is too calm and too polite to describe the battle lines and the stakes of the knowledge revolution. Managers today are being forced to decide which side of the line they are on. On one side of this line is a workplace democracy where all contribute to, vote for, and really support a knowledge revolution. On the other side is the party that uses the tools, the techniques, the language, and even the symbols of the knowledge revolution, but in the service of cynical and nihilistic goals. The knowledge revolution is not just about profits or growth; it is a moral issue. Are we going to line up with the old guard that's protecting the status quo even as it embraces the language of change, or are we willing to turn the model of management inside out and upside down, and really talk about revolution?

Our world's business leaders are powerful agents of change. They have more influence for change than any under-secretary in Washington, DC, and they recognize that a new economy is emerging, one built on knowledge and innovation, with knowledge workers at its core. The task of this new generation of smart people and smart companies is not only to create the next generation of products and services, but to rethink the very way we conduct business, to reinvent the purpose of business. My hope is that each of us will find and contribute to our work, our personal values and efforts to make meaning in the world. But we must also beware not to fall victim to the dark side of this new economy.

The dark side of the new economy

The dark side of the new economy is cynicism, nihilism, and hypocrisy. David Dorsey's book, *The Force*,[1] expresses this dark side. The book follows a year in the life of Fred Thomas, a Xerox salesman who gets mixed messages from his company about how to sell copiers. First Xerox tells Fred that his customers are actually clients; he is not a salesman, but a consultant. His job, Xerox says, is to understand his clients' businesses better than the clients do so he can help them solve their problems – and it really doesn't matter how many copiers he sells them. But the other side of the corporate mouth tells Fred that his team must sell $30 million in copiers to win the prize trip to California for a golfing vacation.

I recommend the book as a case study in the tension, the unpleasant paradox of the new economy. It's an economy where mind games and manipulation and double binds are the stock-in-trade of people inside real companies, who are struggling to be knowledge workers in an environment that tells them that they still have to make all the numbers. The new economy may not be quite that bleak, but we are nonetheless at a moral crossroads. I see the potential for an economy wherein knowledge and information technology combine to create new opportunity. Ironically, this new opportunity is not entirely new; it has been around for years. But in the 1980s, it was hijacked by business reengineering.

The masked bandit: reengineering

Reengineering, was the last gasp of the old economy and it has hardly delivered on its promise. Reengineering was supposed to help companies compete in the knowledge era, but in practice it is anathema to the new economy.

We talk about creating companies with knowledge workers given the freedom to think, debate, and create companies working for real change. But reengineering, in most cases, has served the opposite purpose: it has worked to prevent change, not create it.

What went wrong with reengineering? The problem started with the name itself, which forces a simple, mechanical view of what is really a complex, *human* system. Companies are flesh and blood, yet reengineering tries to treat them like machines. In doing so, it fundamentally misses the hidden issues that guide most companies. The heart of a company is its people, relationships, and values – but reengineering completely ignores these assets. Despite its "clean slate" rhetoric, reengineering most often addresses the structure that exists, rather than what needs to be invented to ensure future success. More deliberately, reengineering is done without the participation of the knowledge workers in a company. If you talk to people in companies where reengineering is going on, they tell you, "We are being re-engineered." It is done to the people, not with or by the people.

All these realities of reengineering expose it as a status quo phenomenon wearing the clothing of change. It offers another technique to cut costs and increase quality when what we need is a strategy to cut costs and increase *knowledge*. Reengineering does not seek to create a knowledge company; it promotes information technology as a replacement for investment in knowledge development. Yet another problem with reengineering is that it promises too much or too little. On the one hand, reengineering promises near-term, measurable change; on the other, it promises complete discontinuous change and quantum leaps into the future. It cannot do both.

More than anything, reengineering is an essentially destructive means of change. It tears the social fabric of a company by stripping out people – the human assets. Those who would embrace reengineering are therefore placing their company's knowledge assets at great risk. In a way it is an attempt to get to the future by becoming less of a company. Whilst these criticisms of reengineering are sweeping and in some cases unfair, they are not merely fanciful. A real example of reengineering gone awry is embodied in Telco, a disguised but true story.

Telco: the dark side at work

Needing change, Telco turned to reengineering. Naturally, re-engineering was intended to make the company better. First, as is typical with reengineering, the consulting firm and senior managers mapped the current operation. After mapping the targeted process, the reengineering team assembled the company employees in a room with the map on the wall and told them to sign the map, to testify that it demonstrated the way the process really worked. In fact, the map was a lie: it portrayed the official version of the process, but not the way things really worked.

The workers signed the fraudulent map anyway because they perceived an implicit threat: sign it, or you impede the reengineering effort. The moral of the story: successful reengineering requires organizational lying. But the story doesn't end here. The next reengineering step was (as it always is) downsizing. At Telco, morale withered as colleagues disappeared. The cause of the depression in morale was more than simply shrinking numbers and fear for personal safety; the workers were seeing people disappear but saw no knowledge-based rationale for the cuts. People weren't dismissed because they couldn't contribute or couldn't give their knowledge to the organization. The community was suffering simply to make the numbers look better.

Following the mapping and downsizing, the reengineering team began redesigning the work. Incredibly, the reengineering team used the latest information technology to transport the company backward in time, to the days of Frederick Taylor.

Famous as the father of workplace efficiency studies, Taylor believed that all work should be broken down into component tasks, and all workers trained to perform each task in the single most efficient way. At Telco, the computer became the enforcer of this rigidity. Each salesperson was given three minutes per call, and fifteen seconds between calls. Period. Customer service received a new computer program, and whenever a customer called for help, the service representative would lead the customer through the information and questions on each screen, without deviating from the protocol. Period.

And what kind of input did people have in the reengineering process? The manager of the reengineering project announced that there would be regular team meetings – but that anyone disagreeing with the way reengineering was happening would be fired on the spot. Reengineering was happening and reengineering was working. Period. No debate allowed. End of conversation. The roots of this behavior lies in the advice of reengineering guru Michael Hammer: carry the wounded but shoot the stragglers.

Perhaps the most unfortunate result of this kind of reengineering is that – deliberately or not – it sided with the dark side of the knowledge economy. While claiming to address corporate problems, it placed more destructive power in the hands of the same old guard that created them. Rather than tapping into the knowledge of workers who knew about relations with specific customers and about the workings of the company, the Telco reengineers viewed these valuable minds as the first targets of headcount reduction.

A knowledge revolution: the alternative to reengineering

All of us will soon choose sides in this revolution. Will we find it most expedient to follow reengineering, which talks about change but actually embraces the status quo? Will we apply its methods, which are essentially anti-learning and anti-knowledge? Or will we follow the path of real change: the knowledge revolution.

If information technology is capable of changing the game, in the knowledge revolution *the game becomes changing the game.* In this next order of complexity, we must acknowledge that all the models we used and embraced and that brought us success in the past will not work in the future. We must bravely strip off the trappings of past success, and create a fundamentally different perspective on how businesses are organized, run, and represented.

Buckman Labs: a study in revolution

Bob Buckman inherited Buckman Labs, a specialty chemical producer. When he took over, it was just another company: it was top-heavy with management layers and bureaucratic regulations, and slow to respond. Today, Buckman Labs is a model of the knowledge-era company. Its 1600 people are not grunt workers, they are knowledge workers. They are knowledge workers because Buckman, in his effort to create a knowledge-managed and knowledge-managing company, first asked himself, "How do I close the gap between my work force and my customer?" He perceived the importance of his workers, and strove to reinvent – not reengineer – Buckman Labs, around people.

In the traditional business model, a company exists and its employees are simply lucky to have a job; the company is first. But Bob Buckman's definition of a company puts the people first. He even carries with him a laminated card with the company code of ethics:

> *Because we are separated by many miles, by diversity of cultures and languages, we at Buckman need a clear understanding of the basic principles by which we will operate our company. These are: that the company is made up of individuals, each of whom has*

*different capabilities and potentials, all of which are necessary to
the success of the company. That we acknowledge individuality,
and by treating each other with dignity and respect, strive to maintain continuous and positive communications among all of us. That
we will recognize and reward the contributions and accomplish-
ments of each individual. And that we will continually plan for the
future so that we can control our destiny instead of letting events
overtake us.*

To Buckman, the company is the people. And the power in the
company is vested in the network of knowledge workers. Decisions
at Buckman are made by people talking: Buckman Labs has two
dozen forums on Compuserve in which its knowledge workers can
learn and make decisions in real time. Authority is fundamentally
decentralized. In fact, not only does Bob Buckman understand that
he doesn't need to participate in all the learning conversations, he
is happy to have others do it, to let them get the work done faster
and better.

Leading a knowledge company

Bob Buckman is a knowledge leader. Because a knowledge-based
company is based on the individuals within it, the agenda of a good
leader changes. No longer the controller of assets or manager of workers,
the knowledge leader must:

+ disperse power, not concentrate it;
+ learn how to create shared understanding;
+ create meaning, not products;
+ recognize patterns, and help others see those patterns quickly
  and clearly;
+ encourage meaningful conversations, including disagreements;
  and
+ focus on values, not technology.

The importance of focusing on values isn't new and it isn't news. In
Eric Trist's 14-year-old book, *The Evolution of SocioTechnical Systems,*

he writes, "Information technologies, especially those concerned with microprocessor and telecommunication, give immense scope for solving many current problems *if the right value choices can be made*." (Italics added.) Therefore, companies must create, share, articulate, enforce, and believe in values.

Every company's annual report says, "Our people are our greatest asset," but few companies are managed as if they believed it. A knowledge company's agenda must support its claims that it puts people first. We must understand that work is intensely personal. Employees bring their best to a company day after day, want that work to amount to something worthwhile, and need a community in which they can relate to other knowledge workers. Every day, knowledge workers grapple with three questions:

◆ Am I in or out of the loop?
◆ Do I belong here, or am I wasting my time?
◆ Can I make a difference in this organization?

Managers must create the context in which knowledge workers can answer these questions affirmatively.

This challenge may intimidate many managers because it requires them to venture into the realm of emotions, feelings, fear, trust, belonging, purpose, responsibility, and opportunity. This realm has been forbidden in the past, but is really the reason people belong, and why they decide to participate in or abandon the knowledge revolution. A successful manager must see the spirit of the enterprise as much as its economics, must create as much positive energy as positive cash flow, must create value for the people in the company as much as create value for the shareholder.

Participating in the knowledge revolution

Successful companies will see the knowledge era as a revolution, not as a fad for redefining success. It won't always be easy. Some of us will have to figure out how to inspire change upwards: I buy into the knowledge revolution, but how do I get my boss to? Others may ignite the flames of change, but find it like a fire of wood shavings that burns brightly but quickly: how do we sustain a revolution based on knowledge? Many of us understand how we're supposed to think, but don't know what to do differently when we go to work tomorrow: how do we implement the changes?

Change may start with something simple. Not all of us need to rush out and hire a director of intellectual capital, for example. But change will happen when we, as managers, honestly regard our human resources as knowledge workers, not drones or robots or numbers. During a tour of a Toyota plant in Japan ten years ago, a proud manager told me, "We have a tool at this plant that your Detroit auto factories don't have." Bewildered, I asked what tool Toyota had that the equally modern Detroit factories did not. The manager held up a pencil. All of Toyota's workers carry one so that they can write down and submit ideas that occur to them.

When I related the conversation later to US auto industry managers, I was met with cynicism. "Half of our auto workers are illiterate," they said, "so even if we gave them pencils, they couldn't write anything." Unlike Detroit, Toyota recognized that even its assembly line workers are capable of contributing as knowledge workers, and saved millions of dollars because it treated them as such.

The knowledge revolution will be a revolution of democracy, a movement characterized by dispersal of power, and by managers who lead through empowering front-line knowledge workers to contribute and to make decisions. It will be a movement led by managers who close the gap between the work force and the customer and who are willing to trust and respect the people who are the company. It will reward companies, managers, and knowledge workers who will accept nothing short of reinventing business.

Note

1   Dorsey, David (1995) *The Force*, Fawcett Books.

Chapter 4

Managing Knowledge Workers in a Changing World

Peter Drucker,

Claremont Graduate School of Business

The knowledge worker in context

I want to start by asking a rhetorical question. Who were the first – and perhaps the greatest – executives of all time? The builders of the great pyramids! Those projects were huge, even by modern standards. They were certainly more vast than any project undertaken before the mid-1800s. Yet these men – and we presume they were men – organized the collective work of thousands of other men, planned, arranged for materials, and did all of the things big corporations do today. But the knowledge to do this was in just a few men – the rest were organized to contribute their physical labor, and that physical labor has changed very little over the years.

Thus, people who know how to manage have existed for centuries. Yet, now society has a need for managers in greater numbers than it did in the past and their skills are essential. Now we have many more people doing knowledge and service work. And what do we know about managing knowledge work? It all comes down to managing knowledge workers, a difficult task to say the least. Why? Well, I would characterize knowledge workers in two ways. Firstly, I would say that they are dismally unproductive, and secondly, that they are not employees, but volunteers, even though they are paid for what they do.

Dismally unproductive?

The productivity of knowledge and the knowledge worker is low. Historically, there was no reason to improve it. Before World War I, 95% of the population were manual workers. For most of history, society ran on muscle power or skilled labor. In 1880, Frederick Taylor looked at manual work and made great improvements in its productivity. Taylor looked at the task being done, and asked "What is the one best way to do this task?" However, he never asked if the task itself was necessary. His efforts had enormous success, resulting in an improvement in productivity of about 3.5%, which is a 50-fold increase over a century.

Previously, knowledge was an ornament. Even up to World War II, almost all work was manual or skilled labor. What we did in World War II, out of necessity, was to learn to enable many people to do what in the past only a few people had been able to do: produce high-quality optics, make machine parts, build complex machines, etc. We did this through discipline, through study, and through conscientious attention to process.

However, all manual and skilled work is programmed by the task. You look for efficiencies by asking, "How should the task itself be done?" But that may not be the right question for the knowledge age. In contrast, knowledge work is not programmed by the task. Knowledge work is driven by the results. The first question must be: "What is the task?"

The major cause of dismal knowledge worker productivity is that we have knowledge workers doing work that we did not hire them to do, and much of which probably does not need to be done at all. This is the severe limitation of classical TQM, in that it perfects a lot of work that should never be done at all. Even today, we are too quick to ask how to do the task better, and not consider whether it can be eliminated altogether. Only the knowledge worker himself can answer that, but all too often his job consists of non-essentials. For instance, nurses spend over 75% of their time shuffling papers. They are therefore overpaid for what they do and underpaid for what they should be doing, not to mention frustrated by having so little time and energy to give to the work they have been trained for and find meaning in. Meanwhile, engineers spend time writing and rewriting reports. No one applied to engineering school because she wanted to write reports. And, incidentally, no one was admitted to engineering school because she was a good report writer. Eliminating non-essential work is the key to the productivity of the knowledge worker.

As no two knowledge workers have the same job, each is responsible for defining his or her own job. What should we in this organization hold you accountable for? What contributions and results should you be accountable for over the next 15 months?

This process is iterative, however. The first attempts to do this will not be right, but they will allow us to learn. The nurse will tell you, for example, that while arranging flowers for a patient is not a nursing task, it is something she or he should do because non-professional contact with patients is integral to building the patient relationships necessary for good nursing care. And what is the nurse being paid for? Patient care! (Not housekeeping, paperwork, or doctor care!)

It is also the responsibility of the knowledge worker to educate others. Every knowledge worker must first be a teacher, creating a wider understanding of their knowledge. It is their job to describe to the organization the power and limitations of their area of expertise. The knowledge worker must be clear about what people should know about their area, especially what they can and cannot produce. Ultimately, becoming a learning organization requires first becoming a teaching organization.

Unlike manual or skilled laborers, knowledge workers are paid to know something we (managers) don't. You have the knowledge, we don't. In the old labor and skill model of organizations, managers had held most of the jobs of the people they supervised. They came up the ladder, jobs changed slowly, the people at the top knew every job in the plant. They were in a position, through their experiences, to specify the information and knowledge needs for employees.

Today no two career paths are the same, no two experience profiles are the same. Knowledge workers cannot assume their managers know what they do. Thus, it is imperative that the knowledge worker educate his associates as to what his job and knowledge are.

Lastly, the knowledge worker must define his or her information needs. In the past this was a management task, because information was scarce. Today, information is becoming a commodity, and the knowledge worker will have to learn and answer the question "What information do you need to do your job?" Usually the question has not been asked, and whatever you answer without checking most certainly will be wrong.

The nature of knowledge is that it makes itself obsolete. On the other hand, skills change very slowly. My ancestors were printers in Holland. The skills didn't change for 400 years. The printer learned his skills during his apprenticeship and never had to learn anything new. There has been no change in stone masonry for 2500 years. The tools are still the same. Socrates, who was a stone mason, could do the work today. Knowledge changes much faster. The problem is that we are not organized to learn; we are organized to preserve skills.

How do you manage change in knowledge work? By organized abandonment – by getting rid of yesterday. New ideas need good people who must be pulled off of yesterday's tasks. There is nothing more futile than trying to keep a corpse from stinking. Managers must plan for organized abandonment, and manage change. Get rid of yesterday; move onto the new. The new always requires able people, who take change for granted and see it as an opportunity.

Volunteers, not employees?

In knowledge work, the means of production is now owned by the knowledge worker. They are mobile and can work anywhere. They keep their resumes in their bottom drawer. Consequently, they must be managed as volunteers, not as employees. Only the unskilled need the employer more than the employer needs them.

Managing volunteers is an American specialty – no other country has a tradition of volunteerism like America. What are some of the things that make for a happy volunteer?

- seeing results;
- knowing what he/she is doing;
- knowing the objectives;
- knowing why he/she is there;
- having responsibility;
- setting the goals; and
- being expected to help set direction.

So, what does this teach us about managing knowledge workers? The job of management is to make them effective. There are a number of ways to do this:

- make demands on knowledge workers and hold them account-able;
- give them responsibility;
- put in stretch goals they can be proud of achieving;
- make sure they have training and education;
- place people so that they are productive;
- give them freedom so that they develop their own standards; and
- ensure they have rewards and recognition.

In short, managers must change people's behavior through appropriate rewards and recognition – the most potent form of which is peer recognition – and by setting stretch goals. It is important for knowledge workers to be involved in setting their own standards for reaching those goals. One way to start is by accessing the job requirements and then reviewing what contribution the knowledge worker can make.

There are three critical areas to consider when managing knowledge workers as volunteers:

1. *Results* are like your box office returns. They are a gauge of the productivity of your knowledge workers. People must be able to produce.

2. *Manners* are the lubricating oil of the organization. Moving bodies touching each other creates friction, but you can function as long as you can interact. Don't allow bad manners, and don't allow people to confuse "freedom" with abandoning manners.
3. *Responsibility* is key to motivation. Demand that people take responsibility for the expectations others have of them. Start with commitments to your boss, then your subordinates. Then be clear about what you need from them. Remember, we do not automatically know what others do and need, and they do not know what we do and need. Talk to each other.

The key to productivity is abandoning work that does not need to be done. To make organized abandonment systematic, I suggest a policy of reviewing all products, processes, and services every three years, asking the question: if we were not already in this business, or performing this activity, and knowing what we know now, would we enter into it now? If the answer is "No," then take action to stop it now – *do not study it!* Near successes can hinder innovation and are dangerous. They encourage the continuation of work that should be abandoned. Organized abandonment must be built into your business.

This also extends to the people. The ultimate test of management is succession. Great leaders are too often followed by collapse of the business, because the issue of succession is ignored. Too often, leaders pick their successors, and they tend to pick carbon copies of themselves, and carbon copies are always weak. Two institutions – the Church and the Military – have endured in part because they do not allow their leaders to select their own successors.

Another strength of these two institutions is a robust hierarchy. I know that this goes against current wisdom, but let me assure you, the "death of hierarchy" is nonsense! Someone must be in charge, and have clear authority. The issue is not "leadership" in the abstract, but "leadership for what purpose?" Great charismatic leaders can spread tragedy. On the other hand, Harry Truman had the leadership and charisma of a dead fish – yet he was an effective executive. He was able to create a structure which acted on purpose, not on charisma.

Now, I am not advocating dysfunctional, bogged-down, self-absorbed hierarchies. The worst thing in the world for any organization is for it to focus its attention and energy internally. It is imperative that you begin your examination of the business from outside. What goes on inside is a means, not an end. There are only costs on the inside, there are no results. Results are on the outside. The outside world is where dramatic social and economic changes are occurring. The pressure to increase the productivity of knowledge work comes not only from the desire of individual companies to gain a competitive advantage, but from our collective need to meet the challenges posed by these changes. Get out there! See how things really work, from your customer's, supplier's, ally's, competitor's points of view. Certainly, you must know your core competencies, but look at the environment, look for gaps that your core competencies can address. Don't start with your current products! You will not see anything new and you will miss opportunities. Don't even be happy satisfying your current customers. They will lull you into obscurity. Listen to the environment and look for those gaps that you aren't taking seriously. Take them seriously before they kill you.

This may sound like a lot of work, and it is, but the nice thing about having an organization full of knowledge workers is that they can all be working on these very issues. The organization no longer has to rely on the executive suite to do its knowledge work. People throughout the firm can be asked, encouraged, and even required to think like a CEO. It is up to the CEO and the rest of the managers to enable these knowledge workers to be productive by getting rid of all of the distractions, and by appreciating them for what they are: highly skilled people who are interested in turning their attention to the achievement of your organization's objectives. Do not squander their knowledge – the most valuable resource your organization will ever see. Executives who recognize the role of information and knowledge in the organization today hold the future of business in their hands.

Part II

Knowledge and the Organization

When asked to rate the significance Knowledge Management has had at the organizational level (e.g. roles, functions of communities of practice, infrastructure), more than half of the respondents chose a 4, 3, or 2 (see Fig. II.1).

This was surprising to us, since we believed that if knowledge management is having an impact (and our graph in Chapter 1 indicates that this group thinks it is), it would be felt at the organizational level. Most of the cases discussed at the Knowledge Advantage events over the years and the work being done by our firms deals with organization-wide issues. It may very well be that, because so much work is being done at the organizational level, it is here that the highest expectations for returns are as well. As with any new practice, there will always be learning and transition costs in any knowledge management undertaking. Plus, it is at the organization level

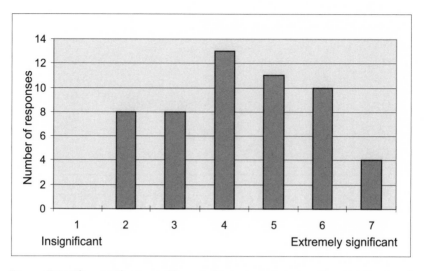

Figure II.1: The significance of knowledge management at the organizational level

where the greatest rubs occur between individual action and strategic intent. "The literature and promise of knowledge management build high expectations," says Vickie Peters, Director of Strategic Planning at the American Heart Association's National Center. "The reality of implementation (cost, changing human behavior and skills, etc.) is beginning to push us from the peak [of inflated expectations]." Richard Armstrong, Manager of Continuous Improvement at Bechtel, echoes these sentiments: "I think we need to better align the people component (which includes organization) with business drivers to make this impact happen."

Nonaka, Bauer, Bartlett, and Quinn all explain *why* organizations need to change, and even *what* they need to change into, but as always the hardest part of any transition is the *how*. Of course, the "how" will be very different for various organizations, depending upon their starting points, other initiatives underway, and the perceived urgency of such changes. It is for this very reason that we have not assembled here a selection of case studies of firms grappling with such transitions. Not because such cases would be uninteresting – and there is much that can be learned from the experiences of others – but this book is about those factors which should remain as beacons, guiding organizations through such churning waters. In the midst of the difficulties entailed in the organizational transformation that accompanies taking on a knowledge-based approach to business, refer to the chapters that follow. They will remind you of the sort of positive organizational impact we know is possible.

Chapter 5

The Dynamics
of Knowledge Creation

Ikujiro Nonaka,

University of California at Berkelely

Introduction

Usually there is not much to discuss about the creation of a professorship and it does not create any intellectual debate. However, recently a new professorship at Berkeley received a lot of attention and analysis from the American and British press. I have been given the title of Xerox Distinguished Professor in Knowledge, Haas School of Business. Journalists joined professors, particularly professors of philosophy, in saying that they could not understand what a professor of knowledge knows or teaches. Moreover, a chair in knowledge could not be more misplaced than at a business school, an institution dedicated to profits. According to them, where profit is pursued, knowledge can only be secondary. *The Economist* echoed these sentiments with the headline; "Mr. Knowledge: America's management industry needs a champion for its latest buzzword. A 62-year-old Japanese academic fits the bill." The article then tracked the rapid growth of the emerging field of knowledge management.

In my opinion, philosophy is not just thinking in an armchair. One has to face reality. On the other hand, practice without reflection does not provide sustainable knowledge advantage. In today's complex world, we need a more fundamental way of thinking. In business or management we need to incorporate epistemology or philosophical thinking in our business practices.

Some years ago I wrote an article on "The knowledge creating company" in the *Harvard Business Review*. The first paragraph says: "In an economy where the only certainty is uncertainty, the one sure source of lasting competitive advantage is knowledge. When markets shift technology, competitors multiply, and the products become obsolete almost overnight, successful companies are those that consistently create new knowledge, disseminate it widely throughout the organization, and quickly embody it in new technologies and products. These activities define the knowledge creating company, whose sole business is continuous innovation."

Since then, several concepts and methods have been developed in the field of knowledge management, and these can be categorized in two ways. The first is the measurement of knowledge. Measuring intellectual capital or assets helps us to understand the difference between the value of physical assets and market evaluation. The second category is the management of knowledge, that is, capturing the knowledge or skills of individuals to increase the efficiency of knowledge and skill exploitation. More than 30 of the Fortune 500 companies have appointed CKOs – chief knowledge officers – to manage organizational knowledge. These advances push the frontier of knowledge management in the way that they develop the "how to" of knowledge management for practitioners.

However, we are more interested in developing a theory of organizational knowledge *creation*. While existing arguments on knowledge management emphasize capturing, exploiting and disseminating knowledge, I think that the most critical process is the continuous creation of knowledge. Knowledge is dynamic and living, thus our research focus is on such dynamic processes of knowledge creation, not static output. Our goal is to conceptualize the knowledge creating process and, hopefully, to measure it to some extent.

The prototype of knowledge creation can be found in new product development processes. We have been observing these processes for over ten years, and have developed the following framework.

Knowledge creation and SECI model

There are two types of knowledge: tacit and explicit. Tacit knowledge is personal, context specific, and therefore hard to formalize and communicate. We know more than we can tell. Tacit knowledge is subjective, experience-based knowledge that cannot be expressed in words, sentences, numbers and formulae. It is very context specific. Tacit knowledge includes beliefs, images, intuition, mental models, and technical skills – like the expertise of the craftsman. The other kind of knowledge is explicit knowledge or codified knowledge. Explicit knowledge refers to knowledge that is transmittable in a formal systematic language.

These two types of knowledge have been discussed since the age of the Greeks in terms of epistemology, philosophy or theology, and visions. Since Plato and Descartes, westerners have tended to deal only with explicit knowledge. In Japan there are not many philosophers, but one of the most famous is called Kitaro Nishida. He states that "perfect truth pertains to the individual person and is actual. Perfect truth therefore cannot be expressed in words, and such things as scientific truth cannot be considered perfect truth." (Nishida 1990). According to Nishida, knowledge is personal knowledge, and it is context specific. Tacit knowledge is individualistic, as perfect truth cannot be expressed in words. Hence, scientific truth, says Nishida, cannot be considered perfect truth.

In Japan, silence is said to be golden because those who talk too much cannot understand anything. Thus, going out to the field and experiencing is highly valued. Consequently, many Japanese companies go into the field in order to gain experience. In short, Japanese tend to emphasize tacit knowledge, crafts and skills.

In our understanding, tacit knowledge and explicit knowledge are not totally separate. Rather, they are mutually complementary.

They interact and interchange with each other in the creative activities of human beings. Our model of dynamic knowledge creation is anchored in the assumption that human knowledge is created and expanded through social interactions between tacit and explicit knowledge. We call this interaction knowledge conversion.

Excessive focus on explicit knowledge leads to paralysis by analysis. Over-evaluation of tacit knowledge tends to lead to reliance on past success. Therefore, we need dynamic interactions between the two to reach beyond experiences. The conversion between the two kinds of knowledge often begins with the individual and is then continuously amplified in quality and quantity.

We have four modes of knowledge conversion:

♦ socialization;
♦ externalization;
♦ combination; and
♦ internalization.

Socialization, which is the conversion from tacit to tacit, is a process of creating tacit knowledge such as shared mental models and technical skills through shared experiences. The key to acquiring tacit knowledge is experiencing, particularly some form of shared experience. Apprentices work with their masters and learn craftsmanship, not through language but through observation, imitation and practice. In the business setting, on-the-job training uses basically the same principle.

The second mode is externalization, that is, the conversion from tacit to explicit knowledge. This is the process of articulating tacit knowledge into explicit concepts or languages. This mode is important for the entire knowledge-creation process in that tacit knowledge becomes explicit, often through metaphors, analogies, concepts and models.

Combination of explicit with explicit knowledge is the third mode. Combination and systemization of concepts through symbols such as language or figures is achieved through media such as documents, meetings, telephone conversations or computerized communications. Information technology can be very effectively used to enhance combination. The recent progress in knowledge management has largely been made by facilitating this conversion mode.

Finally, internalization is the conversion process from explicit into tacit knowledge. Internalization is the process of embodying explicit knowledge, and it is closely related to learning by doing. The new knowledge created through combination is internalized into individual tacit knowledge again. Thus it becomes part of the tacit knowledge base in the form of shared mental models or technical know-how, becoming valuable knowledge assets.

The model with its four modes is called the SECI model after the first letter of each of the conversion types. In the SECI model, all of the four modes need to be realized as an integrated process of knowledge creation. Unless shared knowledge is articulated, it cannot be easily leveraged by the organization as a whole. Sharing and accumulation of tacit knowledge, or isolated combination or internalization of explicit knowledge are only parts of the entire process. Personalized tacit knowledge needs to be shared, conceptualized, systemized and disseminated throughout the organization, and then internalized by individual members of the organization. The process remains partial and incomplete if any of the conversion modes is omitted or no balance among them is achieved.

For example, the comptroller of a company may collect information from throughout the company and put it together in a financial report. This systemization of explicit knowledge does not expand the organizational knowledge base by itself. Only when tacit and explicit knowledge interact can innovation occur.

Organizational knowledge creation is a continuous and dynamic process of interaction between tacit and explicit knowledge. Not many individuals can share their knowledge freely. However, to create new knowledge, it is necessary to transcend the personal sphere. Teams need to articulate new knowledge and to combine it with existing knowledge so that they can share it with other groups or departments to create organizational knowledge.

Thus, knowledge creation is a process of self-transcendence, and organizations are places for the creation of knowledge. Organizations need to support individuals, rather than control them, because they are the source of tacit knowledge.

The SECI model (see Fig. 5.1) describes processes of self-transcendence placed in organizations that facilitate knowledge creation. The individual transcends himself, or herself, through socialization.

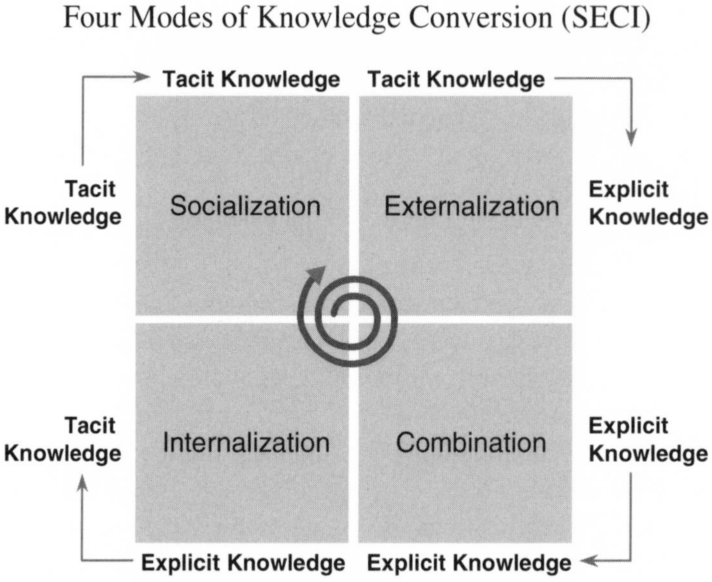

Four Modes of Knowledge Conversion (SECI)

Figure 5.1: SECI as process of self-transcendence

Externalization helps teams to transcend their current knowledge. Combination helps teams to reach the organization level. Finally internalization means to transcend the super-personal level and to reach the personal tacit level again. In short, the SECI model offers a completely different perspective on organizations as places that facilitate self-transcendence of individuals. Thus knowledge creation indicates a paradigm shift away from old control-type management thinking.

Knowledge-creating activity

In reality, it is a silly question to ask a company whether it engages in knowledge creation or not. A typical response would be "this is not a university." In reality – that is, in the organizational context – people do not know whether they engage in knowledge creation or not. Hence, we need to assess knowledge creation in terms of concrete actions. This is a reason why we have been observing and analyzing the innovation process as a prototype of knowledge creation for over

20 years. The analysis of activities has led us to identify several components or factors linked to knowledge conversions.

First, in the socialization process, it is necessary to walk around inside and outside the company to capture tacit knowledge. As knowledge is living and context specific, walking around outside of the company provides access to knowledge embodied in someone outside of the company. We need to be on the spot to acquire tacit knowledge with all our body's five senses, through such activities as direct interactions with customers. Similarly, capturing knowledge by walking around inside the company is necessary to access and acquire knowledge that already exists at the actual job sites in the company.

An example of extensive walking around is Hewlett Packard. HP is said to practice management by walking around or wandering about. According to Tom Davenport (a consultant, and co-author of *"Working Knowledge: How Organizations Manage What They Know"*), one of the problems with reengineering is that it forgets people. People who wander around seem to be redundant, so they are easily laid off. However, their activity is critical to capturing living, organic knowledge on the spot. Further, accumulating, disseminating, and sharing of tacit knowledge directly with colleagues or subordinates are very important components of socialization. Getting rid of people who do socialize weakens the tacit knowledge base of the company.

The second process is externalization, that is, articulating tacit knowledge. The process of expressing one's ideas employs images and words, concepts or forms generated in dialogs, using deductive and inductive methods. For example, metaphor and analogy are important expressions that help to articulate tacit knowledge when no suitable expression for a given image can be found through deductive or inductive methods. In such cases, illustration through metaphors and analogies is useful. Images and stories similarly convey tacit knowledge. For example, experts can support the translation of the tacit knowledge of their customers into readily understandable, explicit knowledge.

Very critical to this externalization process is the notion of dialog. Dialog here refers to face-to-face communication between individuals in which they share their beliefs and know-how in order to articulate their thinking. The articulation of tacit knowledge, even though it is very difficult, can be achieved when we engage in dialog, and communicate with our eyes, features, gestures and even through what the Chinese call KI, that is energy. Metaphors and analogies can be useful for externalization because it may be better to convey images by using a variety of figurative languages.

Dialog is different from debate. It encompasses instantaneous feedback, simultaneous exchange of ideas, and continuous mutual enhancement. Debate means to play a game, to play logic. In dialog, since it comes from one's guts, one represents his/her beliefs, philosophy of life, the way s/he lives. So dialog is real, as one cannot change his/her position like in a game. True dialog means to be sincere, to respect each other, and to collaborate with each other. In dialog, we bet our life. Therefore, trust is very critical to promote real dialog.

The combination process is where new explicit knowledge is captured and integrated. The process of collecting externalized knowledge from outside and inside of the company is what combination is about. Disseminating explicit knowledge and editing existing knowledge are important factors in combination. I need not explain this in detail because combination is efficiently promoted by information technology.

Finally, internalization means embodying explicit knowledge through action and practice. The process includes internalizing, through on-the-job training, in order to actualize concepts and strategies or communications on innovation and improvement. Direct experience takes time and is very expensive. Therefore, we may use a variety of simulations or experiments to enhance internalization. Recently, such instruments have been well developed by multimedia and so on.

The four conversion modes and their components are the essential activities of knowledge creation. By observing these activities we can assess the extent to which an organization is creating knowledge. We have been conducting surveys on several companies, regarding their knowledge-creating activities. The questionnaire we developed enables us to find out the strengths and weaknesses of the company, in relation to knowledge creation. So far, our findings show that high-performance companies usually score highly in all four modes. The companies that score highly in only one mode tend to be low performers.

The knowledge creating process is a continuous process. Stopping at one mode and not moving to the next endangers the outcome. The process seems to lose energy, and becomes weak. However, we can develop a variety of instruments to support the continuous movement through the SECI process.

Knowledge vision

The knowledge creation process is supported in several ways. We need to design the vision, strategy, structure, system and leadership to promote the process continuously. We call these conditions enabling conditions. Starting with a vision, we can propose dreams, aspirations, or sometimes outrageous goals. Visions are images that challenge us to transcend our own boundaries.

3M pursues "innovation." Matsushita's vision is "human electronics." Boeing intends to be at the leading edge of aeronautics, to be a pioneer. This understanding of visions shows that my interpretation is different from that of the "visionary company." The company vision is the one characteristic that differentiates the company from its competitors. Companies can distinguish themselves through the vision and the operationalization of the vision.

At 3M, I spent almost two weeks with the corporate CEO, and at the production center. The continuous striving for innovation is important, but the second part of 3M's credo, "Thou shall not kill an idea," a metaphor taken from the *Old Testament*, is more fundamental. This emphasizes the need for discipline and the need to stick to your vision without interruption. Knowledge creation is a very fragile process. Therefore, in this process we need continuous support through care, love and trust. The easiest way to hurt people is to kill their ideas at the stage of idea generation. I am afraid I have killed a number of students' ideas simply because they did not agree with me. I did it unconsciously. Anyway, if you stick to such nurturing discipline, which is a premise for knowledge, the amount and quality of knowledge you generate over time is considerably larger. It depends on your discipline.

At Matsushita, they are disciplined to see the truth beyond profitability. The greatest enemy today is yesterday's success. Matsushita is an extremely fierce competitor; they are sharp up to a certain point. However, they are disciplined not to imitate, but to make an innovative product. It is discipline that enables us to create naturally developing knowledge. Knowledge creation is a way of life.

Knowledge strategy

The second point is strategy. From the viewpoint of knowledge creation, the essence of strategy lies in developing the organizational capability to acquire, create, accumulate, and exploit knowledge. The most critical element of corporate strategy is to conceptualize a vision about what kind of knowledge we should develop and to operationalize it into a management system for implementation.

For example, NEC first made the connection between computer and communication explicit in its company vision. Computer and communication were projected to be integrated by the year 2000. There were several bridging technologies identified, such as semiconductors. However, mapping the path towards integration was not enough.

Knowledge is by nature self-organizing. If we conceptualize a strategy in terms of a complete visible product, it's the typical way of product portfolio management. We have to see the invisible knowledge that constitutes the finished products. Therefore, identification by knowledge means that once we see a product in terms of core technologies, skills and services, we can see potential relationships and combinations. By doing so, we can identify flexible knowledge relationships that may correspond to the markets. How to incorporate this idea into strategy is a key issue.

NEC viewed technology as a knowledge system when it developed core technology programs at its Central Research Laboratories in 1975. At that time, the company was engaged in three main businesses: communications, computers, and semiconductors. Because it was difficult to coordinate R&D in these different areas, it was necessary to grasp technologies at a more abstract level, that is, knowledge. First, base technologies were identified by forecasting product groups for a decade into the future, including the extraction of technologies common to and necessary for them. Synergistically related basic technologies were then grouped into "core technologies," such as pattern recognition, image processing, and VLSI. Since 1975, NEC has expanded its core technology programs using autonomous teams. Today it has 36 core technology programs in action.

In addition, NEC devised a concept called the "strategic technology domain" (STD) in order to match core technologies with business activities. An STD links several core technologies with business activities. Thus, an STD represents not only a product domain but also a knowledge domain. At present, there are six STDs:

1   functional materials/devices;
2   semiconductors;
3   materials/devices/functional machinery;
4   communications systems;
5   knowledge-information systems; and
6   software.

Those STDs interact with core technology programs in a matrix. By combining core technology programs and the STDs, the knowledge bases at NEC are linked horizontally and vertically. Through this endeavor, NEC

Perspective of "C&C"

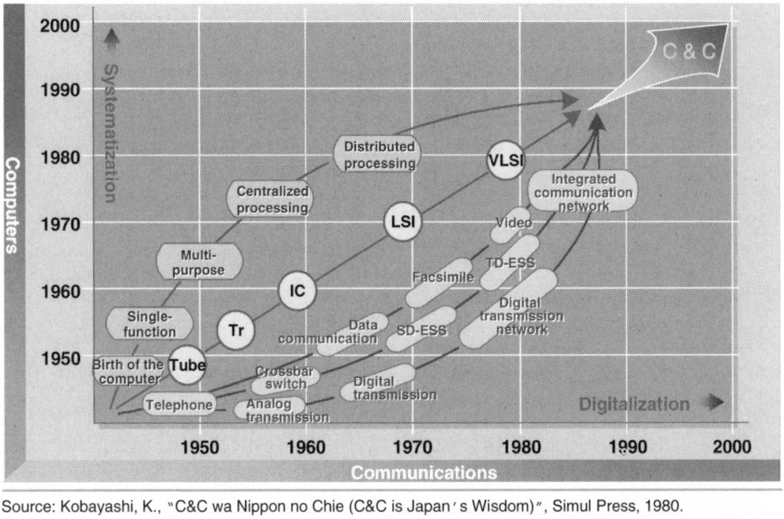

Source: Kobayashi, K., "C&C wa Nippon no Chie (C&C is Japan's Wisdom)", Simul Press, 1980.

Figure 5.2: NEC

has attempted to develop a corporate strategic intention of knowledge creation at every organizational level.

It took NEC almost 17 years to institutionalize this system. However, the fundamental idea behind NEC's style of managing core technologies has been studied by others such as Siemens, who adopted similar techniques. It is interesting to note that at 3M, they manage technology platforms. 3M categorizes its knowledge base into 33 technology platforms. I have no sound theory, but I would guess 30 to 40 core technologies are the limit in terms of managing the knowledge base.

Intellectualizing systems and organization

So far, I have dealt with vision and strategy. Let me proceed to systems. Knowledge is not only embedded within the organization. It is also embedded in the relationships between organizations. Thus, the question is how to create a network of communities of knowledge; the knowledge of the distribution channels, competitors, customers, users, clients, supporting industries, regional communities, subsidiaries, and so on. How to incorporate the knowledge embedded within the market needs to be managed carefully. Perhaps a very capable salesperson will do this even unconsciously. He may have a dialog with a customer during which he shows some prototypes or they share their experiences. Behind such interaction, he has been building a mutual understanding and trust. The purpose of this interaction is, from my point of view, not simply the acquisition of explicit knowledge. Because explicit knowledge is what every company possesses in abundance. The needs in terms of knowledge can be much more precisely described with tacit knowledge. The tacit, individual mental models, gut feelings and the like are needed. To capture and incorporate such tacit knowledge within the organization, the salesperson relies largely on embedded sales skills, embodied mental models that facilitate the conversion of tacit into explicit knowledge.

Sales skills are very important. However, they are very individualistic and personal. Organizations have to strive to build a system that supports the continuous elicitation of tacit knowledge in the markets, regardless of the qualities and capabilities of individuals.

Companies have to construct knowledge conversion systems that mediate processes from the market to the company and from the company to the market.

Let me show you an example, the case of Sharp, to make this easier to understand. There are two interesting knowledge conversion systems there. One is called the new lifestyle-planning group. The other one is corporate technology and developing project team. Let us start with the New Lifestyle Center.

This group was created in 1985, and the first director of the center has now become the CEO of Sharp Corporation, Mr Tsuji. The center was conceived just about the time when Sharp started re-thinking its business domain. The Corporate R&D Group reviewed the company's business domain from a *technical* viewpoint. At the same time, Sharp recognized the need to review its business domain from the *consumers'* viewpoints. It was for this reason that the unconventional center was established. It has the purpose of getting deeply involved with the market and to convert tacit knowledge, to create a

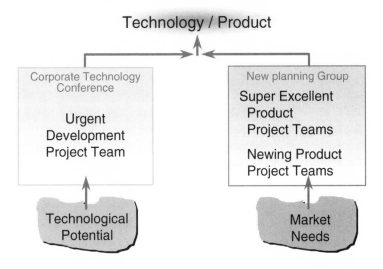

Figure 5.3: Sharp

new concept and to propose this new concept to the other divisions of the company.

There are about 40 to 50 people working in the center. They report directly to the top management. The New Lifestyle Center employs four different systems:

1   the trend leadership system;
2   the lifestyle creative system;
3   joint research in different industries; and
4   collaboration with the corporate design group.

The trend leadership system organizes about 600 leading consumers, ranging from middle-school students to senior citizens, divided into numerous demographic groups. These consumers provide detailed feedback on prototypes within a week. If Sharp were to ask consultants, it would take them months. Sharp prefers face-to-face interaction with these leading customers to surveys. This is important because often consumers cannot articulate what they experience with products. In such a case, face-to-face interaction or other media such as video recordings can tell something about the consumer experience, which will be analyzed later on. Through such forecast groups, the center has access to a large amount of high-quality knowledge and information, from which consumer trends emerge with timeframes of between one and ten years.

The second system, the lifestyle creative system, organizes consumers who are not interviewed on their opinion on a prototype, but are free to provide feedback on their own experiences with prototypes in real life situations. Sharp does not ask them how they like products but allows them to experiment with the prototypes in real life situations as it pleases them. Based on the sometimes surprisingly new ways of using prototypes, improvements can be made that promise to establish a new lifestyle.

Michael Cusumano states that the secret of Microsoft is not really Bill Gates. The secret is the way they develop their software. They use an iterative prototype approach, rather than the old sequential approach. They integrate different prototypes of parts at each of the several milestones when they simulate test runs to understand how well all the different software parts harmonize. In essence, their way to systemize and package this development approach is an important factor in Microsoft's continuing success.

The third system is joint research with companies in other industries. Sharp uses the knowledge and information of competitors or other companies in other industries. For example, when Sharp first developed the microwave oven with a toaster function, it used information and knowledge obtained through joint research with a food processing company. Sharp was able to develop a new product category and the food processing company could improve foodstuffs to be heated in the microwave oven.

The other important system is called the urgent project system. When you create a new concept, from one to ten years ahead, you have to develop some core technology or base technology to realize the concept. Such kind of important projects are organized as urgent development projects. At the corporate technology conference, the teams for urgent development projects are selected and the project is kicked off. The teams are empowered through gold badges that symbolize authority and power. Every member of the team receives a gold badge. In Japanese gold is called "Kin." "Kin" also sounds like the first syllable of the Japanese word "Kinkyu" which means urgent. Therefore, if you wear the gold badge it symbolizes special significance, power and the importance of the project. The mission of an urgent project team is to develop strategically important products or technology within 18 months. Headquarters awards an unlimited budget. With direct support from the president, middle managers heading the urgent project teams are given top priority in the use of company facilities or equipment. Thus all divisional managers and relevant people have to listen to the team members and support them.

One important condition for such adjunct development teams is that they span the boundaries of more than three business groups. This system does not apply to small technology or product developments. It is used to mobilize the entire knowledge and skills embedded throughout the organization. At Sharp about 15–20 teams develop different products simultaneously. If you want to engage in the difficult application of such a system with one or two teams, it does not mean much. We have to gain a critical mass. In corporate design groups, for example, more than 200 industrial designers work together with the planners. Designers can not only draw pictures but they are also capable of visualizing total images or any concepts. The promotion of concepts is a very early stage in the development process. As you change image into reality, tacit knowledge into concrete drawings, you can see the next logical step more clearly. They have lots of dialog but if we include industrial designers, the conceptualizing can happen very fast. What you have been talking about could become a prototype very quickly. Such rapid visualization can facilitate much dialog.

Sharp created the lifestyle focus center and employs the three systems to convert tacit knowledge into explicit knowledge. The role of corporate design is to facilitate the process through visualizing and prototyping.

Combination, the following conversion mode, is done quickly at Sharp by turning the prototypes to the operating systems of specific divisions and employing concurrent engineering to facilitate the start of mass production. Such crystallization of a concept is done quickly. These are examples of how organizational systems at Sharp support knowledge creation. For organizations, it is important to design such systems consciously or unconsciously.

Hypertext organization

The third aspect of enablers deals with organizational structure. Organizational structure at Sharp is similar to hypertext. The analogy of hypertext refers to a layered structure with multiple linkages. Hypertexts provide simultaneous access to multiple layers. The case of Sharp shows that we need to have organizational structures with different layers for task force, bureaucracy, and hierarchy. Hypertext organization is made of interconnected layers or contexts: the business system, the project team, and the knowledge base. The central layer is the business system layer in which normal, routine operations are carried out. The project team layer is where multiple project teams engage in knowledge-creating activities such as new product development. Finally there is the knowledge-base layer, where organizational knowledge generated in the two other layers is re-categorized and re-contextualized. The knowledge base is embedded in vision, organizational culture, and technology.

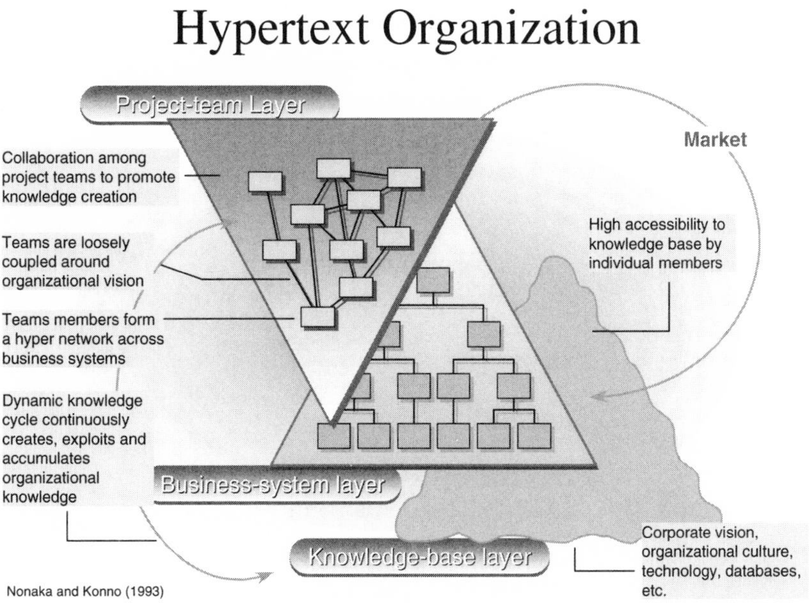

Hypertext Organization

Project-team Layer

Collaboration among
project teams to promote
knowledge creation

Teams are loosely
coupled around
organizational vision

Teams members form
a hyper network across
business systems

Dynamic knowledge
cycle continuously
creates, exploits and
accumulates
organizational
knowledge

Business-system layer

Knowledge-base layer

Market

High accessibility to
knowledge base by
individual members

Corporate vision,
organizational culture,
technology, databases,
etc.

Nonaka and Konno (1993)

Figure 5.4: Hypertext organization

My idea of enablers comes from, or is derived from, interactions
between tacit/explicit and the four modes of knowledge conversion.
That is the basic framework – very simple but strong. To promote
socialization and externalization, it is much better to have the structure of face-to-face relationships. Cross-functional teams are about
such face-to-face interactions, but managing such teams is not easy
because of the variety of different experiences among team members.
Often such teams lack a common language. Therefore, we need someone to coordinate, translate, and lead. Usually the cross-functional
team has 10–30 members. However beyond 30 it is no longer a team,
but becomes an organization in its own right.

At Fuji Xerox, for example, 17 cross-functional teams developed FX 3500. Somehow, they have core members who can do this
process. They may be called knowledge activists. The four guys at
Fuji Xerox all have cross-functional experience. The most important one is personnel – knowing what kind of knowledge information is located where. Market research and quality control take the
longest time. At Fuji Xerox, integrating the four as a self-contained
whole is key. I think the Chinese proverb says that a gang of four

makes a revolution. Somehow it always seems to be along the number four, I do not know why. Because of this, in a gang of four, individuals can represent the organization holistically.

Once they have developed the concept, it has to be crystallized and put into practice. The creation of a division to incorporate new ideas needs to be done quickly. Speed, energy, and agility are very important. The hierarchy, however, takes time to carry out a job.

We need both self-organizing, self-contained project teams and a bureaucracy. Because bureaucracy is very good at combining and internalizing, it excels in terms of efficiency. We do need both aspects. A business system is a hierarchy. When a concept is developed it is quickly converted to the specific division; a strong hierarchy is in place. Between the two types of structures that interact, we can develop knowledge and knowledge-based innovations. The structure should facilitate the creation of knowledge.

Middle-up-down management

We talked about vision, strategy, system, structure, now we need to address the issue of people. People are an important enabling condition. To succeed in knowledge creation, organizations need someone who continuously nurtures, develops, supports and cares. What kind of people can fulfill this role? In my opinion they are middle managers, as top management cannot oversee every knowledge-creating activity throughout the organization. Middle managers are not a cancer, as some management fads claim, but they are the important promoters who initiate activities that lead towards a complete movement along the knowledge spiral.

The role middle managers play in knowledge creation cannot be explained using either the top-down or the bottom-up management model. I call the new model middle-up-down model. In this model, top management creates a vision or dream, while middle management develops more concrete concepts or middle-range theories that employees at the front line can understand and implement. Middle managers try to solve contradictions between what top management hopes to create and what actually exists in the real world. In other words, top management's role is to create a grand theory, while middle management tries to create a mid-range theory that can be tested empirically. They provide their subordinates with a conceptual framework that helps them to make sense of their own experience. This is very, very difficult. Maybe creating a vision is easier than this part. In addition, frontline people face the reality. They do not care about a vision. Hence, middle managers have to strike a balance between idealistic and realistic approaches.

Middle managers are strategically positioned to unify strategic macro information, which is more or less explicit knowledge, with the actual feel of micro information. Many of them have tacit knowledge, create or produce concepts, and live up to being the project leaders using self-organizing distributed leadership. Not all of the middle managers can achieve or sustain such leadership. However, distributed leadership is what we try to address with the educational programs at the Graduate School of Knowledge Science, at Japan Advanced Institute of Science and Technology, which opened in 1998.

Ba: place

I talked about the four modes of knowledge creation:

- *socialization*, that is, sharing experience;
- *externalization*, that is, articulating know how in words or forms;
- *combinations*, that is, systemizing words or forms; and
- *internalization* of word or forms through learning by doing.

I mentioned what kind of concrete activities we can utilize to achieve each conversion. In addition to that, I described the enablers who energize the spiral with speed and agility. Still, it is not clear why it becomes a spiral. The four modes of knowledge conversion and five enablers have to interact in some concrete place with integrated form. Everything interacts but it has to have some place, a concrete place. Knowledge creation does not occur in a vacuum.

What is the place – in Japanese: Ba – for knowledge creation? More specifically, a place can be physical, like an office, or dispersed business space. It can be virtual (e-mail, teleconference) or it can be mental, such as shared experiences, ideas and ideals. It can be a relationship, or people sharing a common goal. Shared mental space is the key for creating knowledge.

Ba is a time–space nexus, or as Heidegger expressed it, locationality that simultaneously includes space and time. The key concept in understanding Ba is "interaction." Knowledge is created through the interaction among individuals and/or between individuals and their environments, rather than an individual who operates alone in vacuum. Knowledge creation is a dynamic process that transcends existing boundaries. Thus Ba is the shared context where individuals interact and realize themselves as part of the environment on which their life depends. The shared context sets binding conditions for the participants as it limits the way in which the participants view the world, while providing a higher viewpoint.

As we have seen there are the four processes of SECI. To create movement along a spiral we need to have a different type of knowledge creating Ba – the physical, intellectual, and emotional place that knowledge workers share. New knowledge may be created by individual minds, but a network of interactions nourishes minds. Individuals share tacit knowledge, that the organization captures and communicates as explicit knowledge that further enriches individual tacit knowledge.

Two dimensions define Ba. First is the type of interaction, that is, whether the interaction takes place individually or collectively. The second dimension is the type of media used in such interactions, that is, whether the interaction is through physical, face-to-face contact or virtual media such as books, manuals, e-mail or teleconferences. Each Ba offers a context for a specific step in the knowledge creation process, though the respective relationships between single Ba and conversion modes are by no means exclusive. To build, maintain, and utilize Ba it is important to facilitate organizational knowledge creation. Hence, one has to understand the different characteristics of Ba and how they interact with each other. The following describes the characteristics of each Ba.

◆ *Originating Ba* is defined by individual and face-to-face interactions. It is the place where individuals share experiences, feelings, emotions, and mental models. It mainly offers a context for socialization, since an individual face-to-face interaction is the only way to capture the full range of physical senses and psycho-emotional reactions – such as ease or discomfort – which are important elements in sharing tacit knowledge. Originating Ba is an existential place in a sense. It is the world where an individual transcends the boundary between self and others, by sympathizing and/or empathizing with others. Removing the barrier between the self and others is important; again there are several philosophies to be considered, such as Descartes versus Nishida. Descartes states "I think therefore I am," thus he clearly separates between subject and object. In originating Ba people become part of the environment. In sharp contrast to Descartes, Nishida's motto is "I love, therefore I am." From originating Ba, care, love, trust, and commitment will emerge, which form the basis for knowledge conversions.

◆ *Dialoging Ba* is defined by collective and face-to-face interactions. This is the Ba where Nishida's world and the Cartesian world interact in thought. It is the place where individuals' mental models and skills are shared, converted into common terms, and articulated into concepts. Hence, dialoging Ba mainly offers a context for externalization. Individuals' tacit knowledge is shared and articulated through dialogs among participants. The articulated knowledge is also brought back into each individual, and further articulation occurs through self-reflection. Dialoging Ba is more consciously constructed compared to originating Ba. Selecting individuals with the right mix of specific knowledge and capabilities is the key in managing knowledge conversion in dialoging Ba. The extensive use of metaphors is one of the conversion skills required. The importance of sensitivity for meaning, and the will to make tacit knowledge explicit, is recognized at companies such as Honda and 3M. Here, dialoging Ba for collective reflection is institutionalized in the company culture. Initiators (conceptual leaders) are challenged to pursue their ideas. Consequently, "Thou shall not kill a new product idea" is a rule (at 3M) that provides an organizational-level, a Ba for dialog where people engage jointly in the creation of meaning and value.

◆ *Systemizing Ba* is defined by collective and virtual interactions. Systemizing Ba mainly offers a context for combination of existing explicit knowledge, as explicit knowledge can be transmitted relatively easily, to a larger number of people in written forms. Information technology, such as on-line networks, groupware, documentation, and databanks, offers a virtual collaborative environment to create systemizing Ba. Today, many organizations use such things as electronic mailing lists and news groups, through which participants can exchange necessary information or answer each other's questions, to collect and disseminate knowledge and information effectively and efficiently.

♦ *Exercising Ba* is defined by individual and virtual interactions. It mainly offers a context for internalization. Here, individuals embody explicit knowledge that is communicated through virtual media, such as written manuals or simulation programs. Exercising Ba is synthesizing Nishida's world and the Cartesian world through action, while dialoging Ba achieves this through thought.

We introduced four types of Ba. In order to provide a platform that supports the entire process of knowledge creation, we need not one

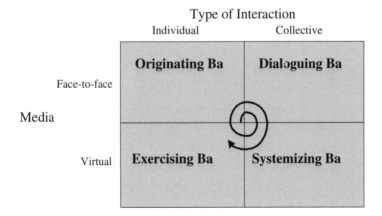

Ba, the shared space for interaction

Copyright: Nonaka, Toyama, and Konno, 1999

Figure 5.5: Four types of Ba

but multiple Ba to support an ongoing process. Why is this so critical? Let us use the metaphor of energy. Originating Ba supports socialization in a self-organizing way. Now knowledge is autonomously accumulated and converted through interaction. Top management facilitates the process by first compressing and concentrating the autonomous energy and then releasing and accumulating it. Thus compressing and reducing alternate. Finally, knowledge crystallizes. It is energy, time, space and energy. The fundamental rule of energy is to accumulate, compress, release and exercise.

We need multiple types of Ba to provide the necessary energy for knowledge processes. Ba exists at many ontological levels and these levels may be connected to form a greater Ba. Individuals form the Ba of teams, which in turn form the Ba of organizations. Then, the market environment becomes the Ba for the organization. As stated above, Ba is a concept that transcends the boundary between micro and macro. The organic interactions among these different levels of Ba can amplify the knowledge-creating processes.

Let me explain finally why a continuous spiral movement occurs. Perhaps the essence of our spiral is similar to Professor Brian Arthur's concept of increasing returns. When I was a student at the University of California at Berkeley I was strongly influenced by Professor Herbert Simon. His concept is basically problem solving and information processing. I still recall his metaphor of ants. It is a beautiful metaphor. He said, when you walk at the beach look at the paths left by ants. Each path is very complex. This complexity does not mean that ants have the capability for very complex cognition. Ants only know the direction to their home but they cannot understand the obstacle just in front of them. Therefore, it is trial and error and finally the ant arrives at home. Therefore the paths of the ants simply show the complexity of the environment. It has nothing to do with their cognitive capability. This metaphor shows that there are limits to information processing capability, hence bounded rationality or cognitive limits. Based on the metaphor of the ant, one could think that human beings are basically like ants. If so, hierarchies need to be established to overcome human beings' cognitive limits. We need hierarchy, division of labor, and specialization. This leads to bureaucracy but from the new perspective of an information-processing paradigm. I was strongly influenced by his way of thinking and I did my dissertation along these lines. However, since I have been observing innovation processes over ten years, I have viewed very different perspectives of human beings. In innovation processes the people involved, and more typically the leaders, had a dream, belief or hypothesis they wanted to realize. To make this dream come true they sometimes put their lives on the line. Arguing, fighting, the political process – these are all ways in which we justify our beliefs. It is part of life, as human beings, that we have cognitive limits, but nonetheless we try to challenge and transcend these limits.

The paradigm of knowledge creation goes beyond the cognitive limits and includes a little bit more of human nature. Human beings try to control and to get out of difficult situations, to be creative. Nonetheless, we have to admit that we surely have cognitive limits and that rationality is bounded. Our theory is different from Professor Simon's. Simon sets out to overcome cognitive limits by building a hierarchy. My conclusion is that to overcome cognitive limits, we need to create a variety of different perspectives.

If many would develop a variety of perspectives to overcome cognitive limits of bounded rationality concept, the shared mental space could be expanded. Mental space is continuously increased when we can somehow overcome the individual cognitive limits. Thus, we grow by creating, expanding each individual's knowledge domain or cognitive space, and sharing mental space. In this growth we transcend ourselves. So creating knowledge is to create continuously a new boundary of a shared mental model.

Information and knowledge

Finally, I would like to make a comment on knowledge. I have been conceptualizing strategy in terms of knowledge, not in terms of product. Thinking about strategy from a knowledge perspective is different, given the fact that knowledge is self-organizing and, despite our cognitive limits, it is boundless. To overcome this contradiction it is important to create a variety of perspectives. Continuously expanding shared mental space to challenge new boundaries. That is what the whole thing is about. However, knowledge is often confused with information. I would like to emphasize the difference between information and knowledge. Information is a commodity.

◆ Firstly, information as you already know, is a necessary medium for eliciting and creating knowledge. Information is a start. Information has to be internalized or embodied through thought and action. Only when it is internalized can we say that it is knowledge. A database is not knowledge, because it contains mere information.

◆ Secondly, information is passive, received from external sources. If we switch on the TV, lots of information comes out of it. In contrast, knowledge is active, generated by commitment and belief. People have something they would like to realize; they want to achieve something. These gut feelings are very important for knowledge creation, that is one of the reasons why I stress tacit knowledge.

◆ Thirdly, information is transient, efficiency concerns dominate. Knowledge is universal, some aesthetic values, aesthetic concerns dominate. Aspirations to be true, good, and beautiful are important in the pursuit of knowledge. We are continuously seeking something external. That is why knowledge is a subject in philosophy. Knowledge is defined traditionally in philosophy as "justified belief." In a sense belief is represented by tacit knowledge in our concept. To justify tacit knowledge it has to be converted into explicit knowledge that is then combined with other explicit knowledge.

I emphasize that we define knowledge as a dynamic human process of justifying the personal belief towards the truth. Organizations are the place for dynamic knowledge creation.

Chapter 6

Turning Knowledge into Innovation

Dr Bob Bauer,

Xerox PARC

The key to successful technologies that support knowledge initiatives is to ensure that they support the complementary "structures" of organizational practice. The organization of the knowledge workscape can be characterized by both the authorized structure within which work is done (designed structure: the structure around the work of organizations) and the emergent structure within that work (generated structure: the structure within the work organizations).

Three types of technologies support the richness of this duality in work practice: tools of the practice; enterprise libraries; and conversational tools. All of these must be present in individuals and communities of practice for the infrastructure to provide sustenance for successful knowledge ecologies. As an example, this chapter discusses activities of a collection of communities of practice that have successfully changed the framework for achieving architected, reusable technology components in Xerox heartland products. The Toolkit Working Group (TWG) is an example of a successful "emergent" constellation of several communities of practice through which "authorized" product programs have made significant advances in both innovation and time to market. We find that the productive use of the intranet by TWG is consistent with the presence of all three technology types.

I have a quote from a photojournalist called Scott Mooder. It's specifically about the issue of knowledge, and I think it captures the dichotomy and the difficulty of the issues around knowledge today. He says: "a culture and what it produces is made possible by, and is reflective of, the knowledge that underlies it." What this represents for me is, in fact, the challenge that we have of trying to connect the information flows that are so vital to the way that industry works today. It's the life-blood of any organization I think, going into the 21st Century. Knowledge itself, sitting in card catalogs or book stacks, is of absolutely no value. That knowledge is, as we say, "knowing at rest." The "knowing" that we really care about occurs where there are people that are active, making sense of it and actually taking action based on it.

Connections between knowledge and knowing

It is these various connections that I want to discuss: connections between the way that people work and the way they're organized into their work in formal ways, the way that they get information, and the way that they use it. Let me start with a definitional approach so that we all have a common understanding about knowledge, and what we mean by knowledge. It is decidedly different from information. This is a fairly common view and I'll show you a way that we actually emphasize this view. If we start with data, which is just the numbers, words, sounds, images, that is, the basic meat and potatoes of all of our work, information processing is about arranging and getting meaningful patterns out of that data in order to have something we can then make use of. Knowledge comes from putting information into productive use, from actually making it actionable. And so in the field of knowledge management, as it's called, or knowing, the challenge of this way of looking at the world and organizing, is really one of action. And if you ask yourself "what are the elements, what are the parameters that, in fact, lead people to be able to take action based on information?" there are decidedly different characteristics that you have to pay attention to. That's where the challenge comes in, where things start to get soft, and where we have to look at technologies differently.

When we move from data to information management we have to organize it, find patterns in it, group it, categorize it, put it in a form that people can comprehend; to make it manageable, if you will. But when we try to make it actionable, then we have to worry about things like, "what is the information related to? What other relationships are there? What's the context in which the information will be used and utilized?" And if that's the case, "do I need it?" "What's its relevance?" When we don't worry about things like that, progress and action slow down as we experience information overload. So relevance is critically important because access is not so difficult anymore these days. In fact, the difficulty of controlling access can be hard, but the relevance of that information is a more difficult parameter. Another point to consider is authenticity. "Can I trust the information? Who is it that I'm getting it from? What is it coming from? Is it a trusted source?" And finally, the experience of "have I done this before?" "What other things have I done that it's related to?" These are the parameters that we have to deal with.

The working definition that we use at Xerox for knowledge is that "knowledge is information put to productive use by people." Each organization or each mission can define what the definition of productivity is. There are economists that try to measure productivity, but I think what we all understand, and what we focus on, is this notion of use, of making the information flow, keeping it active, keeping it so it's actionable. We apply these four qualities:

- context, in terms of trade-offs, culture-related events;
- relevance, the priority, timeliness;
- authenticity, the trusted source; and
- connections, linkage with other information.

It is these kind of attributes that we try to pay attention to when we design new technologies, when we experiment with new infrastructures and systems that we work with. We do this in order to understand, first of all, where is the source? Where does this kind of information exist, and then what we can do about it?

When we talk about managing knowledge versus managing information, we are not just dealing with delivery and accessibility of the content of the information, there is also the process of adding value to that content. You can't just stop at getting the signals. Knowledge management means that each person who touches the information, if it's a knowledge organization, a knowledge generating and contributing organization, adds value by filtering, synthesizing, interpreting, pruning. There are technologies that do that and there are human endeavors that do that, and they're inextricably linked. From my experience of managing the Systems Lab at PARC, I would say that creating artificial agents that can do this by themselves is at best a long way off – well beyond my time of working – and is the least effective way of utilizing the technologies.

Information management is very heavily technology focused. It's about investing in large computers and fast networks, and creating good access to those networks. But that notion of dealing with knowledge, of "knowing" for an organization and its contribution and delivery on its mission, has to balance the work practice and culture of the way that the information is used along with the technology. This means that, in fact, rather than just assuming that information capture can be standardized and automated, there's a lot of soft stuff that goes on in the knowledge game, because it requires ongoing human input, whose variance can't really be automated. So when it comes to technology investment, this is about creating a technological environment for people that takes into account the way that people learn, the way they work, the way they organize, and the way they add value. It's about encouraging and enhancing and promoting the way of doing business, the way of dealing with information, such that everyone is a contributing factor to the knowledge.

Knowledge and ecologies

PARC currently has five research themes for the 21st century. The term we're using now to describe what I'm putting across is "knowledge ecologies." It's a little too cute, but it helps guide our work, and for me at least, it captures the notion better than knowledge management. Knowledge management is a term that sounds like you can take packets of knowledge and spread them around. It's knowledge as a quantity of something that you can pour into somebody's head or that you can pass around, as opposed to some organic utilization of it. If we take an organic model we can, as with any ecology, determine what its care and feeding ought to be, how it ought to be nurtured, what are the bad factors and the good factors that can help it, and then allow it to grow and have its own dynamics. We can observe and encourage it.

This notion of ecology means it isn't just about how we organize the work. It's not just about the technology we invest in, the processes that we put in place or the practices that people have. It's some interconnection, some interweaving of all of these factors, and that's what makes it difficult, makes it soft. I think that we're at the beginning of understanding what it means. What I'll share with you is three or four conceptual frameworks that have been helpful for us. I've learned about them and developed them with people at PARC, and at the Institute for Research on Learning, which is an organization in Menlo Park, California, that was spun out of PARC about ten years ago. It is an independent entity that has tried to study learning processes and practice.

Let me start by relating it to core competencies, a concept that was in vogue about five years ago and which I started working with after Xerox went through a massive change. We went through downsizing, reengineering, and all the other catchphrases that had to do with laying people off and changing our business. In the 1980s the Japanese came in and ate up Xerox's market because we were a monopoly and thought that we were immune to competition. The quality movement, which we adopted in the mid-80s, helped us get out of that hole. But what it didn't do was to change our perception of what roles each of us had. I was fortunate enough to be in the group of half a dozen people working with the CEO of Xerox, Paul Allaire, in 1990, to reorganize the 80-odd thousand people who worked for Xerox after the downsizing. The question we looked at was how to get people to have more of an end-to-end sense of the organization and the business, not just of their particular function.

We were the most highly functionalized organization that any business professor had ever seen. The CEO was the only one in the organization that had a handle on marketing and technology and sales and logistics, and it all came up to the one man at the top, and that clearly was going to be non-competitive.

We were organized that way for a reason, and we had obviously been successful and become a multi-billion-dollar organization, generating huge revenues year after year. At the time our biggest worry was, if we were going to cut up all of these functional hierarchies, what was going to happen to our core competence? This was a Prahalad term that was hot in the literature, an idea that Hamel and Prahalad were promulgating in the early 1990s. The competence, the skill base, and the capabilities of the organization are where we have to start in a knowledge ecology, in a knowledge management world. And the interesting thing is that in looking at core competence, we actually redefined it, giving it a more humanistic orientation than you would typically see in the literature about it. In fact, we have here a notion of creativity and of coordination. It involves concatenation of various capabilities. You have to be world class at what you do in individual functions. But core competence and the advantage one gets from it come from multiple streams of technologies and multiple capabilities. We weren't just competing to have the best marking engine to put black marks on paper against the Canons and IBMs of the time, we were also having to ask ourselves, what did we know more about than others, and how do we harness those two together? That was our business. How do we harness the collective learning knowledge and skills in the organization? That's what we pulled out of the literature: that core competence comes from a shared understanding of markets and customers and technological possibilities. Not by having individual experts – the great geniuses that firms and organizations always like to count on – but rather in the collective.

We developed and extended the notions of core competence, and we defined five technical core competencies for the corporation. In Hamel and Prahalad's conceptual framework this becomes the basis for creating what are called core products, which are delivered to markets. But what's missing in all of this, and in all of the presentations we heard at the time, was how you make that work. Where's the source of the core competence? Where is the collective understanding? You don't just promulgate the understanding and expect things to happen. You have to understand where it's rooted and where it's grounded. That's where the notion of communities of practice arose in our work, which we developed from understanding at the Institute for Research on Learning. A researcher called Gene Lave came up with it in the 1980s.

Knowledge and communities

Let me define for you what a community of practice is. There's a distinct way of looking at communities of practice as opposed to just congregations of individuals and peoples. Networking and understanding does not make us a community of practice. It makes us have common interests. It allows me, for instance, to share with you and hopefully bring some value to your work. But I'm not doing anything with you, *per se.* I'm not engaged, over an extended period of time, in solving your particular problems and mission, and therefore it makes me distinct from performing common work, which is what a community of practice is all about. So there are many types of forums in organizations. There could be task forces that form to solve a particular problem. There could be special interest groups in the computer science world and in other communities. There are Special Interest Groups (SIGs) that in fact share information and try to come up with creating journals. There are standards/bodies that set standards. All of those are groups that have common contributions but they don't perform work together over a period of time. They don't reside in an organization with a common sense of purpose and focus.

Let me make it clear that a community of practice – this root of core competence, this underpinning of where information will flow and knowledge can get used and knowing exists – is actually something that emerges. There are the four attributes that we look at when we try to identify where the emergent communities are.

1   They are *multi-functional.* What seems to make small entrepreneurial outfits work well – to harness advantage – is having strong relationships between the business community and the technical community. To have different functions interact, different

perspectives and viewpoints, is absolutely critical to having a thriving community of practice to generate new initiatives. They work together in a common purpose by engaging in a real output.

2   They have a *sense of mission* and they have something that they have to do where they build things together, or they can solve problems, or deliver service. It doesn't have to be a particular output, *per se*.

3   They require *time to develop*. A group that's been working for a while together actually develops an internal language and new skills of their own.

4   They share a *unique intellectual property*, if you will, that that grouping actually applies to their work. What that does, as a result, is to make lasting changes, both in the people and the community.

One of the things that I discover is that, whenever I go into a new organization, the first thing that I'm sure I'm going to find is that a community of practice exists. They're everywhere, and each has a specific language and use of the terminology. My use of knowledge management may be very different than yours and you'll have your own three-letter acronyms and I won't have the slightest idea what they mean. We certainly have our own at Xerox. In fact, within any organization the case is the same. You walk into a room and you have to sit and observe and only be a peripheral participant, as we call it, before you can actually join in. It takes time to do that because there's a language, there are tools, there are ways of doing business that are characterized by communities of practice. We've all been in them, because that is the way work gets done.

When you're a member of a community of practice, you need to know what other members of the community know, not to get one up on them, but rather to invoke their knowing – because none of us have the skills or the time to be expert at everything. The reason for diversity is to be able to take advantage of cross-skill mixes, and after working in a community of practice one knows how to invoke that knowing and that knowledge, if you will. The group is using its own tools and processes to which you have to be introduced. And the identity is changed in one's eyes and in others' eyes. So no matter where I go within Xerox or the world I will always be a member of the Palo Alto Research Center. Even organizationally, in the formal authorized structure of Xerox I set out to create advanced development technology centers to start bridging gaps between research and the business community some years ago. My identity is forever a part of that community, and when I need to get things done I know who to go to and how to invoke those relationships to get things to happen. That can't be governed by policies and procedures alone.

Implementing change

The sort of questions that people ask are, "where's the lever, how do I manage it, what's the problem?" And that's because people, in their work, have almost a dual personality of where they see themselves and where their work occurs. What I've been talking about and defining is what we call the emergent, which is the structure within the work that gets done. I don't care if it's yours or mine, it can be the government or industry, there are these structures within the work, whether they're recognized or not. It's like when you make the phone call to someone you know that you've worked with before, in order to get something done that you can't get done anywhere else. Or to find out that piece of information so you can add it to your mission. It's a way of working. It's an economy in any ecology that's based on gift-giving rather than on incentives and being in fear that you're going to get laid off in industry, or because you think you're going to get an award. It's based on the fact that if I do good for my partner that I've built a relationship with then I will get it back at a later time. And this emergent property of work is everywhere. The groups are small – they are no more than 50–100, maybe 150 people – because they're social networks. But they are networks. And they can be encouraged and supported technologically in order to create a knowledge-enhancing organization.

But of course that isn't the way we care for people. That isn't where they get their paychecks. That isn't where they get their common mission statement and that isn't where their boss, at the end of the day, gives them performance reviews. There is an authorized structure that we place around the work itself. For instance, there are people who are more comfortable operating in one or the other. I'm sure you have it here, we have it in industry for sure, where there are people that are always rebellious and just want to do their own thing. It doesn't matter where they are, they'll be in another organization tomorrow, whoever their boss is, it's transitory. They're only be there for two years and then they'll get another boss. But they know their mission and work, and they know what the organization is going to do and be. And gosh darn it, they want to contribute to the mission of the organization, which is set at the top. And the structure can just go away and do it's own thing and that's fine. "Leave me alone to do my own work."

On the other hand, there are people who are more like, "whatever the boss wants, that's what I'm going to do ... don't bother me, I've got to get this work done and that's what I'm going to get my performance review on ... and that's what my promotion will be based on, and that's the way I'm going to make sure that I can do what I want to do and what the organization needs ... and I don't have time or authorization to go work on something unless I get my boss to tell me that it's the right thing to do." There are people who in fact thrive and get motivated by climbing the ladder, and there are others that thrive and are motivated to do their own thing. Both of these people exist in all organizations. Both of them contribute to the mission. In fact, each of us do both every day, maybe to different proportions. The game here, and the play is, at the merger of the two. It isn't a matter of "we have too much authorization and we've got to break the hierarchy," because that's not possible. There has to be some predictability, there has to be a way of managing risk, there has to be a way of allocating resources, there are really important valuable, necessary ways that we've organized, based on chains of command. But there's also the fact that we have the people who are doing the work that we count on, after we set the missions, who are actually using these networks and these informal connectivities, and that in fact get overlooked. That's when we have to find ways of also supporting this technologically, as well as with our processes within our organization. And again, it's doing both of these that makes it an interesting challenge. I think that's where the knowledge game is going to be played, but I don't think we quite know what knowledge management means yet. These are meant to intersect, at the interface between the authorized and the emerging. These two properties are present, and we have to pay attention to both of them.

Learning or supporting knowing

My experience is that people are inherently skeptical and cynical about any new movement, about any new way of doing things, and they believe that it always applies to the worker bees at the edge of the authorized structure, rather than to the senior executive. One of the ways to encourage the right kind of behavior is with a rewards and recognition process. What our CEO did at Xerox was that he adapted an existing process. Every year we give recognition to executives, where the chairman picks certain people to celebrate. Traditionally it was always people who exceeded their numbers – who could sell more, who could make more profit, who satisfied the mission sooner than was expected – and it didn't matter how that was accomplished. Some of the worst SOBs in the company were being rewarded. He decided around 1992 that he was going to make sure that he celebrated someone, at least one person every year, who was being promoted and recognized, based on both what they did and the way that they did things.

Jack Welch of GE has this wonderful 2 by 2 that he promulgated about ten years ago now, which talks about performance on one axis and way of doing it, or management style, on the other. We adopted this in Xerox. We like to hedge things so we made it a 3 by 3. So there was not just good and bad performance, but there was mediocre. But the idea was that you could be good or bad, in both how you do it and what you achieve. In general, we bias the system to where, if we have an SOB who's performing, that's okay, because we need performance. But when the performance drops and he's still acting like an SOB, he's out. If we have someone who's performing and is really a good guy, we hold him up and we celebrate him. But if that same person the following year or two years doesn't do so well, for whatever reason and isn't performing, we don't kick that person out. We have private mentors for some senior executives, they sit on their shoulders literally in meetings and tell them what they're doing well and not well, and help them in any way that we can and try to build them back up again. We try to maintain and survive and promote those people, and bias the system that way, although at the end of the day performance certainly still counts in any of our organizations. It's just a bias. It really is utilizing the authority of the hierarchy to make this work and to recognize that you've got to make examples in this view of the world to make this one prosper.

I want to give you a very simple 2 by 2 of how to think about learning and productivity. It comes, again, from my colleagues at the Institute for Research on Learning. If you read the chapter on knowledge management by Ikujiro Nonaka you'll see something similar, which is that the kinds of information and the kinds of dealings we have in going from information to knowledge, are not just the explicit, written-down decoding of messages that come over the network, encrypted or not. That's explicit information, but there's also the tacit information. There is the knowing and the know-how. The important thing to understand is that it's both about individuals and what individuals have, and groups, and how groups, in fact, connect with that information. The groups have both a knowledge and a knowing. There's a paper by Scott Nolan Cook and John Seely Brown called "Bridging epistemologies," about knowing and knowledge and action. What knowing is, is in fact all about transitioning among these different quadrants. It is about moving between the explicit and the tacit and working as individuals and working in a group or in a teaming way through communities of practice and building understanding. This is a framework we use in order to evaluate technologies. Do we have technologies that are contributing to flows among these different quadrants? Do we have ways that we're encouraging the organization to have people come together as well as to have a quiet time themselves, so they're not spending all their days and nights in meetings and task forces, because we do need down time to think and to work by ourselves?

When we look at the technologies that enable movement around that particular cycle, there are various ways of talking about these technologies. We lump them into a management technology framework that involves three classes of infrastructure: computer-aided design, computer-aided manufacturing, and computer-aided data analysis. These are the tools of the practice, which are represented in the work that I do. They are the tools that individual analysts and knowledge workers use to get their job done. It could be a spreadsheet if they're a finance person, it could be a CAD system. They are the computer tools that we use to practice our craft. Then there are the repositories of all of the information that's out there on the Internet.

Where we can find out about competitors and we can find out about design parameters, and we can find out "what the heck is my mission statement, I've forgotten it." The digital libraries that underlie this are a major change in the way the world is working.

There are various ways of enabling collaboration and support and there are various tools that we've developed. E-mail is certainly one of them, which allows for asynchronous communication that is spaced in time. There are chat rooms that allow real time interaction. There are co-presence systems such as the one made by a company we spun out called Placeware.com that allows for people to meet together and have presentations and share information about the presentation with both the speaker and themselves, even if they're distributed. We've used video as well, and the networks all enable that. There is a set of intranet technologies that are going to be vital for allowing individuals with their tools of practice and the data repositories, to find the ways to get the relevance, the context, the authenticity, and the experience-base shared so it becomes a learning organization.

I just want to summarize with two things that I would categorize as organizational learning. What does it mean to learn as an organization? That's the basis, the understanding, and the way of viewing the world and of managing initiatives. We think it is the way that you create ecologies by recognizing communities in the workplace. I've talked about authorized and emergent views of work, and I've talked about this 2 by 2 window of productivity to recognize individuals in groups and the tacit as well as the explicit knowledge. Technology, the tool for knowing, has to afford these opportunities because there's too much information for everybody. We also find that without communities, technologies don't get used. So this is a matter of things going hand in hand, generating new knowledge, new ways of knowing, and creating an actual fabric for teams to interact using these tools for collaboration.

I just want to finish with a quote from John Seely Brown, the Director of PARC. It takes the notion of Descartes, "I think, therefore I am" and turns it on its ear. As John Seely Brown likes to say, "we participate, therefore we are." This is really what this whole game is about. I think doing that with technology, which is what PARC is about and where Xerox has been leading the way, is where the future lies.

Chapter 7

The Knowledge-Based

Organization:

A Managerial Revolution

Christopher A. Bartlett,

Harvard Business School

It's impossible to talk about organizational knowledge without considering organizational structure. After writing the book *Managing Across Borders*, with my colleague Sumantra Ghoshal, we realized that we had dealt with only part of the puzzle – that globalization was just one element of a major organizational and managerial transformation taking place. Observing the monumental restructuring, reorganization, transformation, and trauma of organizations in the 1980s and 1990s, we perceived that a number of factors were causing companies essentially to reform themselves. At the heart of all the delayering, restructuring, and innovative use of information technology, we detected a fundamental shift in the management model, and in the organization that frames it. This chapter gives an overview of past and emerging organizational structures, their basis in management philosophy, and their implications for knowledge management.

The doctrine: strategy, structure, systems

Unquestionably, we are now seeing a major traumatic change in the structure of industry and competition. Companies that once dominated their industries – companies like GM, IBM, and Kodak – are undergoing incredible chaos and change. Outside the United States, as well, corporate icons have been humbled. Recently, the president of Matsushita, Akio Tanii, was forced to resign, confessing, "Matsushita is no longer an excellent company."

Why are so many large, once incredibly successful companies in trouble, if not crisis, at the same time? I believe that the answer lies in what's common to all of them: the way in which they're organized, and their management doctrine.

The beginnings of that doctrine can be traced to the 1920s, when the leaders of several of the nation's greatest companies – General Motors, DuPont Corporation, Sears, Standard Oil of New Jersey – created an organizational revolution. Essentially, they moved from the functionally oriented structure that had until then dominated companies, toward a new, multidivisionalized model of organization.

That model marked an innovation in management philosophy, which has since been captured and embedded as doctrine: the strategy/structure/systems model. It is recognized by business academics, consultants, and practitioners as fundamental to how the typical organization is structured, the way roles and responsibilities are allocated, and how managers think about their work.

The basic strategy that companies pursued was diversification, which allowed them to grow. A divisionalized structure enabled – in fact, institutionalized – diversification in two ways: first by providing a resource allocation process controlled by top management; and second by supplying a management philosophy based on delegation of responsibility but counteracted by coordination and control from the top. Delegation, in turn, required complex systems of information planning and control. This marriage of strategy, structure, and systems framed management practice for the next half-century and was the basis of US – and subsequently other nations' – corporate growth and global expansion.

The divisionalized structure also framed the classic roles of top, middle, and front-line management still seen in most companies today. Top management dominates as the chief strategist and the controller of scarce resources. They are the people who have the deepest experience in their industry, an expertise that theoretically allows them to make the best resource allocation decisions. Middle management's role is to manage the systems vital to the process of delegation and control. Its essential task is to push management objectives and controls down, and to pull information and capital requests up. Meanwhile, front-line managers run the operations and deliver the results.

A structure suited to its time

The strategy/structure/systems model was enormously successful in the postwar era because it was ideally suited to the external environment of the time. The reality then was a booming economy that created more opportunities than companies could fund. Strategy/structure/ systems was the ideal management model for sorting through an overwhelming number of ideas and proposals, and determining which to fund.

But an inevitable product of expansion in this model was additional layers of management. More and more divisions needed more and more layers to create and manage the systems linking the strategy-formulating entrepreneurs at the top to the front-line implementers at the bottom. Companies had to group divisions under groups, lump groups into sectors, and divide divisions into strategic business units, creating six, eight, or eleven layers of management from top to bottom. Complexity increased exponentially.

During the 1970s and 1980s, another wrinkle was added. As well as managing multiple functions and multiple business opportunities, companies were increasingly playing in multiple markets. Companies now had to organize and manage around three dimensions: functions, businesses/products, and markets. Consequently, global organization structures assumed the shape of complex matrices. This was the golden era for academics and consultants, who came in with stages models and contingencies theories, and helped form strategic business units, growth-share matrix models, and global structures. Still, it was increasingly problematic for the managers, who were faced with incredible change and were having enormous difficulty managing it.

The problem: bureaucracy, fragmentation, stagnation

Today, we continue to live with organization structures that were forged in a different time to meet a different business imperative. Our complex and convoluted structures may appear logical from the top, but from the bottom the view is increasingly absurd. Referring to the classic organization chart, GE's Jack Welch once expressed the problem in colorful terms: the typical organization has "its face turned toward the CEO and its ass towards the customer."

It was no wonder, then, that the incredible success of this model began to fray around the edges. In fact, not only was the increasingly complex and bureaucratic organization model becoming obsolete, but so was the underlying strategy/structure/systems doctrine of management. There are three key problems:

- The strategic decisions being made at the top were increasingly separated from where the real knowledge and expertise resided in the organization.

  The sheer diversity of operations at the front line made it difficult for top management to understand what was going on there. Making their job even harder was an external environment that had become much more dynamic. Over time, the expertise that was assumed to be at the top, embedded in experience, had shifted to the bottom and created a very capable group of front-line managers.

- A long series of structural elaborations led to fragmentation and bureaucracy.

  The essence of the divisional organization was just that: division. Organizations were divided into operations that were fragmented and increasingly compartmentalized. This division of assets, resources, and accountabilities prevented any kind of linking and leveraging across the organization.

- The increasingly sophisticated systems needed to manage layers of organizational complexity constrained flexibility and growth.

  Systems grew more bureaucratic and overloaded. Ultimately, all they were able to achieve was the transmission of financially-oriented information.

It's important to stress that it was not simply the organization structure that began to run into difficulty, but also the philosophy it embodied. But in spite of the seemingly obvious difficulty, we often mistakenly assume that organizations are "somehow transcending this."

A case in point: Westinghouse

Westinghouse embodies many of the problems of an outmoded management doctrine. When Robert Kirby took over in 1975, the company's organization structure and management focus epitomized the model that had been successful for the previous half-century. Just before Kirby inherited the company, it had experienced a major crisis. Management had entered into contracts with nuclear power stations, but made the mistake of agreeing to supply uranium at a fixed price. When the price of uranium subsequently went through the roof, the company was exposed to a $2 billion liability.

Kirby's response was classic – perfectly in line with his position's tradition. Firstly, he pulled the strategy lever. He said, 'We've become too diverse, too unfocused," so he purified the portfolio, cleaned out the operations, and tried to rebalance. Secondly, he pulled the structure lever. He said, "We've lost control," so he created strong staff groups at the center, and at the business level, 37 SBUs. And finally, he pulled the systems lever. He increased controls and instituted more rigorous formal planning.

Seven years later, Kirby passed on the organization, declaring, "Westinghouse is a company where there will be no more surprises." But when Douglas Danforth took over, he found a business that was the epitome of business stagnation and organizational gridlock.

What did Danforth do? Again, the CEO played the typical CEO role as chief strategic guru, organizational architect, and systems engineer: he pulled the same three levers. During his five years at the helm, Danforth divested 70 companies and acquired 55, completely reconfiguring the portfolio. He further decentralized the company into 26 strategic business units, and built and managed what he touted as the world's most sophisticated strategic planning system, VABASTROM (for value-based strategic management system). At the end of his term, he declared victory; the company, he claimed, was now in the winner's circle.

A pair of leaders, John Marous and Paul Lego, succeeded Danforth, as chairman and president respectively. They inherited an organization about which Wall Street was beginning to ask the question: is this just portfolio reshuffling? Their task, they immediately understood, was to move from portfolio rationalization to sustainable growth. How to do it? Pull the same three levers that Kirby and Danforth did! So they focused strategy on seven core businesses, reorganized the business structure into seven groups, relied more on financial controls, and measured value creation. Their faith in the traditional levers led them to announce: "We've taken a good company and we're aiming to make it a great corporation."

The most recent chapter – as yet unwritten – in this now predictable tale begins with Paul Lego's replacement, Michael Jordan (formerly of Kentucky Fried Chicken). Westinghouse just took a $5 billion write-off, and is again headed toward crisis. Jordan's actions aren't clear yet, but if I could give him a word of advice, I would say, "Please, Mr Jordan, don't pull the three levers!" Admittedly Kirby's and Danforth's, and Marous' and Lego's reaction was built into the structure. After all, we teach it at business schools and consultants reinforce it. The strategy/structure/systems model of management is deeply embedded in our society, in our values, and in the practice of management. Somehow, top managers must move past seeing themselves as strategic gurus who redesign strategies, restructure organizations, and reengineer systems to solve problems.

Quick fixes side-stepped the problem

As early as the 1980s, companies were beginning to recognize fundamental organizational problems, and undertook a variety of actions to resolve them. As an antidote to hierarchical bureaucracy, for example, they began to create "skunk works" to legitimize entrepreneurial activities outside the main line, and corporate venture units to fund venturing internally. Similarly, they recognized that the SBU structure was fragmenting capabilities, and sought a way to build the capabilities and knowledge they lacked; outsourcing and strategic alliances became major thrusts. Finally, systems and controls constrained the company to only incremental growth, so these companies responded with mergers and acquisitions.

These management approaches of the 1980s were in direct response to the problems caused by the divisional system and the strategy/structure/systems management philosophy it embodied. But the unfortunate fact is that none of these prescriptions deal with the problem, they merely sidestep it. These approaches may have their legitimate place, but as "quick fixes" to the classic problems , they fall hopelessly short. In other words, they're part of the reaction, but not part of the solution.

At IBM, for example, a very successful personal computer business could be created in a skunk works, but when rolled back into the larger organization – with its traditional hierarchical structure and management doctrine – it was plagued by the same problems as the rest of the business. The same has been true for companies who joined the outsourcing or alliance fads. These reactions often compounded problems by stripping the company of capabilities and knowledge. This is certainly the story of the US consumer electronics industry, which now consists of what might be described as "hollow corporations." Likewise, the value of mergers and acquisitions has eluded many companies, who either paid too high a price in a bidding war or ran into problems trying to integrate the new businesses' cultures into the core.

New competitive practices missed the point

As the 1980s slipped into the 1990s, profound forces were at work in the business environment, and people began exploring or reacting to different pieces of the puzzle. Initially, I focused on one component: the globalization of markets and its impact on how companies must develop capabilities and organizations. Other components were equally challenging:

- increasing technology costs;
- complexity and change;
- slowing economic growth;
- changing skills and resources of competitors;
- constraining and pressuring government bodies; and
- shifting societal norms and expectations.

One corporate response to these multiple forces was to tackle a whole portfolio of change techniques. Any seasoned manager has been exposed to all of them: total quality management, time-based management, alliance-based competition, flexible manufacturing, fast-cycle innovation, core competence, service intensity, mass customization, continuous improvement, customer responsiveness, and so on.

As each new source of competitive advantage was layered on, however, the basic strategy model went essentially unchallenged. Why? The notion, developed mainly by Michael Porter, was that companies should compete by being one of two things: low cost or differentiated. Alternatively, they could pick up a niche. But certainly the worst thing management could do was to try staking out a middle ground. At the time, Porter's model accurately reflected the market. But unfortunately, the book either didn't translate well into Japanese, or those guys were too busy exporting to read it. In fact, some companies succeeded in building low-cost positions, then layering differentiated capabilities on top of that, then even picking off the niches. In other words, they didn't do one or the other; they did all of the above.

New organizational forms addressed issues piecemeal

Companies began to recognize that their strategic imperative was not a simple either/or choice; rather, they had to build layers of competitive advantage. They took a hard look at themselves and saw that the organizational implications of this new reality were tearing away at their elegantly designed hierarchical structures and at the classic strategy/structure/systems management philosophy.

This realization led to a whole new round of experiments, focused on organizational forms. It was another field day for management advisors – following every strategic guru at about ten paces was an organizational consultant, looking forward to a lifetime's worth of follow-on studies. The projects focused on various goals and approaches: team management, destaffing, organizational learning, empowerment, delayering, reengineering, entrepreneurships, networking, downsizing, coaching, and so on.

In truth, much of the work to make and integrate these changes carried tremendous value. But it still fell short of complete success.

The problem? Managers attacked the issues piecemeal. Investing incrementally in new models of management, they tried to bolt them onto their old structures and integrate them into their old management doctrines. But empowerment in an organization where the management model is built on autocracy is impossible, as is sustaining networks in an organization designed as a hierarchy, or cultivating learning in an environment constrained by policies and procedures.

In the end, these approaches were thwarted by the huge barriers embedded in the company's structure/systems doctrine and embedded in management practice. Organizations treated them like any foreign body in the blood stream: they rejected them.

Convincing a manager who's made his or her career based on command and control suddenly to embrace an approach that's typified by empowerment and empathy may seem impossible. Inflexibility, rigidity, and arrogance developed a generation of management, yet was an attitude not suited to the management style and organization of the next generation. In fact, if a single lesson could be drawn from the experiences of the 1980s, it would be simply this: you cannot implement third-generation strategies through second-generation organizations with first generation-managers.

Moving to the knowledge-based organization

Over the past few years, I've studied 20 companies that seem to be exceptions to the rule. Some are traditionally large companies, like Intel, 3M, and Kao, that have avoided the widespread problems of their peers. Others have had problems, but have undergone successful transformation; companies like AT&T, Asea Brown Boveri, and Komatsu. The group includes companies of varying sizes, industries, and nations.

What became clear at the outset of this research was that changes in these companies' environmental situations were fundamentally transforming the organizational tasks they had to accomplish. This, in turn, challenged the management model. In the post-war environment, capital budgeting was the key organizational task, and the hierarchical structure and top-down planning and control systems were the ideal. But in a world marked not by steady growth but by structural discontinuity – in the midst of the information and knowledge explosion – the key task is not capital budgeting, but knowledge accumulation. Why? Because the scarce resource for most companies is not capital – it is knowledge and expertise. This environment requires a very different organization structure; one driven by front-line initiative, flexibility, and the ability to link and leverage the knowledge created in front-line organizations.

Elements of a new era of management

From this research, I have drawn conclusions that can be summarized in three phrases:

- ◆ organizational concept;
- ◆ managerial role; and
- ◆ management philosophy.

A different concept of the organization
Managers constrained by the old paradigm of strategy/structure/systems tend to envision organization in terms of boxes and lines. They flip over an envelope and redraw, forgetting that the boxes represent people and the lines represent relationships. They focus on the assets and tasks they're dividing rather than the processes and roles they need to develop.

A fundamentally changing role for managers
The traditional model featured roles for top, middle, and front-line managers as resource allocators, administrative controllers, and implementers. The new model calls for organization builders, management and organization developers, and innovative entrepreneurs.

A new management philosophy
The old doctrine of strategy, structure, and systems must give way to a fundamentally different framing, cast in terms of purpose, process, and people.

Asea Brown Boveri: birth of a global competitor

One company that has undergone dramatic organizational transformation is Asea Brown Boveri (ABB). Essentially, ABB is a group of "also-ran" companies that have been rationalized and integrated into the world's leading electro-technical company. These companies include Asea, the Swedish-based electrical company; Brown-Boveri, the Swiss-based engineering company; Stromberg from Finland; Combustion Engineering; and part of Westinghouse's US power distribution and generation business. In its first five years of operation, ABB's sales jumped from $17 billion to $30 billion and return on capital employed (ROCE) rose from 13.6% to 17.1%. Notably, this impressive performance came in the midst of a worldwide recession and in an industry many had counted for dead.

ABB's feat is not an accident. The company's foundation for success is a highly publicized global matrix built on 1300 front-line companies and a lesser-known philosophy of managing conflicts.

ABB's global matrix: entrepreneurship in a global network

ABB's famous feature is its management structure. It is a lean organization with only four layers. Miraculously, its structure is sufficient to oversee 6000 profit centers in 1300 operating companies in 60 businesses that comprise the four segments of this $30 billion company.

The operating companies are the real core of the organization, and are run very much as independent companies: financially autonomous and legally separate wherever possible. They control their own human resource policies as well as 90% of the company's $2.5 billion R&D budget. They even retain a third of their own earnings for internal development projects. Their managers each report to one of 60 business area managers. The extraordinary feature of this next management level is its staffing. The staff size for one $250 million division? Three. A financial comptroller, a technology guy, and a development guy. That's it. And above this level just eight people constitute the executive committee. Total staff at Switzerland headquarters, including these business heads, their immediate staffs, legal, finance, and so on, numbers fewer than 150 people.

The point is that this is a very, very tight operation. The CEO, Percy Barnevik, applies what he calls the "30-30-30-10 rule" to every business the corporation acquires. In the headquarters operation, he requires that 30 percent retire or move out; 30 percent move down to the front-line units; 30 percent move into some kind of independent service providers; and just 10 percent remain at headquarters.

ABB's lean management structure might be impressive, but isn't it essentially the same as a traditional conglomerate? In fact, the company is able to integrate its assets into something more than just a grab bag of 1300 companies because of the way it is run and its underlying management philosophy. A great deal of management time and attention has been devoted to redefining the roles and relationships among management.

The company's objective has been to counter the top-down bias that's built into any hierarchical organizational structure. ABB does this by casting company managers not as implementers, as in the old model, but as entrepreneurs. This means giving them not only resources, but also a greatly expanded role in decision-making; it is a legitimate shift from mere delegation to empowerment. The difference is critical. To a lot of people, empowerment is just a new-age term for delegation, and often comes closer to abandonment. Real empowerment requires allocation of resources, support from the top, and the legitimization of these people's role in shaping the business.

ABB operating company managers, for example, are strongly involved. They may sit on the board for their business area, and therefore play a role in shaping the strategy, organization, and policies of worldwide business operations. Even below this level, managers within operating companies work on teams to define strategy. ABB's structure empowers them to assume that level of leadership.

In addition to creating mechanisms to promote bottom-up, entrepreneurial initiative, ABB's management sought to remedy the vertical, financially oriented information flows that characterized the classical hierarchy. The old model built information planning and control systems around the resource allocation process, pulling capital budgets to the top, and sending down operating control systems. ABB's goal has been to create a much more leveraged organization built on knowledge-sharing across the company.

In line with this philosophy, operating company managers see themselves not as controllers – they don't have the staff for this, anyway – but as developers: first as developers of the managers running the businesses; and second as organizational developers. Their goal is to set up operations so as to create not only new business opportunities, but also internal capabilities and the ways to link and leverage them.

Besides changing organization structure, ABB has also changed the management process. In addition to the executive committee at the top, a board is associated with every operating company. An operating company manager manages largely through this board, along with counterparts including regional managers and related business managers, technical experts, and so on. More than anything else, it is the creation of these boards that has changed the managerial relationship. The relationship between a CEO and his or her board is very different from the traditional hierarchical relationship of authority and control.

The ABB management process: resolving tensions

Traditionally, companies have had to make choices: should we organize by product or geography? Should we centralize or decentralize? Should we be global or local? ABB's philosophy is that these are not either/or propositions. Its leadership believes instead that the company must be able to manage these paradoxes. To be both global and local, for example, it builds a global presence on an integrated network of small, highly entrepreneurial companies. While supporting a strong philosophy of decentralization, ABB still retains the ability to coordinate control; the company recognizes that decentralization only works when management believes the front-line operations make sense.

Managing such paradoxes requires linking and leveraging, which ABB achieves through a variety of functional councils. For example, it has created "performance leagues," which show companies how they're performing compared with their counterparts, but go beyond comparing merely operating performance to consider strategic and capability performance as well. Best practice transfer is another important element of linkage and leverage. ABB has established a rotating council to capture knowledge, expertise, and leading-edge practice and move it around the world. Similar councils evaluate other practices (like purchasing) across the organization. Above all, these integrating forums serve to create a horizontal process that counterbalances the traditional vertical process.

Essentially, ABB has redefined the roles and relationships of managers. Front-line managers are now entrepreneurs driving a bottom-up process; middle managers are coaches, leveragers, and developers of the organization; and top managers are institution builders and creators of the organization's values and purpose.

When I asked ABB's chairman, Percy Barnevik, how he would characterize corporate's role, he answered, "Well, we're really a company of overheads." Given that the company has less overhead than I had ever seen in a firm of similar size and complexity, I was confused. "Oh, no – not that kind of overhead," Barnevik explained. "I mean overhead transparencies." Barnevik sees his primary role as moving around the company, communicating its purpose, its values, and how he wants managers to behave. "I may be out of town, but," he insists, "I'm never out of touch."

Despite ABB's emphasis on communication and cooperation, this is not management in a T-group. There is an iron fist down the financial side of the organization. There's an ABACUS control system. There are strong operating reviews. In many ways, the hierarchy is alive and well – but it's only a part of how the company is run. ABB is striving to create management by discipline, not by control; every manager is challenged, not by a mandate to constrain, but to stretch.

Emerging perspective: organization as processes and roles
Not only at ABB, but in a number of companies I studied, too much focus on structure is a distraction. Companies must not focus on the division of tasks and activities, but on the redefinition of roles and relationships around three core processes:

- driving business performance;
- developing and leveraging capabilities across the organization; and
- managing corporate renewal.

The first of these processes, driving business performance, is entrepreneurial and largely front-line initiated. Front-line managers have the primary responsibility of pursuing opportunities and building the business; middle management's responsibility is to develop those front-line managers; and top management provides the clear mission and demanding standards to drive the process.

In the second process, developing and leveraging capabilities, middle management plays the central role of linking resources and knowledge sources across the organization. Here, the role of front-line managers is to generate those new capabilities. Top management's contribution is to embed a set of values that encourages cooperation and collaboration. The effective functioning of this process is what keeps ABB from being simply a portfolio of independent operations. Without it, capabilities generated in individual units would remain there, unknown to the rest of the organization and unleveraged.

The third process, managing corporate renewal, is essentially a knowledge-creation process and is led by top management. But an important distinction must be drawn from how this is normally done in organizations. Typically, the front line collects data from the outside and transforms it into corporate information; middle managers are responsible for embedding that information into practices and capabilities to improve front-line management, and top management is responsible for creating the nice, smooth environment in which that can occur. (This is basically the task of aligning people with strategy, making sure the organization's structure is neatly divided so that tasks and responsibilities don't overlap, and managing systems so that performance matches objectives.)

Top management's new role of leading the renewal process is quite the opposite of this "smoothing" responsibility. This new role asks them to challenge the embedded knowledge and wisdom in an organization, creating organizational disequilibrium. At ABB, for example, Percy Barnevik started acquiring combustion engineering companies in the United States because he believed most new knowledge and technologies were being developed there. Immediately after acquiring the first of these companies, he integrated it into his operations to create disequilibrium, to expose others forcefully to American practices that might help them to manage better. For similar reasons, he began acquiring environmental companies; Barnevik believed everyone in the industry needed to become more environmentally conscious. Again, he managed by introducing disturbance. I believe, like Barnevik, that the most effective leaders will be those who generate trust on one hand while issuing challenges on the other.

3M: institutionalizing innovation

Like ABB, 3M is an incredibly entrepreneurial company. But unlike ABB, it did not require transformation. Somehow, throughout its half-century in operation, it has been able to resist the doctrine of strategy/structure/systems and the rigid hierarchical bureaucracy that plague other top management's new role of leading companies. 3M's achievement is all the more impressive when contrasted with another company that started in the same basic business and at about the same time: Norton Company. Both companies started out making sandpaper and grinding wheels, and later diversified into adhesives.

Norton grew up as a family-owned company, run in a very hierarchical fashion. Very early, it developed the classic structural divisions and embraced scientific management. Later, it became one of the first firms to adopt PIMS, the profit/impact model using regression analysis to determine profit. Norton was also one of the first advocates and defenders of the SBU approach. As one of the first clients of Boston Consulting Group, it ran its business in a growth-share matrix fashion. Still later, it abandoned the growth-share matrix for McKinsey & Company's nine-celled matrix.

Clearly, Norton exemplifies the classic strategy/structure/systems, top-down, hierarchical-driven company. Throughout its history, top management has seen its role as controlling and allocating financial resources and achieving growth largely through acquisitions. And Norton has perpetually lagged behind 3M.

How did 3M avoid the same fate? Its direction was different, thanks to two important events very early in its history. First, one of the company's front-line technicians developed waterproof sandpaper, which differentiated 3M's product. Second, someone else on the front line adapted the coating technology used to glue sand to paper and created adhesive tape. These two innovations showed top management that its best course would be to respect the capabilities of front-line managers and to cultivate and protect entrepreneurship.

Implementation of that philosophy took some interesting forms. For example, managers were granted 15 percent of their time to pursue whatever projects they wished, regardless of how they related to their division's priorities. This very deliberate philosophy continues to drive the company. Today, divisions know their prime responsibility is to seed innovation in order to meet management's insistence that 25 percent of sales come from products introduced in the most recent five years. The rule applies even to a division like sandpaper, representing a belief that there is no such thing as a "mature business."

Furthermore, as creativity generates new business opportunities, the organizational structure is allowed to evolve from the bottom up rather than divisionalized from above. If a project grows to a certain size, it becomes a department. If a department grows to a certain size, it becomes a division. And if a division grows to a certain size, it becomes a sector.

Finally, the company places an enormous emphasis on ideas. The saying at 3M is: "The products belong to the division, but the ideas and the technology belong to the company." Accordingly, management spends a huge amount of time creating channels and forums for transferring and leveraging ideas across the organization. Thanks to its ability to leverage knowledge, the company has grown from its modest beginnings in sandpaper and adhesive tape to a $15 billion entity comprising over 100 core technologies and 60,000 products.

The lessons 3M teaches are very similar to those behind the reinvention of ABB and other companies. The company grants its front-line managers an entrepreneurial role in the interests of building effective businesses. The job of middle management is to develop those businesses into a successful company. And top management plays an institution-building role, driving the constant renewal of the organization.

Changing the organizational conception: from control to empowerment

Almost all managers' thinking about organization is constrained by the traditional strategy/structure/systems model and the organization charts that typify it. This way of thinking has to be changed. The truth is that organizations aren't just structure. Structure is just the skeleton. Organizations also have a physiology – the flow of information and knowledge is their life blood – and a psychology, representing people's values and how they think and act.

To suggest a new way of conceptualizing the organization, I want you to imagine a complex pattern of interrelated teams and task forces overlying more traditional hierarchies. The point is to shift the organization's whole way of thinking about the world from the old paradigm of strategy/structure/systems to one based on purpose, process, and people. Companies must focus on creating entrepreneurs at the front line – who do not, in Jack Welch's terms, have their faces turned perpetually toward top management – and on supporting and managing them with a group of people whose roles are development and institution-building.

Beyond a constraining doctrine to a liberating philosophy

The problem with the strategy-dominated model of management is that it continues to view the organization simply as an economic entity; in reality, a company is also a social institution. Managers need to understand this difference and manage accordingly, especially in companies where knowledge is the key asset. Rather than viewing organization structure as an aggregation of tasks and responsibilities, managers must perceive it as a way to redefine roles and relationships around the key tasks of the organization. Rather than focusing on fragmented tasks, managers at all levels must work together toward the common goals of entrepreneurship, competence-building, and renewal. Finally, companies must do away with a systems approach designed purely to eliminate the risk of human error. Rather than managing people as if they were controllable costs and replaceable parts – sources of error to be eliminated – we must recognize them as organizational assets and the embodiers of knowledge.

Biography

Since joining the faculty of Harvard Business School in 1979, Chris Bartlett has focused his research and instruction on the general management challenges faced by multi-national corporations. He is the author or co-author of five books, including *Managing Across Borders: The Transnational Solution* (HBS Press, 1989), and is widely published in management journals. Bartlett's latest research focuses on the changes in new organizational structures and the core roles of managers, and on the new skills managers must have to succeed in those roles.

Chapter 8

Maximizing Innovation Using Intellect, Science and Technology

James Brian Quinn,

Amos Tuck School of Business, Dartmouth College

We used to think about economic growth in terms of land, labor and capital. Not any more. The driving force is clearly intellect and intellect converted into service to create value. An interesting thing about this is that the models used in Washington to measure the economy bear no relation to this. There is no model that measures our intellect capital. The methods for measuring services are utterly lousy. Only 40% of the services industries are actually covered by current economic data.

In addition to that, most of the productivity that's created in the services sector – let's say an increase in productivity in telecommunications – is passed through to the user sector. When we as consultants create greater value for customers, that goes to the customer sector, often the manufacturing sector, and the producer gets no credit for it. So the statistics are just absolutely lousy and part of what we're seeing today and the confusion of policy in Washington is due to this fact. The world has distinctly changed.

Intellect is defined in the dictionary to include three things:

- knowledge itself, that is, knowledge which is knowing;
- the capacity to use knowledge, which is diffusion; and
- the capacity to create knowledge, which is innovation.

Guess where the greatest value is created? Not in possessing knowledge, but in using knowledge.

I'm an engineer, I know pretty well how a car works but I could never design an engine, I could never tell you exactly how it works. Most of us can't tell you how our VCR works. But it's the use of the VCR, the use of the car, the use of the computer that gives us our great value. So as we manage knowledge we need to manage diffusion and to create the highest value we need to manage a process called innovation. I have devoted a great deal of time to exploring the role of intellect in both *Intelligent Enterprise* and, more recently, in *Innovation Explosion*. Those intrigued by the ideas I discuss here might also want to take a look at those books.

The shift to the intellect economy

What's happened in our economy, the reason that it's taken this radical shift in recent years is that the services sector has grown very rapidly since World War II and now 80% of our population is employed in the services industries *per se* – and mostly in the knowledge-based services industries. So most of our activity is in knowledge-based services.

Manufacturing has continued with about the same percentage of employment but produces much better product today, and more of it, because of efficiency increases introduced through services activities. Incidentally, 60–75% of all the people employed in manufacturing are in service activities, like research, development, product design, accounting, personnel, etc, and all of these are knowledge activities. So if you really took a careful read on our economy today it's a 92% knowledge-based economy. It's no wonder that we are concerned about this. It is the primary engine creating new value.

What does this economy look like when you get behind the figures a little bit? It turns out that the services sector is a huge, growing, high-tech activity. And if you look at the various elements of the service sector, financial services alone create value in the economy almost equal to the entire manufacturing sector. That's no knock-on manufacturing, it just happens to be the way things are.

The other thing that's interesting is that all of these value creators are high tech. Financial services are the purchase and sale of information on electrons worldwide. It is a huge activity. Just in terms of scale we transact $6 trillion worth of financial activities per day. That's the entire US economy transacted per day internationally! But most of that is not picked up by the data sets that we use to run our economies with.

Big, high-tech industries are growing rapidly and they're the big users of technology. Other dominant services are health care and delivery systems (worth some $1.1 trillion), and entertainment, our second largest export from the United States. All high tech.

In addition to this, the companies that support these industries are becoming very large. Toys "R" Us at $9.9 billion is three times the size of the next largest toy producer. Why? Because it's closer to the customer, it has more knowledge about toys than anyone else in the world. It can therefore guide the entire industry. So what has happened is that through knowledge we have the growth of very large enterprises. Home Depot, $19–20 billion, is four times the size of Black and Decker ($5 billion), the largest tool distributor in the world. And so it goes.

There are two interesting points to make about this state of affairs:

1   They have knowledge, and knowledge is their coin in trade.
2   The growth of the very large distribution chains – Wal-Mart, K-Mart, Foot Locker and Circuit City – has changed the world. This may sound like a radical statement and it is.

What's happened is very straightforward. Any innovator out in South-East Asia, or wherever they may be, who can get one buyer in Circuit City interested in his or her product instantly has distribution in the world's most advanced market places, and the capacity to update their information constantly from the feedback of these distributors.

What's happened therefore is that we have suddenly tapped into the minds of roughly two billion new people. And if you think innovation has been fast in the past, it's about to take off again. Two billion new minds tapped into the most advanced market place in the world changes the game completely. But that's not all that's changing the game. We've got to learn to manage in this new world. It's a very exciting place to be.

Let's take a look at some of the other dimensions here. We now have grown specialized services companies, like Flour and Bechtel in the engineering sector, both $12–15 billion companies that can design things with very high technological capability. They can hire the best in the world, invest in the best software, have access to multiple best customers, and therefore be creative at a higher level than anyone else before. There is a company called Microsoft that does the same thing.

Service Master is a company that's in the maintenance business. They keep such detailed information on 17 million pieces of equipment, that they can maintain the equipment better and at a lower cost than anyone else in the world. They can do this so efficiently that they can co-invest with you, the client, and make enough on the return on investment in that process for it to pay out for them. So it decreases your investment, lowers your cost, increases your quality, etc.

So what we have now then is a peculiar economy. A peculiar economy creating a peculiar kind of structure and strategy for management. If you are performing a service externally and you are not best in the world at it you're giving up competitive edge. Not only that, if you're performing it *internally* and you're not best in the world at it, you're giving up competitive edge. The interesting thing is that the value chains of all companies turn out to be a linked set of services activities for which there are outsourcing suppliers.

Services can be made anywhere in the world. We can therefore tap into best in the world anywhere. Information, design, systems, documents go across borders in a flash of the eye. So what we now have is a lateral competition for every company competing against the best in the world in each element of their value chain.

In the case of an oil company we used to think of this as the most integrated company. Now the research for techniques can be outsourced, as can structure standing, seismic studies, experimental drilling, developmental drilling, infrastructure development, transportation, plant engineering, even refining and pre-refining. And let's not forget trading, mixing, blending, marketing and distribution. All of these can be outsourced, leaving us with a very interesting company. It is more than just a virtual company. It is a totally disaggregated company tapping into best-in-the-world intellect. And if we don't tap into best-in-the-world intellect we're giving up competitive edge. Not only that, if we don't tap into best-in-the-world innovative intellect we will fall a long way behind.

Outsource everything not world class

So what we're running into today is professional outsourcing on a scale we've never seen before. We're outsourcing intellect, strategic planning, real estate management, treasury functions (some of the automobile companies are doing this today), image creation, application and software systems management, and new product introduction. We outsource to people in the value chain or the distribution chain for this activity to get the product out fast at lowest cost with the highest responsiveness. They have the best information systems for sucking information back into us. We therefore outsource for information value.

What's happening therefore is that we have a new economy that is a services-based economy that is very disaggregated and each one of these outsource units is both a competitor and a supporter. The result of this is that they are innovating like crazy and if we can tap into that innovation we essentially get the benefits of that innovation investment that they make for free. It's well known in innovation literature that at least 50% of the innovation takes place at the interface between the customer and the producer. What we're doing by this outsourcing process, if it is properly managed, is we're tapping into the richest form of intellect that exists from the best suppliers and innovators in the world.

What's happening in dollar terms? The international trade in services is growing six times as fast as the international trade in product. But watch what's happening to small companies. Software and networking IPOs have appreciated in value between 1980 and 1996 more than the sum of all other technology activities. That is one walloping number.

So what we have is a services- and software-dominated economy with the innovative action happening in software. And the core element of our new book, *Innovation Explosion*, is what does software based innovation do and how do we manage it? Because it is a very radical shift in what's going on. This is the most exciting economy ever.

Many people have felt for a long time that the post-World War II era was the most exciting era because we had a whole bunch of highly trained, highly motivated people coming out of the services at that time coupled with a whole store of technology that was ready to burst. What we have today is the tapping into the world of two billion new brains and a store of technology that is absolutely fantastic. And what's about to happen can only be compared to a deluge. We're going to have to run to stand still in this world and this is what we're trying to address in the book. It's very exciting stuff.

The fields are just burgeoning today in every technology area you can name. And this is creating a new economy. Brian Arthur discusses this in depth in his chapter on the knowledge economy and he takes you into the economic side of this a bit more, but let me just make a very brief point. What we have is a new economy where a small energy input in intellect creates a large value output.

The term "entropy" refers to a system where if you put energy into it the energy will always decline until it reaches either zero or ambient levels. However, a negative entropy system self-actuates and creates new energy. How does this happen? It happens through the network externalities that occur in a network-based economy. Look at it this way. I get a great idea. I put it out on a network and say, "Here's my idea." Someone picks up the idea and says, "OK, I like that. I'm going to modify that, I'm going to put it back out." And you add value to it. Now somebody else says, "Hey, that's a great one. I'll take that and that and in my business I can add this value to it over here." We keep going. If I ever give it to Nonaka-san it'll go up greatly in value, of course. He'll take it and add another twist to it.

Now what happens is very interesting. I haven't invested in any of this stuff but the value has gone up enormously. Now I look back and say Nonaka-san's ideas, combined with something else I've been working on, now trigger in me another level of innovativeness back here and this is the positive feedback loop and all at once you get this weird economy.

It's no wonder that Alan Greenspan can't tell you what's going on in this economy. He's as good as they come – a very fine man. But this economy is different from anything we've ever seen and the probability of continuing to have a low inflation, high value added, high employment economy has been dramatically shifted by this type of international service-based, intellectually-based economy. This is what the game is all about.

What we have is a very fascinating, totally disaggregated system. We have little pockets of individuals who aren't connected to each other in any way who are essentially broadcasting ideas outward. And the broadcast mechanism has been made much easier by network technologies, so that these people are able to interconnect more. If you think about innovation, it is the first interconnection of two previously unassociated matrices of ideas. We've expanded the probability of this association out of all previous bounds because people can and do communicate. The depth of knowledge behind each of these areas has become so specialized that we have bunches of highly specialized people exchanging little pockets of knowledge all over the world.

Just recently I've been trying to solve a pension problem. I thought it was a pretty simple problem but I found out that there is a particularly arcane element of the pension code that was holding me back. I kept getting lousy advice from supposed professionals. Then I finally asked the question, "Who is the best in the world in this field?" And I finally got a convergence on who that was. I picked up the phone, called the guy and said, "Here's my problem." He said, "That's no problem. We handle this all the time." In 15 minutes of a telephone conversation this one guy, who really knew, was able to solve a problem that hundreds of people had been working on before and – Presto! – created great value for me. This is the way this economy works.

What's the largest growing segment of our economy? It's the home work professional, isn't it? It's by far the largest growing piece of the economy. So this type of interaction is going to get more and more common. As that happens we will get more and more of these types of intersections, and with them will come enormous value creation.

We've seen the creation within companies of what are sometimes called amoebae organizations. They're very small-scale innovative units. The term "amoeba organization" happens to come from Kyocera and the chairman of Kyocera refers to this as one of his techniques of getting growth. He forms very, very small teams, the smallest possible units, perhaps just three or four people. He gives them – or lets them select – a very defined task, and expects them to solve any problems, implement the assignment, move it into the operation and run it profitably. When you get this happening within companies and you have all of these individuals operating out of their homes creating new value, especially the new software guys out there – remember the biggest IPO growth is in software – the combination of all of these things is creating an absolutely riotous set of new knowledge.

How do we manage in this chaotic world? You didn't hear the words "chaos theory" mentioned until a few years ago, because it just wasn't in the management lexicon. Physicists talked about chaos theory but no one else did. On one side we have chaos theory, which deals with the way that a small perturbation introduced in a disaggregate system self-amplifies throughout the system. It's the old story of the beat of a butterfly wing starting a tornado. You get this amplifying effect in a highly diverse, highly diffuse system. On the opposite side of that is another theory called complexity theory that says while chaos theory may be operating and may create tornadoes, something else is happening too. If we have a reasonably refined set of rules that system, which looks to us like chaos, will become self-organizing.

A tornado may start with the beat of a butterfly wing but once it starts there are internal patterns. Inside your company innovation is chaotic but there is a pattern, a swirling pattern like the tornado, an identifiable pattern which can be managed. Identifying the pattern becomes one of the key methods of managing innovation when it occurs in this swirling chaos. You have to be able to monitor it early. You have to be able to anticipate it, but you may not be able to control it. That's another interesting thing.

The days in which we can control innovation are gone. Forget them. We can do this for extensions of knowledge but for anything new it's not on. Just think of the numbers for a second. Most of the innovation that's done today comes first in software. A 12-step software sequence can produce ten trillion different outcomes. If you think you can anticipate that at the outset you're wrong. Instead, what you have to do is manage in a system in which ten trillion outcomes are possible and you can't know at the beginning what's going to happen.

Government policy has to operate in this same realm. The way to get growth today is to stimulate knowledge generation, knowledge sharing, knowledge accessibility and knowledge use. What's happening in the economy is very profound. We don't know where this is going to come out. Anybody that says they do is out of their mind.

Strategies to compete

How do we develop a strategy? First of all we have to be the best at something. Something important to a customer is an intellect specialty, a capability that is best in the world. Why do we want to do this? For one thing, that's the only way we can get competitive edge. But also, we can't tap into the rest of the system or trade with others out there unless we've got something to give to them. The essence of technological trade is knowledge being traded for more knowledge. But step one is to get to be best in the world.

Then the second strategy that works is continual innovation. We use the word "continual" as opposed to "continuous" because innovation tends to work in spurts. You get an idea, you develop it, you get it out and into the market place. While you're pounding out product you may not be continuously innovating but you are continually innovating because the next ones are coming along.

A third strategy is speed of innovation. Speed has a high premium in this marketplace because it decreases your risk. The faster that you can get to the marketplace with knowledge about the marketplace the less risk you have. Hence you want to attach to that marketplace as best you can and leverage. And the way you get that leverage is through your outsourcing, and through your capabilities to connect with sources other than inside your own company.

This is why core competency strategies came into being and what real core competency strategies really are. A core competency strategy develops two or three – not ten but two or three – intellectually based service activities where you can be best in the world. And notice I said "can be." You may not be best in the world yet, but you can be. The document idea at Xerox came out of this kind of thinking. They could be best in the world at this if they assemble the resources and go to it.

What happens then is you get companies like Sony, which is one of my favorites. In the design and marketing of small electronic products they are the best in the world. In the same industry you get Matsushita who are the best in the world at process design and distribution. You get some companies, like Nike, that are best in the world at marketing and product design but they don't produce anything. Wal-Mart is the same way. Wal-Mart doesn't produce anything, but they are the best in the world at distributing.

Economies of scale

One of the interesting things that flows out of all this is a change in definition of what an economy of scale is. There are three and only three economies of scale today that really count:

1   the economy of scale of information;
2   the economy of scale of distribution; and
3   the economy of scale of connectivity.

Notice that all three are information related.

With those three economies of scale you can identify the companies where it makes sense to grow larger. It makes sense for distribution companies, connectivity companies and information companies to grow larger. Watch out for the other guys because until somebody discovers a physical economy of scale (and there aren't many of those around), they're asking for real trouble. Watch the mergers, acquisitions, and so forth that are going on today with this and that company, because it's a very interesting feature of today's marketplace.

Let's look again at what this core competency business is. It's not where we are best in the world but where we can be best in the world or where the customer is going to insist that we be best in the world. And I mean best in the *world* because, remember, a service can cross borders unimpaired. Therefore it has to be best in the world not best in a country or a state.

How does this look in various industries you're familiar with? In banking, the banks used to be fully integrated and they did all of these things, marketing, distribution, credit approval, fund movement, collections, investments, etc. A couple guys at McKinsey noted that 68% of the cost of banking was in two activities, marketing distribution and funds movement. Then they made an interesting analysis. They said, "Is there any evidence that any bank is best in the world at marketing?" And the answer was no. They said, "Hmm, there are opportunities there." Then they asked, "What is funds movement all about?" The answer to that question was electronics, but that's not something banks typically do well. A lot of other people looked at the same data and suddenly the industry was restructured. A whole industry created itself around funds movement, another one around marketing distribution of banking types of products. And the result is that element by element the banks were disaggregated into specialized groups, syndicated brokers, etc., for things like mortgage services, and the bank itself became a hollow shell.

Now, who survived and who grew in this field? I could give you dozens of examples of the good guys, but let me just take one: State Street Boston. It's an interesting example. State Street Boston saw the coming of the mutual funds business and they said, "Somebody is going to have to be custodian for all that stuff. What does that take? It takes electronics. We don't have the electronics but we'll get them." So they attracted to themselves software types who became the second rank of management. The deal makers, the loan officers, the former businesses of State Street Boston, went away. And in short order State Street Boston found itself with 53% of the mutual custodial business. Now they handle $3.8 trillion under custody.

This gives them more knowledge about this type of activity than anyone else in the world. They can invest more money in the software than anyone else. They can attract the best people into this field – the best stimulating the best. And with that system they can innovate in new products. So what's happened is that through core competency strategy, specializing, getting best in the world depth in a field, they can now innovate in ways that no one else can. So the two go together.

What happens in other industries? I don't care which industry you pick, you'll find the same thing. Application-specific integrated circuits, biotechnology, virtually all telecomms, almost any one of the high-tech fields you want to name today, operate this way. The smaller, highly specialized companies do each stage of the value chain at best-in-the-world levels and the big companies essentially become coordinators and partners, levering their intellect against the intellect of these outside specialists. When they do this they can leverage their intellect enormously, by factors of 50–100. This is now common.

An interesting example is MCI. MCI invests in the system software. It doesn't bother to do application software because all it has to do is open its system enough for the independents out there who will then innovate on their own to connect into the MCI system. MCI gets the benefit of the flow-through. The innovator gets the benefit of some share of the service. And MCI hasn't had to invest one penny in this.

I talked to the head technologist MCI and I asked, "How many technical people do you employ around here?" To which he replied, "We've got 20,000 people working for us full time." I said, "No, you don't." He said, "Yeah, we do." I said, "Your payroll, that just doesn't check." And he says, "Oh, you mean internally? Not many, but we've got 20,000 other technology people working on our behalf and they're better than anyone we can hire." The small specialists can hire the best. They can give them the specialized software backup to perform at best levels. By tapping into that you can really leverage your intellectual capability.

These are the exciting things that are happening. Their payoffs are not in lowered cost. They're in better quality, access to the most knowledgeable specialists – hence being on the frontier where you couldn't be otherwise – and access to multiple specialized knowledge bases. What MCI has, through its suppliers, is access to all of the specialized knowledge bases of their customers. When Ford outsources it no longer just relies on the knowledge of its internal division because the guy who Ford is outsourcing to has other customers and hears of their problems earlier than Ford does. He therefore innovates earlier than Ford could have done, and Ford gets the benefit.

Champions for innovation

This is a very exciting, very important portion of the innovation business. And we could go on with this. Better strategic anticipation, faster, more flexible response, and higher long-term return on investment. Investment goes down, and return goes up. That's a great combination.

I should talk some about managing innovative intellect. Intellect itself consists of:

- cognitive knowledge or "know-what," which is knowing the rules;
- advanced skills or "know-how," which is being able to take those capabilities or rules and apply them to multiple situations;
- systems knowledge, which is knowing why things are happening; and
- motivated creativity which is caring why, and then doing something about it.

This is why you still need champions in innovation. Nobody innovates without a champion because you've got to care and caring really counts. Getting people together to the point where they intensely care is part of this creating process. Notice, however, when you're managing these knowledge systems we're talking about, look at the way we make our investments. Value increases as we move down this chain but we invest in training in just the opposite fashion.

We spend all of our money training in know-what and maybe a little know-how, almost none on systems knowledge. And teaching people how to create and work together for creativity, none. This is where we've got to start reassessing how we invest in knowledge, one of many areas.

When you're developing professionals, you have to realize that a professional is a person who is at the frontier of knowledge. They have the command of a discipline or field. This means depth. What we pay professionals for mostly is perfection. Do you really want a creative surgeon? Not on yourself, you don't, right? This is one of those "Not in My Back Yard" operations. Do you really want a creative airline pilot? 99% of the time the answer is no. However, the other 1% of the time you want them to find new solutions for you. The guys I was working with on this pension plan were looking for new solutions, but the professional said, "Heck, we do this all the time." So to a professional the problem might look like same old thing but he can deliver enormous value to you.

Consider this: great intellect enterprises are built by the few. Cambridge University was essentially built by one person, Isaac Newton. Yale was built by Willard Gibbs. McKinsey by one person. Microsoft, two people. Intel, three. Netscape, one or two, depending on how you look at it. The interesting thing here is spending the time to find the few. The great intellect companies spend their time finding, recruiting, bringing on board and nurturing these few. Because the others will come. The best in the world want to work with the best in the world and once you get the best in the world you're off and running. If we want to build a business school we get three good people, the best people. Otherwise, I don't care if you hire 50 of the others, you're never going to get there. It's only going to work when you get the best two or three.

You recognize that knowledge grows exponentially. Therefore you systematically expose this intellect to more and more complex problems, and no one is more complex than the customer. So you get them into contact with the customer quickly and repeatedly, and then you up the scale. Notice that the great intellect-based enterprises also absolutely push their people to the extreme in terms of their physical tolerance.

In the great medical schools, you work 100 hours a week. When you've finished you go on into internship and you work even more than that. I don't know how you can work more than that but you do. You go to Microsoft, you work 60 to 80 hour weeks. You go to the great consulting firms, you do the same thing. Why? Because during that period of time you're exposed to complexity, complexity, complexity, need, need, need and you are intensifying that knowledge you have and you are moving up a steep curve. The person who goes to work for Joe Jones consulting is not developing at that rate.

If you can capture that knowledge, if this person can begin to feed that knowledge into the system then you get a second compounding as it goes along. We need to organize to do that. Most organization concepts are based around power – who has the resources, who has the right to give orders. Now we need to organize around the locus of intellect. Where are the smarts in this enterprise? Where is the locus of customization? That is, where is the point at which we modify this for customers? What is the major direction and flow of intellect? Is it unidirectional, back and forth on the same channel or is it cross directional? The mode of leverage then falls out of this.

Intellect and organization

When a company is organized around the locus of intellect it changes the aspect of the hierarchy. It produces a type of flat organization. The flattest organization I've ever seen is 1 to 18,000. This is called reasonably flat. You see organizations every day that are 1 to 400. But if you tell somebody, "Why don't you make your organization 1 to 400" they panic. You can do this very easily if the intellect, the dominant intellect, is at the center, customization is at the node, or the contact node, and these people are independent of each other. I'll give two examples:

◆ *Financial services.* Complex products created at the center are distributed by software to the nodes, each node is then tailored to individual customers. Very simple, very straightforward.
◆ *Large fast-food chains.* The product concepts, the way in which the product is prepared, the sourcing, everything is done at the center. The modification is done at the point of contact, the fast food outlets. These are independent and you can get a tremendous amount of innovation leverage – 400 to 1, 40 to 1 and so forth – out of this type of system. It's powerful stuff.

If the contact node and the point of innovation are the same and both are at the customer level, and the creators are independent, then you can invert the organization. This is highly motivational. In essence they give full power to these people to order the organization. We have lots of these organizations around. Merchant bankers operate this way, hospitals operate this way. Under these circumstances you invert the organization, put the power in one place, and then provide support software at another level to spread knowledge.

Spider's webs are true networks where the knowledge and the modification are at the same place. But the people require contact with others. This is different from an inverted organization where some people don't have to be in contact with others. When contact is essential, you can put them together with a network. Each of them requires different software and a different motivation system.

Under this motivation system if you get the power of the network you have to give incentives based upon network output, and these organizations work best when there are four levels of incentives. One is for professional knowledge, done by peer review. One is for customer performance, done by customers. One is for company profitability, done by value added measure. And the last is team, done by members of the team. If you can get all four of those together, it really works.

Now why is this so powerful? Because in the types of organizations where there are reporting structures that are say, 1 to 20, when you add one person you simply go to 1 to 21. However, in a network when you go from eight to nine you go from a power of eight to a power of nine, meaning that in this type of system, it goes up by an exponential factor, two to the N minus one. So that when you go from a grouping of seven to a grouping of eight you go from two to the seventh power to two to the eighth power, which is essentially a doubling of power.

These dynamics are very powerful. This is why people love these organizations. They are wonderful for seeking problems, they are wonderful for analyzing, they are wonderful for creating options. However, they are absolutely lousy for making decisions. So what we find over and over again is people are saying, "We've got our new network organizations and boy, do they strut and move." But if you ask them what they're doing with them and they tell you they're making decisions, be prepared to go inside and find out that the decisions have either slowed down or significantly modified by the powerful group pressures that tend to form in such networks, to the point where they can't get any really dramatic decisions or quick decisions out of the system at all.

The last one of these organization forms I'll discuss is one which is really a core competency type, a starburst organization, where you have a deep complex core competency which has to be modified with a market core competency in order to go to the market. Who uses this? All of the movie houses, all of the venture capital firms, a lot of the high-tech firms that are moving into multiple markets. Thermo-electron is a great example of this. Deep core competencies can split off. Then you can actually finance these things independently as they do in the mutual funds, as they do in the movie business. Then one person might drive the marketing half of it, with another group driving the core competency.

The new startups are using a modification of these organizational forms. They're essentially three-level organizations in which the knowledge depth is created in functional types of organizations because in order to get maximum knowledge depth you've got to work with other experts. A person who is at the frontier has to work with others who are as close to the frontier as he or she is.

So you keep them in this kind of a structured organization. Link them to user problems where the group moves into a network form in order to find, analyze, and solve them with greatest rapidity and then move back to its base. In between, there is a software base and the software base includes all of the knowledge captured by the system. External models, technology models, customer data and operations data.

A lot of companies leave such knowledge bases wide open to anyone in the company under the theory that if you make it accessible to only one group or another in the company you create a disadvantage for all others and hence tension. These knowledge repositories are very potent and very powerful and almost all the new startups are doing this, and in these the virtual organization becomes a real organization. We move beyond teams into a mode called independent collaboration.

W.L. Gore is an interesting example of this. Gore operates with what they call a lattice non-organization where each individual operates independently as an associate. If he or she wants to go to work on a problem that requires more associates they jointly select a leader. The leader is not selected by the company. If the thing moves into a transaction mode and becomes a product and it starts going out the door, a champion volunteers to take over certain responsibility for certain portions of that and coordinate with the other champions. This is all held together by a communications system called Gorecom and by software which allows such complex interactions among elements of its organizational network.

As demonstrated by the companies I have mentioned, software has become the dominating factor in business innovation. It captures the knowledge, it manipulates the knowledge, it creates new knowledge options and, embarrassingly to many people, software now goes beyond our knowledge capabilities. If you look at some of the great discoveries of the last decade you'll find that they were actually made by software. They were not made by human beings. This is unsettling. There is absolutely no way that large-scale systems, like the human genome project, could work without the knowledge that software itself creates by identifying patterns that are occurring in the incoming data.

What we now have is an extension of human intellect that is extraordinarily powerful and it not only solves the problems but disseminates the knowledge about the problems. Technology is not an answer, it is an enabler, but what it enables allows organizations to leverage human intellect to produce astounding, breakthrough results that were never before possible – a true innovation explosion.

Part III

Knowledge and Strategy

Where we were surprised at the relatively low impact people believed KM to have had at the organizational level, we were pleasantly surprised at the high ratings people gave to the impact it has had at the strategic level (e.g. the firm as knowledge-based business). (See Fig. III.1.)

While 1 (Insignificant) does show up here, we were encouraged by the number of 5, 6, and 7 ratings, indicating that people did feel that knowledge management was striking a chord at the "higher" levels of business, a finding consistent with the Baldridge CEO study mentioned earlier. This is primarily good news, but there are some dangers with this outcome as well. Knowledge management may be more significant at the strategic level because it is easy to understand and buy into, but then less significant at the organizational and individual level since it is hard to actually do. Although this indicates

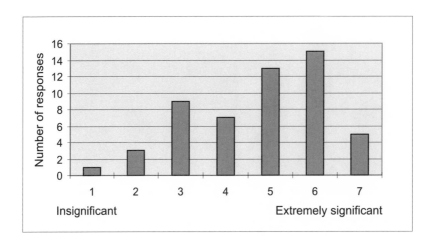

Figure III.1: The impact of knowledge management at the strategic level

that the discussion about the impact of knowledge has risen to strategic proportions, and hasn't been bogged down at the purely tactical level, if it stays at the strategic level it risks the "fad" brand. Still, there are organizations that have embraced knowledge management at both levels. Mark Mazzie, Chief Knowledge Officer of Barnett International, says that for them "knowledge management is becoming a key driver in the strategic planning process. Many clients are using knowledge programs to increase process efficiency and employee productivity."

If a strategic shift to knowledge-based business is what this knowledge-centric set of concepts brings about, we would consider that a great success. In the chapters that follow, Steve Denning talks about a transformation in the World Bank that could have worldwide quality of life implications for millions. Stan Davis talks about the total reconceptualization of the marketplace, its participants, and its products. Finally, Karl-Erik Sveiby discusses how even the way we think about measurement and corporate performance needs to change dramatically. These are all excellent goals and would be wonderful outcomes from this shift to a knowledge-based model of business. If knowledge management is truly significant at the strategic level, its impact will be sweeping and dramatic. That would be fine with us.

Chapter 9

The Knowledge Perspective:
A New Strategic Vision

Stephen Denning,

The World Bank

Knowledge management can be seen in two ways: first, as a way of making the organization do what it does better, and second, as a way of redefining the business. For better or worse, the World Bank is very much in the second category. We tend to think, like an article I read recently in the *Harvard Business Review*,[1] that "If you are not thinking strategically about knowledge management ... your future competitor is." I would recommend the article if you're interested in the economics of information. It's a terrific overview of how knowledge and information, among other things, are really transforming organizations around the world.

I'm going to present a few facts about the World Bank, explain what we're doing in knowledge management and convey the story of what's happening in our organization. I'm also going to draw some comparisons with the ideas of other writers, and I'll be throwing in a few knowledge nuggets.

About the World Bank

The World Bank is an international organization and is owned by the governments of the world. It's traditionally been a lending organization – it lends around $20 billion a year – which provides technical assistance and advice on the side. It has an administrative budget of about $1.5 billion, and profits of around $1 billion a year. So it's a commercially run organization. It's probably worth repeating what is often said in the press, that the World Bank has not been perceived over the past 10 or 20 years as a very change-oriented or agile organization. In fact, it's often been seen as the epitome of a change-resistant organization. It's known for stolid, entrenched management, where successive presidents have come with great ambitions to change it and left with their tails between their legs. So it's an organization that doesn't have a reputation for change but where knowledge management has now become a central strategic thrust.

The mission of the organization is this: to reduce global poverty and improve living standards by promoting sustainable economic growth and investments in people. Often, in private companies, this would be regarded as the quintessence of an unrealistic mission. In fact, when one is doing planning sessions, it is sometimes cited as an example of an unrealistic mission. But this happens to be our mission: reducing global poverty and improving living standards in the poorest countries of the world. And it's important for knowledge management to keep this in mind because we have to be thinking: "is what we're doing helping the mission, or not helping it?" If it doesn't help the mission, it should be discarded.

When we talk about knowledge in the World Bank we are asking questions about what works in development:

- How do you deal with world hunger?
- How do you get kids into school?
- What do you do about the Asian banking crises?

We're *not* talking about transaction information:

- How much money have we lent?
- Which organizations have we lent to?
- What is the repayment situation?

We're talking about the know-how of the organization: what really works and what doesn't work. The problems that we face are so difficult that they are sometimes described as wicked, in the sense that understanding what the problem is, is often more difficult than finding the answer. Once you've figured out the problem – why kids are not in school – then you know how to solve it. When one is not really sure of the problem, knowledge management becomes very complicated.

A promise of change

In October 1996 at the annual meeting of the World Bank, in front of 170 finance ministers, the president of the World Bank announced that we were going to organize our know-how, experience and knowledge, and share it not only with our staff to make us more effective but, using the Internet and other means, share it directly with our clients around the world.

He obviously chose a very public forum to make this announcement, and when he made it probably only about 15 people in the organization knew what he was talking about. It's also true that there was no extended process of consultation. The time since then has been spent dealing with the implications of this announcement.

At the time, we really only had one thing going for us in addition to a president who had announced we were going to do this. We had a couple of small pilot projects in the organization that had been going on in a very small sphere. And they were perceived as successful, so we were able to draw on these pilots and use that success for other things. But all the other elements required to go forward with an organization-wide strategy were not in place. These principal elements of going forward across the organization are now in place. In

"We need to invest in the necessary systems, in Washington and worldwide, that will enhance our ability to gather development information and experience, and share it with our clients."

President Wolfensohn, October 1, 1996

the past year, the pilots have continued to gather momentum and new pilots have come on stream and they seem to be working. They are perceived as being successful.

For about six months after the president made his announcement, there was an argument in the top management about the *strategy*: was this going to be the strategy or not? In March 1997 it was finally approved by the board of directors, with plans for its organization and implementation. So there was an initial struggle at the upper part of the organization to get agreement that, yes, we were in fact going to be doing this. More recently an alarmingly large budget has been put in place and there is now a governance structure to steer the strategy across the organization. There is also a tracking and monitoring system in place. So we have made quite a bit of progress to put in place the elements to make this happen.

How does one person persuade many?

One might ask, or you may be interested to know: well, how did you move this change-resistant, big, old organization to make this sort of transformation? One way I *thought* when I was trying to get this launched was, well, I'll prepare some charts and boxes. That's what management consultants do. And I told people, "I've just read this exciting book by Nonaka and Takeuchi; it's got a terrific picture of what knowledge management is about." While intriguing, theoretical diagrams didn't work. I also thought, since our organization is a rational, technocratic organization I'll present rational arguments. I'll write reports. I'll show people why this makes sense. This was also wholly ineffective; people just couldn't focus on it. Dialog could work one-on-one if you could get enough time with people, but if you're one person trying to convince thousands, dialog is going to take you hundreds of years. So as a way of changing the organization, it was impractical.

Stories have proven tremendously helpful for us, for me. Before I explain why, I'd like to relate one story in particular that was very helpful. In 1996, I was talking to someone at lunch and showing them the charts and reports and he said, "look, I met somebody in Zambia the other day ..." And he told me a little story. And I said, "oh, that's great. I'll put that in my presentation." That then became a centerpiece of my presentation. I would get to a certain point and then I would ask, "What is the future of the World Bank? What does it look like?" And I'd say, "the future looks like today, and this is a true story: in June 1995, a health worker in Kamana, Zambia – 600 kilometers from the capital – logged onto the Center for Disease Control Web site in Atlanta and got the answer to a question on how to treat malaria. Now, this is June 1995, not June 2015. It was not the capital of Zambia; it was 600 kilometers away. It was not a rich country; it was one of the poorest countries in the world. And the most important part of the picture to us is that the World Bank is not in it. We are not organized to convey our expertise and know-how in this fashion. And this is the future; this is the way the world is going to work. So why don't we get ready for the future?

That story was enough for people to get it. Once they have the idea of the future they can then relate to all the charts and boxes and the analysis and everything else, but until they get it, they can't relate to those things. And I believe that stories are a tremendously powerful way of conveying tacit knowledge. There are huge amounts of tacit knowledge in that one little story. It's only 29 words long, but it taps into the personal experience of managers and staff in the World Bank. Everyone in the World Bank has been to a place like Zambia. Everyone has been to a place 600 kilometers from a capital. Everyone understands how know-how is so important. And that little story links up with this personal background. So it may be only 50 bytes in a computer but it has hundreds of megabytes of background material that it hooks into, and that becomes the driving force. It shows the interconnections, and people can immediately relate to this health worker in Zambia and the CDC, and what it would be like for the World Bank to become like the CDC. It's easy to remember. And stories are living. You listen to or read Plato's stories – they're still living a couple of thousand years later.

Stories have all of these things going for them that boxes don't. Boxes have no tacit baggage. They don't connect things. They're straight lines. And there are no straight lines in nature, so one immediately knows one is talking about something artificial. Stories have no straight lines, they have no edges, and they can get through people's mental guards. All of the defenses that management had built up to resist change were undermined by a story.

Here's another story we used a lot this year. Our stories started to become a bit slicker, and this story turns now to the World Bank. And it starts out as a true story. We had a task team in Chile. The minister of education there said, "Quick, give us the global experience of the political economy of education reform." So the team contacted the network and got the instances of this around the world, quickly synthesized that and gave it to the minister. He was delighted, gave it to the cabinet: "Just what we wanted!" And in one sense this is the way the World Bank has done its work at its best, even in its traditional mode. But knowledge management can take it further. The synthesis that is done in Chile, and the inputs there, are edited for further reuse and put into the knowledge base. When a new client, say in South Africa, has a similar question, that team can go into the knowledge base, find the Chile synthesis, adapt it to the South African situation if it's appropriate, with minimal rework, and so meet the client's needs faster and better.

This works if:

1   There is a classification scheme that enables you to find things in a very large knowledge base.
2   You have a live human being whom you can talk to, who will answer questions, and who can help guide the search.
3   There is a technology platform that enables material to move across organization boundaries around the world.

And so, as the story continues, the South Africa synthesis is edited for further reuse and put into the knowledge base. Further inputs come from inside and, we hope, from outside the organization into the knowledge base. And by the year 2000, we plan to have this available externally, so that anyone around the world can log into the database, get the Chile synthesis, or the South Africa synthesis, and use it themselves or ask the World Bank's help in doing it. And this slightly more sophisticated story has helped the bank management and staff to understand the flow of knowledge management and how this would unveil itself in the context of our organization.

80% brainpower, 20% information technology

The story also tries to make a couple of points. One, that technology is a relatively small part of the story: perhaps 20%. It's a central part, a crucial part for the external access, but a relatively small part. It's like saying blood is only 8% of the body or something. You've got to have it, but it's not the main thing. What it's really about is human brainpower. Gathering information, synthesizing it, individual thinking, discussing – this is the guts of knowledge management, and the technology has to support all of these four different types of activity.

And these are kind of messy processes; knowledge typically begins with this discussing process, is supplemented by individual thinking, and gathering information relevant to the problem – then analyzing it and synthesizing it through real-life actions and solutions. It's important to recognize that knowledge doesn't ever become final. It continuously incubates and grows. And one needs to keep supporting all of these messy processes in knowledge management if in fact it's going to be a living system.

A number of others have in different ways referred to this element: that more is less, that getting more information about things is not the answer. What our staff and our clients want is not 500,000 things on something, and not even 100 things on something, nor even 10 things on something! What they want to ask is: "What is the best analysis of the finance of the education sector? Don't bother me with all that other stuff – I just want the best. And give it to me now!" And, in a sense, that's the comparative advantage of the World Bank – at least in its image. And we need to make it a reality that we can deliver what is the right way to do this. Many IT people tell us, "Well, we'll give you these great search engines that can look through all of this and catalog all of these documents." I don't think that any search engine will be able to tell that the best piece on the finance of education happens to be chapter four of the report we just did last month on Vietnam. There is no way I can conceive of a search engine that will be able to make that kind of call. So it's human brainpower that is driving this whole thing.

Benefits of managing knowledge

Once you've got people hooked on the story, then you do have to explain the benefits. And so, yes, we have charts explaining the benefits. And it's mainly three things. One is faster cycle times, particularly on getting this know-how. When we were mainly doing lending, and advice was something on the side, then to get the answer on a know-how question might take one month, two months – might take forever. We might just say, we're not going to do it. Now, with the help desk, we're delivering those kinds of know-how answers to clients in one to two days. But the idea of the Internet is to get it down to one or two minutes! So dramatically more rapid cycle times. And a much larger group of clients benefiting from the World Bank. At present, to get much benefit from the World Bank you have to be having a transaction with us – some kind of lending transaction. And that means a small number of people around the world benefit. The idea here is to open the whole thing up and, through the Internet, make the whole thing accessible – and at the same time improve the quality of relationships and become a completely open and transparent organization.

A three-part process

Of course, people say you've got to have a model. Well, we've got a model. It has three parts. Knowledge management is creating, organizing, and applying knowledge. And in some ways, the most important part is the creation part, because unless you have high-quality knowledge, there's no point organizing or applying it. So it starts with interacting with clients, learning on the job, identifying knowledge gaps, doing research and analysis to close those gaps, and then reaching outside the organization where better knowledge exists. Organizing means putting that into a knowledge base, which is mainly staff and managers in operations, supported by a relatively small information technology platform and an even smaller group of knowledge organizers. Applying knowledge is making that know-how available very rapidly to bank staff and external clients and partners. And our Economic Development Institute is looking around and interacting directly with clients and partners.

A three-segment model is what we needed. And for us, curiously, models that go in circles or loops throw our management off. You'd think – here's a bunch of economists, and economies work in cycles – they'd love circular models. No way. They hate circular models. Models have to flow from left to right and when you do that, people say, "yes I understand." You put a loop in and you just lose them. So that didn't work for us. It was important to use labels that people in our organization could understand. Simple words were more helpful. "Tacit knowledge" doesn't work – you have to say "knowledge in people's heads."

So we have moved along quite rapidly. When we talked with our board of directors in February 1997, we said we'd be active in half of the sectors during the fiscal year. As it turned out, the momentum was such that we became active in all the sectors of the organization.

How did it all happen? Below I've summarized some of the things we're proud of, and some lucky things that happened. I've taken the three biggest of the hundreds of blunders that were made, and I describe some of the bad breaks we've had. Lastly I look at some unexpected lessons that we learned, and the four toughest issues that we're still working on.

Seven (slightly) smart things

In terms of what helped make this happen there is one underlying thing that is absolutely essential: you have to have a simple *compelling vision* that people will buy into. Hence the idea of the World Bank as an organization that would make its know-how available to external clients, partners, and stakeholders around the world. This was a very simple vision and once you got it, you could buy into it. So having a vision behind it that is compelling, and then being able to explain what the benefits of it are, is very important. We did *build a robust coalition* of interested vice presidents. People at the upper middle level. We had six people who really believed in it, who thought this was the future and who were willing to fight for it when the going got rough, as it did quite often. And we were able to get the president on board and he adopted it with gusto. He also publicly announced it before any details were worked out, and that was helpful because there was no going back after he'd made that announcement.

One thing that may be more controversial in the knowledge management community is defining and putting into a system what is involved in knowledge management. Basically, we took the knowledge management activities and, after the staff involved in it had been floundering around for about nine months, we said, "Let's define what it is we're doing." And they collectively defined what they were doing in the following seven categories:

1   *Assembling a large knowledge base.* You have in the knowledge management system (KMS) the high quality know-how that people had gathered together, things that past teams say that they did in their work.
2   *The help desk.* Having dedicated staff who can answer questions. Initially, this was conceived as a second-best type of thing that would become a temporary phenomenon. It has become almost the centerpiece of the whole system; having a human being who can help you find the thing that you need is a critical part of it. And it has been much more immediately successful than the first KMS that came online, and in fact that is much more difficult and takes a lot longer time to become a success.
3   A *directory of expertise*: "who knows what." Also a rather tricky thing to develop but very important in a large organization, as you find out who is who in the organization.
4   *Development data.* This is statistics about what is happening in development. It's not just data, in the sense of, say, stock market data, but each figure in development data is a judgment about the situation in the country. So there is a particular technology and approach that is needed surrounding that.
5   *Engagement information.* This is the links to the transaction information in the organization: what is happening in that operation in water supply in Mozambique in 1996 and the ability to be able to bring that into the picture.
6   *Dialog space.* This is still embryonic but potentially one of the most powerful aspects of the KMS. The ability to ask questions around the organization and get answers and have a dialog is a tremendously important thing.
7   *External access.* This is making the information available externally to clients.

So we mapped these seven activities and then also mapped the whole organization into five global sector networks. We split these up into 15 sectors, and split them again into 76 knowledge domains. Then we mapped the seven activities against the 76 knowledge domains, so that one can see at a glance what is happening at any one time in any sector or knowledge domain, which activities are underway now, which will be underway in December, which will be underway in the middle of next year.

Some people in knowledge management would say that was a terrible mistake, because it's kind of bureaucratized knowledge management. For us, being a bureaucracy was actually terribly important, particularly trying to secure the large budget for this to happen. Because once you systematize the activities and are able to put them into a timeframe and you can describe them, then you can justify to management what the $50 million is going to be spent on. Management had this idea of a kind of an anthill of people wandering around in a random fashion. Once we'd characterized the seven activities and the 76 knowledge domains we could map it, and say, look, it might look like an anthill but here's what's happening, this is what the various ants are building and how it all interrelates. And that was very important for us. So, though it does have some dangers of becoming a bureaucracy, it's had such tremendous advantages that it deserves to be called one of the slightly smart things that we did.

And it's not been smooth going throughout this period. I would say that now the opposition has gone underwater. Some of them have parted but there's still a good segment of the middle management that's skeptical about whether this will work. And learning from other organizations, like Ernst & Young and anyone else who can help us on this, has been very helpful. We're very much in outreach mode, and trying to learn from everyone and not reinvent the wheel.

Four bad breaks

We've had some bad breaks. For one thing, it has been fairly tough going with the upper middle management. You can tell some people the Zambia story, you can tell them the Chile story. They just don't get it. You can beat them over the head and I think some of them will just never get it. They just have a different idea of what the organization is all about. Another unfortunate break is that this is taking place in a downsizing environment, so sharing all of that becomes very difficult when people are worried about their jobs.

Third, we are constantly struggling with stakeholders skeptical that the World Bank could change. And lastly, the legacy information in existing systems is really a mess. Fortunately an effort is underway now to clean up that backroom mess. It's not absolutely essential for most elements of knowledge management, but obviously it would be a tremendous help if you can clean them up.

Six pieces of dumb luck

Conversely, we also had some lucky things going for us. We did have a *leader who wanted change.* He was looking around for a good change idea. In fact, that's how we got onto this whole thing: he rang up one of the coalition of people on knowledge management and said, "there must be a better idea out there. I'm giving this annual meeting speech: I need a better idea." And it took two days and he got it and he never looked back. With our previous presidents, that wouldn't have happened. A task force would have been appointed to look into it and after five years they would have decided that it would be too expensive. This guy just said that's it, we'll do it.

We do have a *highly motivated professional staff* who are very enthusiastic about the whole idea, and there is this tremendous *untapped knowledge potential* in the organization. People ask, "Why didn't we do this before? I mean, we're in the knowledge business – how come we didn't see this?" I think the Web is one reason. The *invention of the Web* created this external possibility that just wasn't there before. This was happening in small units on a paper basis, but once you have the Web you can suddenly start to think on a global scale, and it makes all the difference. The *organizational change that is underway is a good fit with knowledge management.* And actually it was a good thing that things sort of floundered around during that time. There was really *no one in charge* from the time the president made his announcement in October 1996 until the following July, so there was a 10-month period where the organization sort of floundered around.

And that was good because it grew up in a kind of organic mode without anyone being in charge, and so the kind of "friends of knowledge management" would meet and figure out what to do next. And that was helpful because now that there is a formal arrangement, those friends of knowledge management are a big factor and the fact they have been active in this informal, organic way is quite helpful.

In terms of what's happening organizationally, basically we had those six geographical regional groupings: Africa, Latin America, Eastern Europe, etc., and a sort of a matrix organization over that, with global sector networks, so that each staff member in operations is both a member of the geographical region and of the cross-cutting sectoral network. And knowledge management fits very well with horizontal, global knowledge, so it was a kind of perfect fit for this organizational change that was underway anyway. And the knowledge management board, which is 15 people – each of these geographical regions and each of the global networks has a representative – these 15 people are charged with making decisions about the implementation of this scheme across the organization.

Our three biggest blunders

In terms of our biggest blunders, we've got hundreds of these, but these are my top three.

1   Putting knowledge management in the computer department, which is where I happened to be located. I think this is about operations so this is the wrong place to build this. In one sense, it's kind of neutral. The problem is: where do you put it? You put it anywhere, it's going to be a problem. And one benefit of this is at least it's relatively neutral. And the idea has such a force now, it could be in the janitor's department. It hardly matters where it is, because it's underway on such a large scale. All of these sector boards and networks have sectors and counsels they have a lot of bureaucracy associated with this and this is quite a big problem. We've really gone overboard: too many boards.

2   Having a large decentralized budget. We have this large budget for knowledge management but it's quite hard to access. It's not

in any central pot. It's been given to all different units across the operation; it's in about 100 separate little pots. To spend it, each segment has to reach agreement with the network as to what they're going to spend it on – so it's a bit like scratching your right ear with your left hand. Now it may turn out to be a genius idea. The thinking behind it was that it would encourage decisions to be made in a communal spirit. It could still work out the other way, but at present, I would say it's not the brightest.

3   There really is a tremendous amount of discontinuity and disruption of the work. In the year after the president's announcement, we changed all the managers and shuffled everyone around. Implementing a knowledge management policy, whilst people are trying to figure out their new roles and what companies they should be dealing with, is not the best combination.

Our five most unexpected lessons

We thought we had things figured out, but each month we keep finding that we're really still discovering or inventing – that we're staggering along. We have to keep revising our thoughts on what it is we're trying to do. The central idea that "what we need is knowledge" is something – well, at least *that's* strong: this *is* about knowledge, right? Umm, no. We're not so sure about that anymore. In fact, something that is really solid knowledge in our organization – and many other organizations – means that it's true, it's reliable. But by the time it gets to be that solid it is ancient, even out of date. Most of the really good ideas are not solid, they're not reliable, they're not proven, they don't have much evidence behind them. Yet that in fact is what is proving really valuable. In fact, knowledge management itself, I would suggest, is an example of that. Something that isn't proven, that isn't solid, that isn't reliable. There's hardly any solid evidence that this is actually working. Yet here we are making it a central pillar of our organization for the future. So we think that what is valuable is not just knowledge, in a solid, reliable knowledge sense, but the high-value ideas, which may turn out to be knowledge, but some of them will definitely turn out to be wrong. And our job is to track both of them. So it's not just about knowledge and you shouldn't be totally focused on that.

It was a surprise to many of our managers that the Web really doesn't solve everything and that help desks are much more valuable and immediately helpful in the short run, as was systematizing knowledge management. We hesitated over doing this but I think it turned out to be much more successful than anyone imagined. Systematizing it has helped people get comfortable with it.

And also, learning that – we thought, well, if we put this material on the Web, and people have Windows and there's a big N and they can just click on the N and they'll get into the knowledge base – in fact it's not that easy. Even that little distance is too far. I really think we're going to have to get something like the Cigna Casualty Company has, where they have a workspace and all of the tools that the underwriter needs to do their work right on the same desktop, and they do their work in the middle and all the tools are gathered around the outside. We have to get to the situation where knowledge management is embedded in the way the work gets done.

Our four toughest issues

These are the four toughest things we're struggling with.

Making communities of practice work
We buy into all the romance of the community of practice, and it's a wonderful thing, because it does actually fit our business, and because our clients don't just want the expertise of the team that happens to be assigned to their country. They don't just want the expertise of the team that they are working with. They want the best in the world. They want the best expertise across the whole world, and the only way we can provide that is, in fact, to have a community of practice. But breaking down these barriers of their vertical, geographical organizations is not easy. Furthermore, the distribution of our knowledge is very untidy. There was one thing that happened a while back. One of our clients, Indonesia, wanted the global experience on the private sector providing vocational and technical training. It went to the education help desk, which you might think was the right place for this. However, it turns out that the expertise for this particular thing comes from within the social protection network. There is someone there

who just happens to have done a study on this. *Plus* we've got this guy in the private sector who has a lot of expertise on this. So what does this do to our community of practice? The knowledge doesn't fit into any kind of obvious sort of groupings, so pre-slicing it doesn't seem to help. As Nonaka would say, "Knowledge is self-organizing." Maybe we should relax and let it happen, and try to make this one, huge community. I don't know. I don't think you can make a community of 4000 people. We're going to have to think through what it does mean. We do have to strengthen some of the groups that just aren't interacting very well at all – where there are individuals squabbling with each other. But this question of how to sort out a community when the knowledge itself is scattered throughout is one of our key problems. I'm not sure I can just learn to relax, and live with the self-organizing philosophy.

Making the organizational culture shift

Everyone talks about it, and in fact our president is always saying, "We have to get people to share. We have to get people to share their expertise. We have these people hoarding their stuff." When you talk to this team that's actually been working on this for four years, they say: look, this isn't a problem. You can go to anyone in the World Bank and say, "Look, I understand you've got some expertise on this subject. Would you mind sharing it with me?" The problem is getting started. We've got these intellectual introverts sitting alone in their offices and they're just sort of bursting to tell what they have. So who's right here? I think there is a problem of sharing, but it's not on the supply side of sharing. And in fact, I'm very worried that if we create incentives to share we're just going to be deluged with tons and tons and tons of stuff, much of it of mixed quality. But there is a problem on the demand side. What the surveys and other evidence shows us is that actually getting people to use other people's knowledge is the real heart of the problem. The fact is that we can't get senior management to talk about that – they're much happier talking about the "evil hoarders" and saying, "We're going to create incentives to share." Well it's no wonder everyone wants to create incentives to share, because that's what they want to do anyway. When people are willing to talk about the culture problem, then you suspect that maybe it isn't the problem. One of our difficulties here is to get people to agree on what exactly is the culture problem that we're talking about.

Getting best practice

This is like the crown jewels of knowledge management. We can tell you what works and what doesn't work, but in our business there's hardly anything that works all the time. There are a lot of things that never work – and some of them are very attractive to our clients. So identifying those is going to be a big part of it. But an awful lot of our work is figuring out what works in some contexts and some situations and then figuring out what those contexts and situations and conditions are. Traditionally what we'd do is, we'd write a report. But what happens is that a lot of these insights – the things that aren't yet knowledge, the cutting edge material – doesn't get into the report. Also reports can't be kept up to date. So what happens is, you look around at all the information resources and you think about the Web. And, yeah, we're going to do a knowledge base, and only high-quality items will go in. Well, what starts to happen is that people start collecting these various things that they regard as high-quality items – key readings, ideas, examples, frequently asked questions – and pretty soon, they have a rather large collection. So then they think, well, we better distill that into something and learn some lessons from it. And then they look at *that* and it turns out to be rather large collection, so then they say, well, let's distill *that* – and we seem to be going up a pyramid that never reaches a point.

What seems to happen when you try to build best practice, is that you start out developing a pile of things, and people look at that and they say, "Let's at least sort it out and put it into drawers." It's better than the pile, but it's still a bit of a mess. So what we're struggling to do now is make a tree, where the trunk and the branches are solid knowledge and the cutting-edge ideas and insights and the evidence – the pros and cons – are like the leaves attached to the tree. And the idea would be to update it dynamically, as a way of trying to get in on top of the question: how do we present what works? If we can do that on several levels, we might be able to present the field of knowledge in an intuitive way, and then enable you to drill down to different levels to get to this other material.

External access

External access is going to be a huge problem for us. Copyright, confidentiality, and who gets access to what are all major issues. A lot of people want to charge for our knowledge – rather prematurely, I'd say. We actually need to build it before we can begin to charge for anything. A lot of the senior managers wonder what will be the internal impact of having outsiders looking around at our internal know-how. The president loves it: "That's going to be wonderful: we'll get lots of feedback. If we've got low-quality stuff, they'll tell us – and we want to know that." But not everyone is so keen on that. And there are language issues, as everyone starts wanting everything in 16 languages. If things can be translated with software, and I'm told they can be, that would solve or at least enable us to deal with this problem as it's getting big. In any event, this is going to be a huge problem area for us.

Global knowledge management: weighing the risks

This is a question we have asked ourselves: is it riskier for us to do this or not to do it? The president and I think that for a global organization, it is much riskier for us *not* to do it. I strongly believe that unless we do this, we will not survive. We will not be able to meet the needs of our clients, who basically want global knowledge. They want the best there is. And unless we get organized to do this, we will not be able to meet their needs. And although people in the press are starting to talk about what a risky thing this is for us to do, not doing it, we think, is even more risky.

So I have presented to you seven slightly smart things, six pieces of dumb luck, four blunders, four bad breaks, five unexpected lessons, four tough issues … a total of about 30 knowledge nuggets. But in one sense – and this is sort of a paradigm of how knowledge is communicated – each of these nuggets is not worth much. They only make sense if you see how the story fits together. And so, in a sense, conveying knowledge is not the business of conveying nuggets in little pieces; it's the business of conveying the connections between things. And what I've tried to convey to you is the story of what's been happening in the World Bank.

Note

1 Evans and Wurster, (1997) "Strategy and the economics of information," *Harvard Business Review*, September/October 1997.

Chapter 10

Building Knowledge

into Products

Stan Davis

Economic life cycles

Let me set the stage by giving you a few of my thoughts about the economy and the businesses therein. First, economies have life cycles and any of you familiar with my work know that I believe that this economy is going to have a life cycle of about 75 years. We've passed through several cycles throughout history – hunting and gathering, agrarian, industrial and the current information economy. I believe this one is going to be about a 75-year economy, plus or minus five years.

It began in the early 1950s, and it will come to an end somewhere in the decade of the 2020s, putting us in the early third quarter of this economy. It will be replaced by yet another one, which is in gestation now and which has yet to hit take-off. I believe that this next economy will be based upon a biological infrastructure replacing the information infrastructure, which will in turn yield a bio-economy. But that will be when most of us are, at the very least, retired.

The way I look at this current economy is that it has gone through its early period and is now at the beginning of its late period. The industrial economy had an early industrial infrastructure built on the steam engine as the basic technology. The early applications of this technology focused on railroads and the late ones on automobiles.

Well, in the same way that you had an early and a late industrial infrastructure, you have an early and a late information infrastructure. Instead of the steam engine you have the computer, and the first half of the lifespan of this economy was focused on the computer as a crunching tool. The second half is going to be the focus on the computer as a communicating tool. The major shift here is from crunching to connecting.

So all the stuff you hear about networks is really turning out to be the dominant theme of the impact of the technology on the infrastructure for the second half of the current economic life cycle. The shift from crunching to connecting will be as powerful a shift, in terms of the implications and consequences that flow from it, as the shift from railroads to automobiles for the industrial infrastructure.

It's essential to understand that and not just pass over it, because it ought to be the touchstone for understanding all these phenomenal shifts. It's even possible – if you want a marker event or a year – to pinpoint 1995 as the year when the shift occurred. In 1995 the Internet reached its critical mass, with more PCs being sold than TV sets. (Incidentally, the first experiments in replicable DNA-based computing were also carried out that year – glimmerings of the beginning of the bio-economy – but that's another story that I won't get into now.) We're at the beginning of this connecting era – that's my first point.

The difference between a business and an organization

Let me now turn to those entities which function within this economic environment by drawing a distinction between a business and an organization. A corporation – the enterprise you work for – is both a business and an organization. They're not the same thing. To put it simply: a business is *what* you do and an organization is *how* you do it. It may seem semantic, but the difference is very important.

A business identifies needs in the marketplace and provides products and services to fulfill those needs. Products and markets make up two of the pillars of what business is about. In order to bring a product to the market you have to apply resources and you do this in relationship to a defined set of competitors. This gives us the four basic elements of a business:

- the product;
- the market;
- the resources; and
- the competition.

This list makes no reference to anything about how the business is organized, managed or administered. This is the *organization* side and it includes the people, the processes, the structure, and the culture.

If business is what you do and organization is how you do it, then that sets up a cause and effect relationship: you cannot possibly know how to do it until you've got an "it" to do. So, by definition, the business comes first and the organization follows. Any statement about the organization has to be in relationship to something that affects the business. Therefore, how can you possibly have a learning organization or knowledge management until you have a knowledge business or a learning business? It's putting the cart before the horse.

There is the danger of latching on to a buzzword, embracing it as the hot next thing, developing all kinds of concepts about it, and letting the organizational focus take off so damn fast that it leaves the implications for the business in the dust. That is a sure way to have it blow up within fairly short order and be just a fad. That ought not to be the case with knowledge, and I don't think it will be.

I'm focusing on the business, because of the causal relationship in which the business comes first and the organization follows. As the business is climbing that life cycle, it's growing, maturing, and declining. The organization, by definition, has to follow. Now, how far behind or closely does it follow? Ideally you want it to follow about a nanosecond behind. That would be a real-time organization, which at this point is an oxymoron. Such a thing just doesn't exist, at least at any unit larger than one. What tends to happen is in the very beginning of the life cycle there is no organization. Then, as the business takes off and grows like crazy, the organization is running like hell to catch up. People are hired and systems, controls, and structures are put in place.

If you fast-forward to the end of the life cycle when the business has slowed up, what's happened is the organization's got this incredible head of steam and it overtakes the business. Then you get the period in which you have re-engineering and outsourcing and all of the reaction to this dilemma, where you have to put on the brakes to say, "Whoa, organization. It's time to get back to your appropriate place, not ahead of the business." That's the tail wagging the dog. That's a bureaucracy. That's where you've got a business that exists to run an organization. It's an inversion of the proper relationship.

If you're looking internally at how to improve the organization, you're looking in the wrong place. What's the best place to look to how to improve your organization? The answer is not inside your organization. The answer is in your future business. What is the business you are going to become? If you understand what the business is that you're going to become, and then you can ask yourself, "Well, what kind of an organization is it going to take to run that business?" By the time you get that organization in place, you've got a shot at it being more real time, closer to what that business is going to need.

Chips with everything

In a speech in New York given a little over 20 years ago, Danny Hillis, who is one of the gurus in the computer field, said, "One day there are going to be more computers than people." And despite being in a room full of techies, he was so roundly jeered that somebody in the audience said, "Yeah, what are we going to do, put them in every doorknob?" And, of course, that is exactly what has happened. There are more computer chips today in doorknobs and tennis sneaker heels and washing machines and the like than there are in PCs.

This would not work unless we were in a connected economy, with the connectivity occuring at all sorts of levels. It occurs in terms of hooking the PC up to its peripherals, including the mouse and the keyboard and the screen. It includes hooking all of that up into intranets, the Internet and the like. It involves the connectivity between people and machines, between businesses, between nations, and across continents.

So, we have established that the mother of all characteristics for knowledge-based products and services is electronic connection. Some people may take that for granted in some areas of business, but many won't. Have you thought about the uses for an electronically connected box of cereal or an electronically connected automobile tire? Think for a minute about what this kind of connectivity means – this electrical connection. First of all, every time we check into a hotel we get a customized door lock. The next generation of door products are going to be interactive so that when you open the door it is connected to inside the room, to the HVAC system, the security system, the lighting system, and so on. Increasingly it's going to move in that direction.

Let me give you another example. Coca-Cola has 800,000 vending machines in Japan alone. Every one of those vending machines has a chip in it. Here's a wonderful question: What might a vending machine want to know? Well, it might want to know,

◆ the internal temperature;
◆ the number of cans that are left;
◆ the type of cans that are left;
◆ the time of purchase; and
◆ the denominations used.

Remember that every piece of information extracted is particular to the machine from which it comes. Also the machine needs to be electronically connected to be truly useful, to be smart.

We're looking at the knowledge revolution as it pertains to business on the one hand and organization on the other. We're all familiar with the term knowledge management, and we've also all heard about smart products, but it's as though these two concepts inhabit different worlds. What I'm saying is that they are not only first cousins, they are genetic twins. Knowledge management is to organization what smart products are to business in terms of this revolution.

The smart car

Let me take another example with a smart product that gets a lot of press – the automobile. Today there are 50 chips in the high-end car and the average car has over a dozen of them. In the high-end car they are worth twenty percent of the cost of the car. They are worth more than the steel or the plastic, glass or rubber.

Let's take one piece of the car – a really simple one – the gas gauge. The first cars had no gas gauge. You had to look in the tank. The next generation had a little light that went on when the tank was nearly empty. The big divide came in the early part of the electronic era, and the gauge displayed the gallons left in the tank. The next thing was how many miles you had left to drive before you ran out of gas. What's the next iteration likely to be? Remember, this is the connected economy. So what is it going to be connected to? Well, computers are going to take over to maximize the fuel efficiency as to how many miles you can eke out of what you've got left and it's going to be linked to a GPS – a Global Positioning System.

The in-car computer can give you all sorts of information based on data from a GPS: the locations of the nearest gas stations, hotels, banks, etc. It's going to progress from there. It's going to tell you the nearest gas station that it knows is open, or that you have chosen (for credit card purposes, say) – the nearest Texaco or Gulf or Mobil. Today you can rent a car and plug in your destination – it already knows where you are because of the transponder – and it's going to direct you how to get from point A to point B. Map Quest provides free, detailed maps for over three million places and gets more than two million hits per day. And that's before people can dial-in from their cars.

Now take some of the other chips on the car. You've got chips to monitor and control rear wheel road grip, anti-lock brake systems, the drive train in the suspension, the ignition, the traction and the fuel economy. My point is the same whether I'm talking about cars, doorknobs or vending machines. I'm talking about the attributes that are embodied in any knowledgeable offering. I use the term offering to mean product and/or service. With any of these products, what you have to ask yourself is: what is it that the product or service wants to know? Remember that one of the key points to consider when putting knowledge into products is the connectivity aspect. A good example in the automobile industry is a cooperative agreement that IBM has with Mercedes. They're going to be connecting, monitoring, and controlling all these interconnected systems to make the driving experience better and safer. You've got information being gathered on the outside of the car regarding weather, traffic, road conditions and the like. This information is being processed, and sent to the inside of the car, not only to the driver but to the chips that control the engine, braking system, lights, windshield wipers and so on.

Take another example, you've got a knock in your automobile's engine and you bring it in to be serviced. Of course, when they take it for the test ride, what happens? There's no knock. Wouldn't it be neat if when it's making the knock you use your cellular phone and you're on-line with your garage? The next generation is going to have your garage calling you up while you're driving to tell you about the knock.

My brother-in-law retired and, God bless him, he bought an RV. He's cruising around the country in his RV and he realizes that he needs some work done to upgrade the engine and the transmission. Now, in the industrial paradigm, that was a total headache. In today's world, what happened was that a guy in a suit and tie appeared with a PC that he plugged into the steering column, and he downloaded the new software. In fifteen minutes he had upgraded the transmission and the engine.

The RV is an example, but it could as well be a dishwasher, or a toaster. If you're in the business of developing a smart product you have to ask yourself a number of questions: what does it want to know? Why does it want to know it? How does it know it? Knowledge is not new stuff. It's just that you use the technologies that are available. In an industrial economy you used industrial technologies. So how did a car know that it wanted to shift gears? It knew because you had an industrial technology that created an automatic transmission. A thermostat is another example. What would a room want to know? Of course these products aren't always successful the first time round – remember the fiasco of the smart buildings? Architects were going to build smart buildings and that never happened. But home banking failed for fifteen years, and now everybody's doing it. It doesn't mean it's not going to happen. It means that we expect too much in the short run and not enough in the long term.

Spend some time getting to know what your product wants to know, how will it know it, and why. We come up with questions like, is it aligned or misaligned? Is it available or busy? Is it charged or discharged? Is it clean or dirty? Is it current or expired? Is it day or is it night? Is it early or late? Is it fast or slow? Firing or misfiring? Fit, misfit, or unfit? Is it free or pay? Is it fresh, stale or spoiled?

You can imagine all the products on the shelf, instead of having inert date expiration, they have electronic dates on them so that all the packages become electronically connected with one another in the supermarket. "I'm about to expire, I think I'll lower my price." It's not wild. This is exactly what the people in that business are dealing with and thinking about all the time. By the way, my list of questions is only up to the Fs. Is it fresh or stale or spoilt? Is it full or empty? Is it hard or soft? Is it high or low? Is it hot or cold? Is it important or unimportant? Instant or lagging? Light or dark? Light or heavy? Live or dead? Or not live? Locked or unlocked? Is it loud or quiet? Matched or mismatched? On or off? On time or late? Open or closed? Present or absent? Profit or loss? Pure or impure? Pure or blended? Ready or not ready? And I'm in the Rs now. You get the point.

TV Guide: *converting information into knowledge*

The largest-selling magazine in the United States is *TV Guide*. *TV Guide* has had a wonderfully long run, but everything that begins has an ending. It's great if you've got five stations, thirteen stations, sixty-eight stations, but now with a hundred stations and growing, *TV Guide* is going to look like the Manhattan yellow pages. What's more, *TV Guide* is a paper-based information product, not a knowledge-based smart product. The only way to create real growth is to shift on to another curve. You can prop up the declining curve through more efficient operations of *TV Guide* (through, say, better knowledge management), but bringing out a knowledge-based *TV Guide* creates the opportunity for real growth. This is exactly what is in development in Murdoch's outfit, and similar offerings by three others are already on the market.

What would the characteristics of a knowledge-based *TV Guide* be? It would know what you're interested in. How would it know what you're interested in? It would know what you'd watched before and when you watch. Now, how would it know what you watched? It's electronically connected. How would it be electronically connected? It's on your cable, or possibly on your TV set – in the distribution string or in the delivery can. It's electronically connected and in order to get to know what you like, it has to have memory.

So, it's electronically connected and it has memory. Does your product learn its user's behavior? If so, how? And what does that mean? You might say the more you use this knowledge-based *TV Guide* the smarter it gets, the more it learns about you. So another attribute of a knowledge-based product is that the more you use it the smarter it gets.

Now, lest we pass over that last point too quickly, that alone is an entire revolution. The whole industrial era paradigm was that a product was as smart as it was going to be the minute it was manufactured and shipped. A knowledge-based product gets smarter with use because it is electronically connected, interactive, and it has memory. The product gets smarter with use, the customer using it gets smarter, and if it's got a feedback loop, the provider who created it also gets smarter. You bring that car into that smart garage and the garage gets smarter, Detroit gets smarter about how to build those cars, the customer gets smarter about how to operate those cars, and the car gets smarter too.

This is a very bizarre world, where things don't get used up. The industrial paradigm is one of diminishing returns. You buy something and it starts off complete and then it gets used up. You go to a library to look for a book. The book's not in the library, because somebody else has borrowed it. You go to an information era library and take the book out of the library, the book's content is still in the library. This means a whole new set of economics.

We've said that a knowledge-based *TV Guide* would be electronically connected, interactive. Now, how does your *TV Guide* upgrade work today? You get a new one every seven days. You don't have to wait for the annual model change, you get a weekly model change. Well, how would a knowledge-based *TV Guide* work? Updates would be downloaded, or upgraded if you will. The guide gets smarter with use. It learns. Because it learns and has memory, it can also, therefore, anticipate.

So a knowledge-based *TV Guide* will know that Chuck likes sports and Barbara likes nature shows and Junior likes cartoons, and it begins to make recommendations so that knowledge-based offerings anticipate the user's behavior as they learn. They're customized – there's no finite list of characteristics or attributes, because they can be scalable and reusable.

The paradigm of the information era will make things like the Nielsen Reports obsolete, because the information is on-line, real time, all the time. I'll take it further. A great slew of intermediaries will become redundant. Companies that are essential today will be superfluous tomorrow. However, new categories of intermediaries – what I call infomediaries in *2020 Vision* – will be born.

New wine into new skins – strategies for a new economy

The marriage of knowledge and connectivity is going to do nothing less than change the economic rules for how a business – any business – is conducted. I will walk through some fairly logical steps as to how we get to that kind of conclusion and then go on to discuss the characteristics and implications.

First of all, I want to propose this as an axiom: all businesses are becoming more information-intensive. The next step being: the more information-intensive your business becomes, the more it will behave like an information-intensive business. That sounds almost self-evident, tautological even, but beware. One step leads to another, and another, and they all sound very rational until you lose your balance and fall down.

So, the more information-intensive your business becomes the more it behaves like an information-intensive business, and if the most information-intensive businesses are software and other information-related businesses, the more you become information-intensive the more you're going to begin to operate like a software business.

Have you lost your footing yet? "You mean to tell me that a chemical plant or an automobile company is going to run like a software company?" Well, the more it informationalizes and the more information-intensive it becomes, and the more the intangible value of the company grows relative to the tangibles in the company, the more that is exactly what's going to happen.

Companies are not simply going to throw away the diminishing returns model of the industrial era. It's been the bulwark for decades, if not centuries, and it's not just going to disappear. It's going to be very gradual. In most cases it's not going to be volitional or intentional or even conscious. It's going to happen so slowly that most companies won't even be aware of the changes until it's too late for the majority of them, but the few who understood it are going to capture the redefinition of the economic model and drive the others out of business. If you can identify a piece of your business that can operate on an increasing returns model rather than a diminishing returns model, you can redefine that piece of the business. Once you've redefined that piece and you get one or two of those pieces then it's going to begin to snowball.

The increasing returns model

What is an increasing returns model? *Nothing succeeds like success* is an example of an increasing returns model. Another example is *the rich get richer*. What are the elements of an increasing returns model? One, which again I put in my book, *2020 Vision*, can be expressed as I/T (I over T). The numerator indicates the Intangibles and the denominator the Tangibles. We're talking about the ratio of the assets of your company, the value-added in your company. More and more the value-added is coming from the intangible, not from the tangible. And your job is to grow that ratio faster than your competition is growing that ratio.

Second of all, focus on ubiquity before profitability, not vice versa. The old model was you got profitable and therefore grew and therefore became ubiquitous. Not now. First, you establish ubiquity and down the road you realize profitability. That's why market share is everything for today's software firms. The consequence of that is that you may as well give the stuff away, flood the market, become the standard, and then make money off the peripherals, off the add-ons, off the related services and the like.

You want to establish a standard and then let other people build upon it, and that gets into the connected economy again. In terms of the Oracle/Sun Microsystems effort to get people to be writing in the Java language. They're giving the stuff away. They don't quite understand the economic model for how you make money from Java , but they know that what you've got to do is get it to be ubiquitous so that it's a standard in a platform that everybody uses. That was Apple's crucial, strategic error in staying proprietary, based on the industrial mind-set that says if you've got a competitive advantage, you keep it privatized, patented. The new model is, "Here, everybody use it, use it, use it." It's counter-intuitive.

There are a whole set of rules that are going to change totally in terms of how software or information-intensive companies operate, such as lock-in and switching costs, time-based competition, and so on. Archimedes said: "Give me a lever long enough and I can move the world" – an epithet for the industrial-mechanical principle. In the knowledge economy, connectivity is the key.

If you want it in other terms, consider Moore's Law. That was the law for how the infrastructure operated in the crunching era. It talks about price curves, about things getting cheaper and cheaper. That belonged to the crunching era, but whose name is attached to the law for how the infrastructure operates in the connecting era? Metcalf. Metcalf's Law says that the more connected it is, the more valuable a given node is. So, for the first person to have a telephone, the telephone wasn't worth very much. The more people there are on a telephone network the more valuable it is to have a telephone. That's the principle of the connected economy.

In *Future Perfect*, I talk about something which I call my one-thirds, two-thirds rule – if more than one-third of the energy/talk/focus is on organization and less than two-thirds is on your business, then what you have is a business that exists to run your organization. We've got to put more energy around knowledge-based business than we're putting around knowledge-based organizations. Right now I think it's the inverse, which is inappropriate. There's too much focus on knowledge-based organizations and knowledge management stuff, when we don't yet have a clear sense of what knowledge-based businesses we're trying to run.

If we become too hung up on the organizational side, all we're doing is trying to be more efficient. It's just the next variation after re-engineering and all that other stuff. It's trying to prop up the declining curve of a mature business when what we should be focusing on is using all these smarts and these great ideas to get on to the next curve, which is more a focus on revenue growth than on cost cutting. This is where I think the focus ought to be.

Chapter 11

Designing Business Strategy in the Knowledge Era

Professor Karl-Erik Sveiby

Let's start with a small exercise. Close your eyes and then try to find your nose tip with your index finger. While you're doing it, think about what you're doing very, very hard. Take 20 seconds to do it.

How did it go? Did you find the nose? Now, can you explain in words exactly how you did it? No? How come something that is so easy, like finding your own nose, is so difficult to explain? This is the difference between tacit knowledge and information; tacit knowledge being the knowledge, in this case, about the body. And we know a lot about our own body. But most of it is tacit and we don't think about it. However, when we try to express what we know in words, that's information. And then it becomes very hard indeed.

To try to make a computer do exactly the same thing is a very, very difficult task. It's been made easier by a trick. When you program a computer or a robot to do these kinds of movements, you don't instruct it in words. You use a glove or a hand to make the movement that the robot is supposed to make, and the movement is copied by the robot. This is similar to explaining something to someone without words. So what you do is patterned by the conscious intellect. Then it becomes much easier.

Returning to the nose exercise, did you use your best hand? (That is, the right hand if you are right-handed and the left hand if you are left-handed.) Now, ask yourself why you did that – you didn't think about it, right? This is one of the features of tacit knowledge: that not only do we not quite know what it is, but we don't know what we know – so we don't realize when we are using it. Thus knowledge is not necessarily "good." Just think about how many times we let our own knowledge or expertise prevent us from creating something new and prevent us from having a new experience.

If, like the majority of people, you used your best hand, you involuntarily missed the experience of using your left hand. If you had, it would have been a very different experience for you. Perhaps it doesn't matter too much in this case, but think about all the times we're doing exactly the same thing when it does matter. In the context of knowledge and information, we are used to thinking that knowledge and information are, to some extent, similar. However, when we are managing it or creating strategies for it, it makes good sense to think about knowledge and information as something dissimilar.

Another perspective may help here. Let us regard knowledge and information as different; so different, indeed, that they have no relation at all. Let's explore what that means in terms of strategy. The first thing that I would like to do is to link some of the work I've been doing, in strategy, to knowledge and information. I'll start off with a well-known American company, Intel. Intel has $24 billion dollars of assets and a very big chunk of equity. When the shares are traded on the stock exchange, however, their value is much, much larger than this equity – about seven to ten times, depending on when you're looking at it. The market value of Intel, although worth $17 billion in actual tangible value, is something like $93 billion. Now, beneath the surface there has to be something to make up the difference, and it's equity too because the shareholders own it, but it's invisible. If Intel were to be acquired by another company the accountants would force that company to enter this amount of goodwill into the books and not really discuss what it is, but demand that the company depreciate it by a certain amount.

My work in this field has been to try to figure out what is this goodwill and how can it be managed; because it's essentially not something which is just there as an accounting term – a lot of assets are represented by this value. They can be defined as three kinds of intangible assets:

1   *Individual competence*. Everything starts there. Everything we have created in the world once originated from one person or a few persons' brains.
2   *External structure*. When we work outside an organization, we create relationships, networks, with other human beings. These can be with suppliers, customers, competitors, government environments, etc.
3   *Internal structure*. Some of us are working inside the organization creating internal structures, also through relationships.

I created this threefold categorization in the mid-1980s when I was trying to figure out the value of my own company, because we had zero in net book value. In fact, it was minus when we started out. When we became profitable, our profits were something like 1200 percent on the equity. But, the equity was minute, so really what did that kind of figure tell us? Well, it told us that there must be some other assets there that were actually yielding these profits. I was very bewildered in the early 1980s trying to figure this out. So I searched for answers from my fellow executives in other companies. I read books looking for it but have found nothing. I found one book called *Understanding Media* by Marshall McLuhan and I learned one thing that was quite important here: Marshall McLuhan regards everything we do in the world as a medium of ourselves, extensions of ourselves. That's how I got the inspiration – seeing these extensions of ourselves as assets.

In those days I used three categories – customer capital, structural capital and human capital – which have become well known through the works of Scandia Insurance Company, a Swedish firm that has been using this concept. I have actually abandoned the use of words like capital because knowledge and capital are very, very unlike each other. If I give you something in a capital sense, I lose it and you gain it. If I give you some knowledge, we both keep it. Every time we share knowledge it grows; every time we share capital it depletes. Knowledge is also opposite to capital, because if capital is in a physical form it depreciates when it's used. But try to think about knowing something and not using it. It depreciates. Knowledge grows when shared and when used. It's absolutely opposite to capital.

The dynamics of intangible value are very tricky, but extremely important to understand. Suppose that Intel were to increase their intangible assets by $1 billion. It's a lot of money. But in terms of a percentage it's not much. It's less than one percent of their total intangible assets of $110 billion. If we divide that billion dollars with the book value of $17 billion, then it suddenly becomes six percent. So if we measure it related to the visible, tangible book value of our companies, it seems to be very big. And this is a kind of leverage. Working with intangibles means that we're leveraging the tangible net book value, because we are not measuring the intangibles at all.

Let's look at another company, Sun Microsystems. Let's analyze the development over a period from 1994 to 1995. The net book value trends slightly upward over this period. It's because Sun is making profit and because it's adding to the equity. There was one quarter where Sun posted a loss. The share price dropped very dramatically, just prior to the actual loss, in fact it was when the market got wind of the fact that Sun was about to announce the loss. In just a few weeks, the market dropped the total market value of Sun by 50%, so changes in intangible values precede changes in the financials. But it soon turned up again. The main reason for this was Java.

When Sun announced Java it dawned upon the shareholder community and the financial analysts that this might be something which would change our way of doing business on the Internet. They immediately started pushing up Sun's share price. But you know, Sun Microsystems is still the same company. They are doing the same things. They're manufacturing workstations, although they now call them servers. And they are manufacturing in '95 and '96 in pretty much the same way that they did in '93 and '94. Nothing, or very little, has changed. The only change was in the market perception of what these intangible assets can do for Sun. And that perception changed the view on what kind of value there was in the firm. This is very important for you who are thinking in these terms. By actually changing someone's perception of what you can do, you can dramatically increase the share price. But it can also cause dramatic decreases.

Managing internal structure

Let's leave the measurement part and just look in a bit more detail at the internal assets of a company and how they are managed – because that's the strategy part. The internal structure contains things that are very explicit, like patents, copyrights, trademarks, etc. But also more fuzzy stuff like systems, processes, software, and of course, culture. The internal structure of an organization contains both tacit and explicit elements And it has one origin: the competence of the people. The competence I'm referring to is having knowledge and being able to do something with it. It's an effective action. So it generally contains some experience, education, skills, etc. These are the things that we both have to measure and manage, and make a strategy for, if we want to create value from our intangibles.

In one of the subsidiaries of my old company, a publishing firm, we managed knowledge for a very long period of time. We used what we call a knowledge-focused strategy for about 15 years. We tried to manage very specific kinds of assets. Not only the assets themselves, but more particularly the links between them. Let's look first at the assets. In the area of individual knowledge or competence, we did team writing. Team writing consists of writing articles in teams rather than as individuals. Anyone who has tried to write an article knows that if you're writing something in teams, it's very difficult and inefficient. So why did we do it?

The idea here was not so much to increase the value of the article itself, but it was to enhance the tacit knowledge transfer. Everyone who has to write something is crystallizing a lot of tacit and explicit knowledge into something on a piece of paper. And that is an incredible learning process for the writer. So we tried to expose as many as possible to these kinds of learning processes, even if they were not in charge of writing the article. To be able to do team writing, of course, we have to have a collaborative culture, which is probably one of the most important features of any knowledge management system.

We can use any process or system we like in terms of our team. But if people are not encouraged to put something into it that is worth something, then the system will just be assigned a cost. I'd say that the trust between people is the crucial link to whether any system of this kind will work. I equate trust with the bandwidth in the computer system. Trust is the bandwidth of communications.

If we have a lot of trust for the person we work with, we can exchange a lot of the deeper, inner feelings, about what we know. If you have a competitive climate in your firm where you're encouraged as an individual to make your own way, then knowledge-sharing is not encouraged because it's looked upon as giving away an advantage.

If you have a competitive culture like that, where you are not quite sure how a bit of information you're going to give someone is going to be used against you in the next career move, you certainly wouldn't feed it into a computer system and then a database.

We also incorporated another important aspect of internal structure: open office space. Professor Ikujiro Nonaka talks about the Japanese concept of *Ba*, meaning place. For me, his thoughts are very enlightening because a lot of what we were trying to do, at least when I was in charge there, was to manage *Ba*, to manage the space where knowledge was created, rather than manage knowledge itself.

So when we manage knowledge itself we are more or less automatically forced to treat knowledge as an object. But if we manage the space, the environment and let people create – that's an entirely different approach to management. Office space is a very important part of that.

We designed our office space to make it most appropriate for knowledge transfer. For instance, we had open office space. We had no walls and we put the coffee machines in the center. Coffee machines can be very strategic!

What we found was that the coffee machine was actually designing the communication channels in the company, at least on a given floor. So we put a lot of thought into who was located where. We positioned the weakest communicators close to the coffee machine, and those who were talking away all day, the furthest away. We put the managers in the corner office. This meant that if you're going to open up the space, you don't have to have so many meetings because we can learn what's going on just by walking around. So a space like this is conducive to tacit knowledge transfer, and we don't need any technology to do it. All we need is to invest in a space that is conducive to knowledge transfer.

Managing external structure

In order to grow by managing the external structure, we focused on high-image customers, with the notion that their image would rub off on us. If a CEO would read our journals, it was worth millions in advertising – and even more if the CEOs would recommend our journal to others. We focused on building relations with the best executives, by meeting them as often as possible. Most importantly though, when our senior writers went out to interview these top executives in those high-image companies, they didn't go alone. They always took with them two, or three, or even four other people of our staff, actually to visit that CEO.

This often came as a surprise to the poor CEO who got a whole delegation interviewing him. But this process was for the people who were not writing; they were there to observe. They observed what the senior editor was doing and how he conducted interviews. They observed how he approached the interviews and how he followed up. The observers also asked one or two questions themselves, thereby creating a relationship with this CEO. A relationship that, maybe a few weeks further down the line, would enable this writer to get past that tiger in front of his door, who was checking all the incoming phone calls.

So, by having several people participating in the interview, we built not only the relations externally, but we transferred some of it back into our company and increased the competence of our staff. Of course, a mission for us was to write articles using all our intangible assets in the best possible way to create value for the readers. The next point I would like to emphasize here is: think about what customers bring us. They actually bring us a lot more than money. They bring us a lot of intangibles. They bring learning; they bring new product ideas; they bring competitive intelligence, R&D projects; they are leveraging solutions for us.

You should make every effort to monitor your knowledge flows like this. They are revenues just like dollars and cents; they are intangible revenues. But we generally don't measure them, even though they're pretty easy to measure. You can install a system for measuring these things, albeit not in dollars and cents, but you can at least get an idea whether the flows are increasing or decreasing. Intangible revenues are much overlooked, particularly in the knowledge-management arena where we tend to be fairly inward focused. And is it worth it? Well, we beat our competitor every year from 1979 to 1994 except the first year, when we started, and one year when we were more or less on par. It's such a big difference over such a long period of time, that there must be something there.

In managing for intangible value, one of the most important factors for us was that our people had a higher education. Higher education meant adult people had better skills in processing information than the general journalists have. That's what you learn in university. So they were working smarter. I calculated that our journalists wrote articles at twice the speed of our main competitor. That accounts for more than half of the difference in profit margin. Higher education meant that we didn't have to turn around our competence so often.

Furthermore, encouraging close relations with selected customers – the ones that could bring us intangible revenues – meant that our people were learning while they were working. They were increasing their assets at the same time as they were exploiting them.

Knowledge-focused vs. information-focused strategy

Let's look at McKinsey, a consulting firm, and the strategy they use. McKinsey recruits bright, young, highly-educated people. They work juniors in teams with seniors. This creates a rich environment for tacit knowledge transfer. On top of this, they have a collaborative culture, by having a one-firm concept, and they have a partner ownership arrangement. Plus, they have a lot of cultural indoctrination, so that teams of people will be on the same level. They focus on high-image clients and establish close relations with selected clients – but not with all. They have close relationships with universities to recruit new talent; they develop their own concepts; and they share information on all projects in their business. They also have job rotation. That's very important, because by doing job rotations they share tacit knowledge between their partners. They also leverage information between assignments.

One interesting thing is how they treat former employees. The day after an employee leaves McKinsey, he can become your client. And that's how they regard them. They have a very strong alumni network and they regard someone who has left McKinsey as someone they want to relate to. There is nothing lost from their point of view. This is a system for working a whole set of knowledge-based assets. They're trying to give advice to clients based on their own concepts and their own experience.

With a knowledge-focused strategy, we assume that knowledge is a process and that knowledge is in people. So what we have to transfer is a process. We have to sell the process. And this, of course, means that close client relationships are paramount. Because that's where knowledge is created, when we're working for a client. And it means we have to invest in those relationships. And because of people, we have an unlimited capacity to create.

In the terms of Brian Arthur, we gain "increasing returns" from intangibles. I've found that increasing returns are based on revenues and intangible assets, not on cost efficiency measures. With a strategy like this we regard people as revenues rather than costs. And, of course, that makes it easy to invest in people. This becomes kind of a self-reinforcing cycle.

Let's contrast that with what I call an information-focused strategy. In an information-focused strategy, the assumption is that knowledge is an object, which we can transfer and send around. So we sell a knowledge object as a derivative of knowledge. It could be a software program or a book or a piece of information, but it's something which can be sold over the counter. This means that we have to invest in information technology (IT), because that's what IT is good at. We get economy of scale in the production. But this also drives the competitive behavior because, of course, everyone is trying to do the same thing. It's very easy to invest in IT. It's very straightforward, so everybody can do it. So, really, increasing returns come from being the first. If you're the first, you can become the biggest and then the winner takes all. Which, of course, means that if you can reduce the amount of costs involved here, you would gain more profits. Which usually means investing in more IT.

This is a pretty straightforward circle too. But it's an entirely different one. And notice the difference depending on how we regard knowledge. Is it an object or a process? The information focus strategy offers control. It's an established industrial age framework. It's efficient and people are seen as costs substituted for by IT. But it's not effective, because we do not use people's fullest capacity to create. A fundamental feature is that it's easy to copy, because IT is regularly available for everyone who is willing to pay. So it's very hard to create a unique competitive strategy based on an information-focused approach.

Let's look at Goulds, the maker of pumps. The pump is one of the world's oldest technologies. Goulds has been around almost 150 years. Over the last 10 years Goulds has been able to improve their net book value from $5 per share to $10 per share. They have not been able to improve their intangible assets, so the stock price has gone up from $15 to about $22 per share, over a period of 10 years. Now, that is not a very good result.

Until the mid-80s, they were a leading pump manufacturer, having a unique knowledge that made them able to produce solutions for their customers. However, they were starting to question the cost. And because the pump technology itself is commoditized – there aren't many patents around for it – they were being increasingly driven out of the market by low-cost producers.

They've done what almost every manufacturing firm in the US has done: downsized, brought in IT and high-efficiency drivers, and focused on standard products and standard solutions that can be delivered fast. But it hasn't given them much. They are still profitable, but not by much. This is the same in the whole pump industry, actually.

Let's look at what they could have done with a knowledge-focused strategy, to prevent some of the knowledge leakage. First, downsizing is not a very good idea if you want to retain competence. It reduces the cycle. If you reengineer the processes and substitute IT for people, people disappear and you get an IT system which is as efficient, but it's static. It doesn't change. So when you get into trouble, when you want to do special solutions for customers, your people are no longer there to do it for you, even if you have a very efficient process. You're focused on high-volume customers to gain maximum revenues, which is not a very good way of increasing your external structure. The high-volume customers are not necessarily the ones that increase this asset. In fact, they may be the ones that are decreasing it.

The biggest mission for Goulds was to produce and sell standard pumps in large volume. The alternative knowledge strategy focus for Goulds might be something like the following, which involves using all their intangible assets:

◆ employ well-educated salesmen and engineers;
◆ put juniors in teams with seniors;
◆ educate and train;
◆ build a collaborative culture;
◆ introduce a stock options scheme;
◆ build close relations with selected clients (don't call them customers, call them clients); and
◆ most of all, develop your own products, share information, and rotate sales people and engineers, internally.

Now, this is an alternative that essentially focuses on the intangible assets as the main assets of the business, and which focuses on managing those assets. There are quite a few advantages in doing this. One of the biggest is that when you do it, you will create a unique strategy. No one can copy you. Because the relationships that you create with your people are unique to those individuals and those situations you are in. This means that a competitor will have problems getting in. Once you are there, it will be very hard for the client to move to the competitor if you have good relationships between yourselves. It's effective because it utilizes the intangible revenues. In fact, its focus is actually on the intangible revenues, rather than the tangible ones.

It creates new business opportunities. Each relationship with a customer means something which possibly could be leveraged to someone else. It's flexible because people are the only dynamic force we have in organizations. That's important to remember: people are the only dynamic; everything else is static. The only one that can change anything is a person or individuals, but if we make the whole company dependent on IT, we're creating a static organization. It is important because it leverages people for unlimited creative capacity.

We have to change our way of looking at the business and use new kinds of indicators for measuring it. And that's hard. It's an undeveloped area. I'd say that in this field of measuring intangibles, we are roughly two years from the start. Compare that with the accounting system popularized in about 1494 by Luca Pacioli in Italy. We are therefore in the equivalent of something like 1496 in our development process. There's a lot of work to be done.

This is a new paradigm so it's perceived as risky. But I believe that in a world so full of information, tacit knowledge is a competitive advantage. Things that have been talked about as disadvantages, can just as well be an advantage. When we're talking about tacit knowledge not being easy to transfer, it's a problem to be solved, but it's also an opportunity to utilize. It's up to you to determine whether you see the opportunity or the problem. Now, the dilemma about this is that if we divide all companies on a scale that measures distance and closeness with customers, we've got the industrial organization model as the archetype for distant customer relationships; and the knowledge organization model as archetype for the close ones. The industrial archetype is the factory. With products, mass markets, efficiency, people with other costs and focus on tangible revenues. The archetype of a knowledge organization is the consulting firm. So, in a sense, what I'm saying is that if you're not currently a consulting firm, consider becoming one. Or learn from the consulting firms how they are managing their revenues. The consulting firms have been forced to manage their intangibles for a very long time. Otherwise, they would be out of business. They focus on processes – or at least they should. We certainly know that they've very focused on close relationships with clients and creativity. People are revenues – because it's very obvious in a consulting firm when you downsize the consultants. What else have you got?

Therefore, intangible revenues are of utmost importance for these firms. However, most companies are not like this. They are somewhere in the middle, with a bit of both. In fact, if they tried suddenly to become one of these firms they might actually be torn into pieces. An industrial organization with an information focus, is "Taylor-continued." That is, it is just the old paradigm dressed-up in silicon – really no different from what we've been doing all along. However, I believe that the knowledge organization with a knowledge focus is a new paradigm. I'm relying, as an indication of that, on the idea that most firms that are founded today are founded in this model: small firms based anywhere in the world, not producing anything tangible, and based on the competence of those individuals that are founding it or forming it at that moment.

To be an industrial organization with a knowledge focus is what I argued that Goulds should try. But it's uncharted water. We really don't quite know what that brings. Further, I believe that to be a knowledge organization with an information focus is outright dangerous. If you do that, you will substitute your valuable knowledge workers for IT. I don't think that it will work in the long run.

For most companies, getting this right is really difficult. The only solution is to bring this topic up constantly and discuss it in the various cells in your companies. Don't just embark on one route without thinking about it. That's the worst thing to do. You have to start by changing mindset. You need to see your organization as if it consists of nothing but knowledge strategies and knowledge flows, and then move from there. Start a dialog by asking questions. This is the way to explore: to ask questions and then seek to find answers within your own organization. The answers are there, but be careful not to miss them because of knowledge comfort zones. Like using your non-dominant hand in the opening exercise, sometimes forcing yourself to try the unusual will allow you to experience a whole new set of opportunities, opportunities which may hold the keys to your success in the new knowledge economy.

Part IV

Knowledge and the Economy

Our final section looks simultaneously at the impact of knowledge on economics and on the economy. The responses to our survey indicate a belief that knowledge management has indeed been significant at the economic level (e.g. the economic impact of the increase in knowledge work; see Fig. IV.1).

Again, while certainly not universal, we were encouraged by this strong showing of support of the impact of knowledge at this highest level of analysis. Certainly the information/knowledge economy has been talked about in much broader circles than has knowledge management itself, so there is quite a bit of reinforcement for this perception. For instance, Brian Arthur's work on increasing returns has appeared in *Harvard Business Review*, taking it out of the economic closet and bringing these ideas into the general business discussion. Lester Thurow's book *The Future of Capitalism: How Today's Economic*

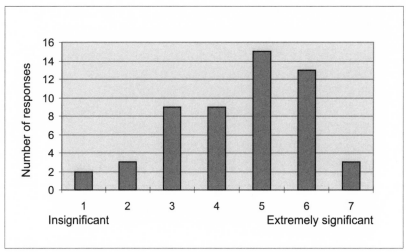

Figure IV.1: The impact of knowledge management at the economic level

Forces Shape Tomorrow's World is also no "knowledge management" book, but discusses clearly how a world filled with information-intensive businesses will be an altogether different one from the one we inherited only decades ago. *Blur: The Speed of Change in the Connected Economy*, by Davis and Meyer, also takes on the large-scale macroeconomic changes currently underway and soon to come due to the new world of knowledge-based business. Knowledge management and the connected economy are in fact reinforcing concepts. Knowledge work has always taken place, but it's when connectivity among knowledge workers increases that minds working independently can be brought together, across the traditional space and time barriers which held them apart. So knowledge work benefits from connectivity, but it is a firm's connectivity that benefits from knowledge work, since distributed manual labor is not made more effective, in and of itself, by higher connectivity. When these impacts are aggregated, the economy shifts, allowing new ways to conduct traditional business and giving rise to altogether new ways to create value.

As the economy shifts to favor a highly connected web of people doing "knowledge" work, this will have implications that reach down through, and up from, all of the areas previously discussed. Individuals will be required to build and use their personal knowledge to generate value. Organizations will need to change to encourage and enable such contributions, and to be able to bring them together in ways that create outcomes more powerful than the individuals could develop on their own. Furthermore, strategies must accommodate, and benefit from, such organizational capabilities in the complex, evolving economic context of tomorrow. As we learn how to get all of these elements working smoothly, that is when we will move beyond knowledge management and truly benefit from the knowledge advantage.

Chapter 12

New Economics for a Knowledge Economy: The Law of Increasing Returns

W. Brian Arthur,

The Santa Fe Institute

Introduction: does the new economy really exist?

If you drive down Route 101 in California, coming down from Oregon, you go through the Pacific Northwest economy. It's dominated by pick-up trucks, and lumber. Around about Santa Rosa you come out of that economy and you go into another economy, in San Francisco. This is dominated by service industries, finance, tourism to some degree. You then leave that economy on 101 South travelling to South San Francisco and San Mateo, and you're into standard industry. And then somewhere around Menlo Park you go through a weird transition and you're into an economy that's somehow different. If you try to get a motel room there during the week, you can't. You have to book two or three weeks ahead or you may as well forget it. If you go to the movies there, the ads aren't for Coca-Cola or for candy or anything like that.

All the ads are for engineers and designers and programmers. This is at the regular movies. There's something very different, very big going on in Santa Clara County in California – otherwise known as Silicon Valley – the air crackles with excitement. So what is happening? Is this just the Web or the Internet? You can smell the fortunes being made here and it feels like there's a new gold rush starting – except this one is electronic.

If there is such a thing as the new economy it's probably starting in Silicon Valley. I taught there – at Stanford – for about 15 years and I watched the economy in the Valley slowly transform itself. When I was there I sometimes felt as if I was a volcanologist on the side of a volcano, and the volcano was *erupting*. What amazed me was that if I turned around 180 degrees and looked at my colleagues in economics at Stanford – my fellow volcanologists – they were all busy perfecting their instruments and maybe too busy to notice that something very interesting was happening just across the road. At any rate, I think there is something happening – and I think that what's happening in Silicon Valley is an early form of what's going to happen in the rest of the United States economy. I'm going to describe things you might recognize that are starting to happen in your own company, whether you're in Rochester, New York, or Cleveland, Ohio. So what is going on? Is there a new economy?

The old economy

To put the new economy into perspective, let me just start by considering the standard: the "old" economy. There's nothing wrong with it, it's worked very well. In the standard economy think of products like commodities – processed food, plywood, steel, beer – the raw materials go in at one end, and the finished product comes out at the other end. Like all products, there's a lot of work in between and an awful lot of ingenuity.

But with those sorts of products (as we're told in all our economics courses and in the textbooks), if one company expands enough in commodities it runs into what economists have long called "diminishing returns." It runs into difficulties. If you're the biggest plywood maker, say in New Hampshire, and you start to expand and expand, then as you start to eat up more of the market across the United States you run into higher transportation costs for your plywood. If you're Coors and you started to expand beer, or if you're Millers, there's only so many people who like Coors over Millers and Millers over Anheuser-Busch, or some other type of beer, and you run into diminishing returns on the demand side. To summarize, we can say that in the old economy, growth is constrained by the following:

♦ stable markets;
♦ established competition;
♦ increased costs at the margins; and
♦ decreased demand at the margins.

The high-tech economy

I want to argue that high-tech industry is different. High tech operates not according to diminishing returns, but according to increasing returns, at least the significant part of it, the design part of it. In the so-called standard industries, a lot of raw material goes into a product and a relatively small amount of knowledge or information. In high tech an awful lot of knowledge, information, and technology goes into a product and not that much raw material. Think of a microprocessor: very little material, only a little bit of silicon, and some other chemicals added to dope the silicon, but a huge amount of engineering, and knowledge.

High-tech products are complicated. There is a lot of knowledge poured into them. This means that if you look at the cost for a high-tech product, a lot of the costs are up-front R&D costs. Think of Windows 95 – it's just one small disk. The first Windows 95 disk cost Microsoft $150–200 million. The second Windows 95 disk cost Microsoft next to nothing – just the cost of reproducing the first disk; the third disk cost the same – a few cents. So for high-tech products, like software – or even a B52 bomber – the first item that gets produced costs a huge amount of money. The subsequent items are copies of the first so they cost much less. The more you get out in the market, the lower your per unit costs. If you produce five B-52 bombers, collectively they cost an awful lot, but if you can produce 500 or 5000 you can amortize the big up-front costs and the unit costs are relatively small.

Another important consideration with high-tech or knowledge-based products is that of networks. For instance, if everybody's using Java as the downloading language on the Internet, then somehow I have to be able to receive Java programs on my computer and I need to use Java as well. So I will join the Java network. The competitor is Active-X: if everybody is using Active-X, I have to use Active-X too. So, again, there's advantage to a product getting ahead through these network effects. The larger the network, the more likelihood I'll find that network useful and that I'll have to join it.

There's a third reason why there are increasing returns in high tech, and that is that many of these products are complicated to use and to learn. For instance, if I'm running an airline and I've invested heavily in Boeings, I know how to use them, to maintain them, and to fly them. I know how they function, and how they work for my passengers. So the more I use Boeing the easier it gets for me to work Boeing into my operations. The same can be said for software, hardware, or even pharmaceuticals. However, this isn't true for high-tech commodities such as DRAM (Dynamic Random Access Memory). These things are just stamped out on a production line.

Now remember that high tech tends to have this quality that whatever gets advantage gains further advantage to some degree. It may be a very high degree if it's software; maybe a rather lower degree if it's close to a standard commodity. At the outset of these markets, you might say there's a reasonable balance, and no single product has significant advantage. But then events (and they may be quite small events: who talked to whom in the plane; who put in initial orders; who was smarter than whom right at the outset) can cause a kind of tipping phenomenon and these markets will tilt. As soon as one company or one product or one way of doing things gets far enough ahead, it tends to get farther ahead. What often happens then is that the market will lock in to a single product for a time. We've seen that happen in the software industry with Lotus 1-2-3, MS-DOS and Java. We've also seen it in the passenger aircraft industry with Boeing, and in the pharmaceutical industry with Prozac.

The more Prozac that's out there, the more doctors know about Prozac; the more doctors know that other doctors are prescribing Prozac, the more comfortable they feel recommending it. Everybody knows about it, they know the side effects. If they prescribe the standard, they're not going to get sued. So you see lock-ins of these markets temporarily – maybe for only two or three years, maybe for as long as five or even ten years – until the next wave of technology washes in and a new order is established.

Notice however, that during that time, companies are going up against each other. One company may initially achieve lock-in like Lotus did for three or four years with their 1-2-3 spreadsheet. Lotus did extremely well and got very, very fat. But it is still possible for some other company to come in and steal the market – as Microsoft did in this case. In fact Microsoft then made a bundle on Excel. It also happens that some new technology comes in and pushes out the old – the old horse buggies and automobiles story.

In the standard commodities market, if you have 35 percent market share and profit margins in double figures, you're doing well. High-tech markets are different – they're unstable, they're not shared, and they're bitterly fought over at the outset. But when your company locks in a market, perhaps for several years, the profit margins can be extremely high. You can be making gross margins of 50 percent, 80 percent, 130 percent. Why? Because, the unit costs are low, and if everybody's using your product and you have no competitors, you can price usually at whatever the market will bear. So there are temporary monopolies in these markets and the margins are very high.

Digital did this with their mini-computers in the 1970s and 1980s. They locked in the mini-computer market and got very, very fat on the proceeds. When the next wave of technology rolled in, in the early 1980s – PCs and workstations – Digital got caught between the two and had to do something very different. In fact, it nearly went under during that time.

So under increasing returns, whatever gets ahead gets farther ahead. Whatever's successful gains more success. And that means if you're the lucky company that starts to dominate a market you can do extremely well.

The culture of high-tech

There's a big difference in the cultures of the new and old economies. If you're stamping out widgets – let's say you're Ralston-Purina and you're producing dog biscuits – the culture there is to keep product moving and keep quality up.

You can look upon running an industry in the old economy as a lever and dial thing – fine-tuning and adjusting and making sure everything works just right. This is what I call a culture of optimization, where the key issues are:

♦ maintaining quality;
♦ keeping costs down;
♦ keeping product moving; and
♦ managing crises.

The whole idea is to keep your margins all right and make sure everything is moving along nicely.

High tech doesn't have a culture of optimization at all. You think it would because it's technical, it's mechanical. Perhaps it ought to have a culture of optimization – but it doesn't. High tech has a culture of missions or quests. And the quests are for the next big thing. If you go into Silicon Valley and you say to somebody like Intel's CEO Andy Grove, "what are you interested in these days?" he's not talking about getting everything operating just right. Of course, he has to do that but that's lower down in the company – the responsibility of the chief operating officer. At the top level, they're thinking two or three product cycles ahead and the key issues come in the form of questions:

♦ What is going to be the next big thing?
♦ How are we going to be a part of it?
♦ How's that market going to work?
♦ How are we going to lock in the market?

These are the kind of questions being asked if we're Intel, if we're Boeing, if we're a pharmaceuticals or bioengineering company. That creates a very different culture. It's the culture of the next big thing, and it's what everybody's looking for in Silicon Valley and in high tech in general. They're asking themselves: how can we capture it and how can we lock in those markets?

This leads to a very, very different set-up. It leads to all-nighters and it leads to parts of the company developing products in secret, because they don't want new product to be hampered, compromised or destroyed by the standard money-making part of the company. It leads to Friday night beer busts because you really have to make sure that you innovate and innovate, and you may only have three months to do it to catch the window, if you want to tilt the market in your favor.

It also leads to flat hierarchies. There's been a lot of talk in the last two or three years about the flattening of hierarchies in America; hierarchies all over US industries are starting to flatten. Now I thought to myself: is that true? Is it true in the Marine Corps? Not that I can see. Is it true in other large organizations, like churches? Not that I can see. Is it true in meatpacking? I don't think so. Is it true in processed food and plywood?

Hierarchies in high tech

What is happening in high tech that makes it different – that has reduced hierarchical structures? You can argue that democracy has suddenly hit the workplace, like it has in Eastern Europe – but I don't believe that. You can say that computers have cut out middle management, and there's some truth in that. But the main reason that they have disappeared in high tech is because the folks who are going to be coming up with the next big thing – the deliverers of the future of the company – aren't the CEOs, they're the designers, the people who are cooking up the new products.

Where do the deliverers of the next big thing park their Harley-Davidsons? Do they park them in the executive parking lot or in the workers' parking lot? They park them wherever they want, because they are the people who are truly important to the company. If you look at Hewlett-Packard of if you look at Sun Microsystems, you don't see that much hierarchy, except when you go to the parts that are producing commodities – stamping out calculators – you will still see traditional company hierarchy there.

If these high-tech and knowledge-based businesses aren't organized in strata or hierarchies, how are they organized? They're organized like an army. But we're not talking about regular army units here, we're talking about commando units, the Navy Seals. They have a definite mission to take that market. And the folks that take that market are very elite and they're treated as elite.

That's all very well for high-tech companies – a different market, a different work culture, a different economic model – and you can argue that the effect of these changes is pretty much confined to one county, in one state, in one country, Silicon Valley. Maybe it's only happening there, and maybe we don't need to worry about it in the rest of the economy. I fundamentally disagree.

The law of increasing returns

There's a second feature of this new economy that I'm proposing which is absolutely, totally obvious. That computing is starting to cost us next to nothing. Information transmission – IT in general – is starting to cost next to nothing. Bandwidths aren't infinite, but transmitting data costs little, relative to what it cost 20–30 years ago. The result of this massive reduction in cost, as far as I can see, is that the US economy is transforming itself from lots of little delivery firms – think of, say, 10 or 15 thousand local banks – to a few in US-wide or global networks.

Let me explain this further. If you want to go to a bookstore, there are several in every town. Your local bookstores are fairly generic – one bookstore is pretty much like another. What we're seeing now, with cheap computing and next to costless information or data transmission, is the phenomenal success of the electronic bookstore – Amazon.com or Borders – with personalized delivery to you sitting in front of your computer. It can be very highly customized to you, because you can customize it on your computer. Likewise in the future, your favorite newspaper – whatever that is – can be personalized to you, or customized for you, and delivered to you personally on the net. In fact, part of that's already available. So what we're seeing as part of this new economy is old businesses that looked like service industries – say, bookstores – re-emerging as large nationwide and global networks. And the networks have their tentacles going out and they reach you as a person and can be customized to you.

So what we're seeing is industry after industry – bookselling, insurance in the next five years, banking, legal services – redefining themselves in the light of the new technology. Take the legal industry for example. There are many small law firms, but a lot of the paralegal work, nearly all of it, is being done on a centralized network called Westlaw which operates out of Minnesota – in the middle of the country. If we come back to the concept of increasing returns, by and large, the larger a network gets the more advantageous it is to belong to that network. Compuserve, Prodigy, and America Online are network providers for Internet access, but as one of them gets larger, in this case America Online, it tends to offer deeper services and to accrue more advantage. And as it gets more advantage or offers more, I'm more likely to join America Online, and so on. And finally, one, or maybe two at the most, are dominant networks. So what's happening in industry after industry in this new economy, as I said, is a reorganization into competing networks. By and large, as one network gets ahead, it tends to get further ahead.

The increasing returns in book selling, Amazon.com versus Borders.com versus Barnes&Noble.com, are not that strong. It's not the case that if Borders builds up a huge network it has a marvelous advantage. So sometimes competition might mean that several networks can keep going for some time. But in other businesses, this is not the case. In banking, for example, there are maybe 15,000 retail banks, and my forecast is that 10 years from now they'll be two or three banking networks. They may have names like the First Microsoft Digital Bank, or First Digital of Citibank, but there won't be many players. 30 years ago there were hundreds of credit cards, each issued by local banks. Now there are only two, Visa and MasterCard. (It turned out American Express and Diners are in a slightly different business, real credit cards.) Why two? Why not one? The United States government will not tolerate one. That would be a complete monopoly, so there has to be two.

Exactly how many digital banking networks will there be in 10 or 15 years' time? My forecast: any number from two to five, depending on the whim and the mode of the government more than anything else. But the economics means that the larger the banking network gets, the deeper the services; the deeper the services the more I'm likely to join that network; the more I join, the bigger the network under increasing returns or a positive feedback loop. There might be some small players, but they will be niche players – the Southwest Airlines of the banking industry.

I want to argue that the law of increasing returns is spreading right across the economy. When I first cooked up the idea – and this was in Stanford – it was the early 1980s, and I routed that around my colleagues and they said, "You know, what you're talking about is theoretically possible. But just give me one example?" And I couldn't think of anything. I said, "Look, you know if there were increasing returns, the opportunity would be arbitraged away by somebody with a computer in New York in 10 to the minus-24 seconds, or something. You know, it's theoretically possible, but you're not going to see it," was the story. Then, a couple of years later, I asked, "What about high tech?" They said, "Well, yeah, but high tech isn't very big, is it?" This was 15 years ago.

So now I know it doesn't just stop at the borders of Santa Clara County. The mainstream economy is starting to reorganize itself into large competing networks. Think again of the airlines – there were many small airlines in 1981, but since deregulation five or six large carriers have emerged, each with its own hub and spoke network.

I have my own vision for this: I was reading an ad in an airline magazine for a product where you can sit in front of your computer with a camera, and the camera looks at your face. And you can see your face and you can try different hairdos. What would I look like with dark hair? What would I look like with a beard? There might be many more options if you're a woman. Now, we used to have barbershops for men and we have hairdressing salons for women. Think – and this is very whimsical – of what this will look like in the future if it keeps going. You can imagine when you sit in front of your computer and you can try 10 to the power of 25 different facial possibilities, combinatorial numbers, "yes, I want my hair this way, I want to color it that way." "I'm thinking of growing a mustache, well, not like that …" There are many combinations. You can try them out on your computer, and when you like one you hit the return button and it locks that one in.

That all goes back, say, to some computer server, some machine humming away in Akron, Ohio. And that does all the computation. And then you sit down under something that looks like a hair dryer – and this is in the future. But it's really kind of an *Edward Scissorhands* affair, and it's clip, clip, clip and there's all sorts of hair flying and there's color added and everything. And you take that off, and, wow, you look like the computer screen. Of course, it's too late to redo it for a few months.

The point is that in high tech this is called push technology. It's kind of in your face. It's literally customized to you, but it's totally centralized. How many barbershops will there be in the country? How many hairdressing companies will there be doing this? Answer? Very few. This would be a centralized network. Likely, there will only be two or three or four.

The casino of technology

So let me to turn to the game in high tech. What game are we really playing here? Let me give you two images. Think of the Ralston-Purina dog chow, or the Michael Porter economy, whatever you want to call it. It's actually what I call the Marshallian Economy, after an English economist, Alfred Marshall, who wrote about this a hundred years ago: the Standard Commodities Economy. It's no easy trick to manage in that economy, as you know. It's an art and it's not always done beautifully, but sometimes it's done very well. The metaphor for that is, I think, some very large humming factory, stainless steel everywhere, quite wonderful machines humming away, people getting everything right, and occasional prices popping up.

What's the metaphor for this new economy? The one I use and that appeals to me most, is that the new economy is like a casino. Imagine a huge marquee. Inside this marquee is a large casino. And in this casino are many, many tables. Each table has a sign which tells you what game is getting played there, or is about to start there. One sign might say Digital Insurance. That really hasn't started yet, but Digital Banking is just about to start. Another sign might say Net Browsers; another might say Downloading Languages; another might say New Mood Drugs; another Property Law.

You're wandering around – and you can only get in this casino, by the way, if you're a CEO of some sort of knowledge-based company, or if you're the strategic person in command – and also wandering around are Lou Gerstner, Bill Gates, Scott McNealey and John Reed, amongst others. They're looking around at the tables and let's say John Reed, who is the chairman of Citibank, sits down at the table called Digital Banking. He starts to talk to the croupier, and the conversation goes something like this:

JR: *"You know, I want to get into digital banking, I know it's going to be here to stay. I understand banking is going to become networked and so on, so where are the guys who think we can pull this off, because I want to play at the table? So how much do I have to ante up?"*

Croupier: *"Monsieur, we are very glad to see you at our table. For you, it will be $2 billion to play the game of Digital Banking."*

JR: *"Hmmm, why $2 billion?"*

Croupier: *"We have to totally reposition your company or start a very different one. And to do that will cost you $2 billion before the game is even started."*

JR: *"Fine, we're prepared to do that. What are the rules?"*

Croupier: *"We do not know that until the game starts, do we?"*

JR: *"Who is going to play?"*

Croupier: *"Well, we'll see who joins the table, won't we?"*

JR: *"What are my odds of winning?"*

Croupier: *"I do not know. I have no idea. The odds totally depend on how smart you are at the beginning and how well you've positioned your firm. More than that, I cannot say."*

JR: (Silence)

Croupier: *"Do you still want to play?"*

The point I want to make here is that in the casino of technology the stakes are very high. You might have to ante up $10 million – $200 million if you're Microsoft and you want Windows 95 – and it goes on up from there to billions. These are not zero-sum games.

It's not that your take is what the other people have lost around the table when the game's over. Your take is what the consumers put into the game on the outside – who has bought the products. You might put up two billion dollars, and in 10 years' time, if you're lucky, you might be worth $40 billion, like Bill Gates apparently is today.

You don't know what the rules are, but you've got to sit down and play anyway. You don't even know who the other players are. But in the high-tech knowledge-based economy, you don't have the luxury of waiting to see how the game works out, and then wander up to the table and say, "I want to play." By then somebody will have locked it in. So these are huge games with huge stakes and huge debts and they're not for the faint-hearted.

I want to point out two things about these high-tech casino games. One is how to strategize, or how strategy works in some of these games, and the other is the nature of the game itself. I want to stress that these are rarely like traditional games. There is a hidden player at each table. A player that's not doing much talking, but murmuring and whispering – and that's the United States government regulatory body – departments like the Department of Justice.

And they're changing the rules as the game goes along. So digital banking gets started and it's well under way, and suddenly they say, "Oops, you can't do that." You say, "But why?" and they reply, "Look at the rule book." You open the rule book and discover it's blank, and there's only one party writing the rule book and that's the government. There are a lot of unseen rules that are actually getting used as well.

But let's say life is comfortable and you think, well I'm in insurance and I don't have to worry; or you're in book-selling; or you're running a beauty salon. In five to ten years' time you will probably be in some network, or computing network, type of market and you'll be playing the game, whether you like it or not.

In other words, you don't know who the players will be. You're not quite sure whether the public will want to subscribe to the game, and if there's any money to be made – you don't know what the rules are. You don't know what new regulations are going to be issues and, above all, you don't know who will be in this game with you. It is a very different state of affairs from managing day to day in standard manufacturing. And it's producing totally different challenges for management from the challenges faced in the standard economy.

I have a friend, John Seely Brown, who runs Xerox PARC. And John puts it this way. He says the challenge in the standard economy is making stuff, making things. It's a big enough challenge for any of us, it's difficult. The challenge in the new economy is different. According to John, it's making sense. It's figuring out what on earth is about to happen – how these games will shape up.

So the challenge to John Reed, the chairman of Citibank, is not to keep his consumer banking humming along. The challenge for him and his team is to figure out how digital banking will actually work when that game gets going. But nobody knows the rules yet.

Seeing through the techno-fog

Let me change the metaphor. Imagine everybody in this new economy, in any particular industry, is on a ship. The ship is moving forward through a fog of technology. And through this fog, can vaguely be seen the outlines of a city – the outlines of the new game shaping up. And there are people who can see better through the fog. Bill Gates is one. He's a marvelous visionary. As the vision is revealed, others are better able to position their companies for the new game that is unfolding. But this is a particularly nasty type of vision because you'll notice that if you're looking through this fog, at this silhouette of how this game is going to work, the silhouette keeps changing as different players change their intentions, and as the government starts to change the rules and regulations. So you're looking at, and trying to make sense out of, the Rorschach ink-blots that keep changing with the interpretations that other people make.

There are people who are good at this and people who are not, but what is sometimes difficult to understand is that there is no officially correct answer to envisioning how these games are going to shape up. Because the shape they're going to take depends upon the visions of the other players. It's as if you were trying to enter a game of football and the rules aren't quite laid down and each team has a different interpretation of how football should be played – there is no consensus, no correct answer.

This shifts the entire emphasis in the new economy, from the managerial challenge – of making things, of getting things right, of optimization – to the visionary challenge – of seeing through the fog, and of accommodating others' interpretations of what lies ahead. This gives a very, very different set up. The people who win in the new games are the people who have better cognition, the people who can figure out how these games are going to work. The people who lose are invariably those who wheel out the old frameworks.

IBM is a classic case. There was a new game and it was called personal computing. IBM said, "We don't know how this is going to work, but we think this will be an extension of what we're doing already. This will be an extension of our mainframe technology that we understand very well." The year is 1980. They wheeled out the wrong cognitive framework and blew it in that market. They practically went bankrupt, as you remember, or at least got into severe trouble by about 1987.

The same happened with Encyclopedia Britannica. Another new game – this time called the multimedia encyclopedia – the year is 1990. Britannica says, "Well, yeah, we can see that coming –and *you* can see this coming – we'll interpret that to mean that everybody wants leather-bound volumes, and in the back of the last volume we'll have a little CD, hastily put together on a computer." Wrong – wrong – wrong. That's not the way this market works. Moreover, you can't sell your encyclopedias for $1500 and hope that anybody's going to pick a CD up for $1500. They just don't do it. Bill Gates interpreted that market as people being willing to pay $90 for a lot of data. And what's a lot of data? It's a lot of software and very much in his business. And by 1995, Britannica was in Chapter 11.

So the whole game now, in this new economy, is a cognitive one. It's figuring out how each new industry is going to play. And we usually do that by wheeling out our old cognitive frameworks. And if those cognitive frameworks are too narrow, we misinterpret the market and totally blow it. That's why whole management teams are thrown out when things go wrong, you don't just throw out the CEO. The reason is that the whole team had an old way of looking at things, and what you need is a new way of looking at things.

If you come up with an over-simplified framework for a game that's just starting up, say like Digital Banking, and you think you understand it before it happens – you're wrong.

Again, if you want another illustration of the point I'm making, imagine that you're charged by the United Nations with going into Bosnia. The game there is not to optimize in Bosnia; the game, before you go in, is to figure what on earth is happening in the first place. If you go in with a cognitive framework that's too narrow or inappropriate, you're going to blow it totally. Where I come from, which is Northern Ireland, there is a famous saying from the movie *The Devil's Own*, "If you're not confused you don't understand anything." If you find you're not confused in high tech, chances are you're wrong.

In other words, confusion is what we're all going to have to live with in this new economy. It's not comfortable, but it's the price of not having premature closure on an inappropriate framework. In other words, you have to keep a completely open mind as to how the new business will work.

Again, think of digital banking. I talk to my friends in banking and they say, "What's the cognitive framework for digital banking?" So I say, "How do you see it?" and they say, "Digital banking, that's an extension of the ATM machine into everybody's desktop." I say, "Really?" Then you ask Gates and his friends: "What is digital banking?" They say, "Oh, digital banking, well, it's software, software, software, satellite servers, networks, encryption … and at the tip of the match we'll have a little bit of financial software."

Well, that's a totally different cognition. Which one would you bet on? As that game is opening up, and you're sitting down to the table, which cognitive framework would you like to be armed with as you're just starting to play?

Strategy in the new economy

As I've said, in many of these markets whatever gets ahead tends to get farther ahead. This gives us some pretty obvious moves in strategy. It's not just a matter of getting prices right, costs down, quality right and so on.

Timing matters a great deal. If you come into the market at the right time, neither too early nor too late, and build up a large user base, you can lock it in, in your favor. As it turns out I was in a position to see what happened with Java with Sun Microsystems recently. I came to the conclusion they're doing everything right and that I must use them as an example for my ideas.

In other words, they'd given away Java for free and they had created a Java consortium of developers to develop products for Java. So by the time Java became available, everybody who had applications would be able to use those, and we could all seamlessly integrate Java, it'd be up and running and the whole market would be locked in before anybody else got a start. I thought they're doing everything just beautifully, and I was going to use that as an example.

Some time later I got a phone call from the chief technology officer at Sun. He said, "Would you come and have lunch next time you're in Palo Alto?" I did. And I said, "What's this about?" He said, "Well, we launched Java according to your ideas. And we've made a bundle ... we were wondering what we could do for you in return." Well, I should have said, "Well, a seat on the board would be very nice." Modestly, I said, "Well, you could give me a new computer." So I have the Porsche or Ferrari of computers, a Sun Workstation sitting on my desk. It's so powerful that I can't even use it.

So it turned out that Java was an example of my theory on that. So I asked the CTO, I said, "What happened?" He said, "Well, you know, we had spent $150 million in Java. We went to Scott McNealey who runs Sun, and we said we want to give it away for free." And Scott just stood there looking puzzled. As you can imagine when the accountants came in and they went ballistic: "Give it away for free? What are you, crazy? Look at all the money we spent. We need to be charging people an arm and a leg."

Then Scott McNealey says, "Why? Our product is a wonderful product. The technology is marvelous. Everybody would be willing to pay for this technology. And we spent so much." All of this is wrong. Nobody wants your technology even if it's marvelous, if you're on the wrong side of increasing returns, if you're spiraling down. Think of Apple. It's my favorite computer. And nobody wants to think of TWA and Pan Am who spiraled down, because they didn't have sufficient momentum. So McNealey made the right decision. Sun gave the thing away for free, they've built up numerous users and developers. Everybody lived happily ever after, maybe, except the folks in Microsoft.

Summary

So let me just finish here by asking what I asked at the beginning: is there a new economy? We haven't seen the total eclipse of the "standard" economy – there's plenty of the old manufacturing economy left. Is there a new high-tech economy? Yes there is and it operates according to increasing rather than diminishing returns. The principles are totally different. It's like operating beyond the sound barrier, rather than beneath the sound barrier. As economists we've had to completely rethink how these markets work. If you're in those markets, and you start to think, "if I gain advantage, I might be able to gain further advantage," you're on the right track.

Strategy is totally different. The markets? It's more predictable who will take what share. If you get far enough ahead, you can get the whole market. And that means that there's all sorts of strategizing to do with timing, building up your increasing returns advantage, and levering product from one market into another.

Moreover, this is not just in high tech, it's filtering down into airlines; it's filtering down into fast-food chains and into franchising; and into service industries; into insurance; into banking; into pharmaceuticals. This is slowly becoming the economy of the next century. And it works according to entirely different principles.

Chapter 13

Brainpower

and the Future of Capitalism

Lester Thurow,

Massachusetts Institute of Technology

I believe that in the 21st century it will be completely obvious that we are playing a very different economic game, with some brand new rules requiring very different strategies to win. I believe, no matter how successful you have been in the past, if you want to be successful in the future you will have to be something quite different. I also believe nobody can predict the future, but at the same time you can understand the forces that will shape the future – and it is always better to play with the forces than against them.

I would like to start with an illustration. I want you to go back to 1990 and imagine you are John Akers, CEO of IBM. Your company has just had the best decade any company has had in human history. For that ten-year period of time, you have averaged between $8 and $9 billion worth of profits per year. To put that in context, the two most profitable firms in America in 1998 were General Electric and Exxon, each of whom just made $8 billion. Seventeen years ago IBM was making the kind of money they are making today. In 1990 your company makes almost $11 billion worth of profits. No company has ever made anything like that in the past, and no company has ever made anything like that since. You are the most profitable firm that the world has ever seen, you are the most admired company in the world and you have the best known brand name. And if you ask the students at any of the world's leading universities, Harvard, Tokyo whatever, what company would they most like to work for? You are number one on the list. The world has never seen anything like it.

Now, like Moses, God comes to you and says, "John, come up the mountain with me. I want to show you the promised land. The year of the mainframe is over. The PC is here and next year if you do not do anything, your profits will be zero, after being $11 billion this year. The year after that they will be minus $9 billion, the year after that they will be minus $9 billion, the year after that they will be minus $5 billion; in the next four years you are going to lose $23 billion, which is more money than any firm in human history has ever lost before or since. Now, John, it is your job to go down the mountain and persuade 420,000 employees of IBM who had the best decade in human history, the best year in human history, that they have to rip it up and do it differently."

Do you think you could do that? I do not think *God* could do that. That was an impossible management situation and I will remind you that Moses had to bring the 10 Commandments twice. The first time the Israelites did not believe them, and they were broken.

Failure to adjust

Now, I do not believe that everyone is going to fall off a cliff like IBM but I believe that everybody is going to have an IBM experience that will turn their world upside-down. If you do not believe that, let me read you a list of names to drive it home. This is a list of the 12 largest industrial firms in the USA on January 1, 1900, the beginning of the century, in alphabetical order. There are two interesting things about the list – see if you can guess them:

- The American Cotton Oil Company
- The American Steel Company
- The American Sugar Refining Company
- Continental Tobacco
- Federal Steel
- General Electric
- National Lead
- Pacific Mail
- People's Gas
- Tennessee Coal and Iron
- US Leather
- US Rubber.

First of course, 10 of the 12 companies were natural resource-based companies. It was an era of natural resources and for a hundred years that has been true. For a hundred years, starting with John D. Rockefeller and ending up with the Sultan of Brunei, the wealthiest person in the world has been associated with oil from the late 19th to the late 20th century.

What is the second most interesting thing about that list? How many of those companies are alive today? The answer is one: General Electric. That is why people write books about General Electric. And if you were to write the obituary for the other 11 companies it is exactly the same obituary for every one: a revolutionary technology came along and they could not adjust to the new reality. That is even true for General Electric. The General Electric laboratories invented the transistor one day after the Bell laboratories, independently. They almost won the Nobel Prizes that the people at the Bell labs won. One day difference: that is the literal truth. General Electric, however, was the dominant maker of vacuum tubes. General Electric gave the transistor to the vacuum tube division. Guess what the vacuum tube division did with it? They spend three years proving it would not work, because it meant the end of the vacuum tube division. There were five companies in America that made vacuum tubes and not a single one of them ever successfully made transistors or semiconductor chips. They could not adjust to the new realities.

Of course, it is not just ancient history. Wal-Mart is currently America's biggest retailer. I would be willing to bet that 20 years from now, Wal-Mart will not be America's biggest retailer. According to the *New York Times*, a few months ago Wal-Mart opened up an electronic Internet store, but they carefully priced everything on the Internet store a little bit higher than it is in the real physical stores because they cannot afford to have you go to their Internet store; because if it was 20 or 30% cheaper as it ought to be, what you would do is go look in their real stores and buy electronically. And they have 800,000 employees in 25,000 stores! All they do for the next 10 years is downsize and lose money. Apparently, it is better to be driven out of business slowly by your competitors than rapidly by yourself. How would these guys get paid? They all get bonuses based on profits and there would be no profits for 10 years if Wal-Mart was to go aggressively into Internet retailing.

How about the pharmaceutical companies? Why are none of the old-line pharmaceutical companies leaders in biotechnology? They all had to buy their biotech companies. Their scientists knew what was going on, but they could not adjust to the new reality and they could not be leaders in the new reality because they were too committed to the old technologies.

The third industrial revolution

When we talk about economic revolutions, we are not just talking about something that creates a big industry. For example, the automobile industry was created in the 1920s and 1930s, but nobody considers that a revolutionary device because it did not change things radically. It was an improvement on the train, it was an improvement on the electric street railroad, but it was not a thing that caused everybody to do things differently. Revolutions occur when everything gets turned upside down, or almost everything.

Take the first industrial revolution, led by the steam engine, introduced in around 1800. Napoleon and Julius Caesar ran armies around Europe 2000 years apart, but Caesar could actually move an army from point A to point B slightly faster than Napoleon. They both used horses and carts, but roads were slightly better in Roman times than they were in Napoleonic times. Two thousand years of history and not a single improvement in land transportation, but 50 years after Napoleon died, steam trains were traveling at 100 miles an hour. The industrial revolution was here, 8000 years of agriculture was over, and one country, Great Britain, already had half its workforce out of agriculture and into industry – and the world is forever different.

If you took a serious course in economic history you would also learn about the second industrial revolution. The second industrial revolution occurred about 100 years later, at the end of the 19th and the beginning of the 20th century, and it had two key ingredients. First, the Germans in the invention of their chemical engineering industries invented the concept of systematic industrial research and development where you deliberately push technology forward. You do not wait for the brilliant thinkers to appear out of the sky like the Watts and the Bessemers. That spelled the end of Great Britain as the dominant economic power in the world because, for a variety of reasons, the British could never make that transition to systematic industrial research and development and to this day they are not leaders in systematic industrial research and development. Brilliant scientists occasionally, but not leaders in industrial research and development.

The second component of the second industrial revolution was electrification. Electrification did not just create big industries like the electric power industries. It created opportunities for brand new industries, like telephones and movies, and it changed the way we do everything. For example, if you go to the National Industrial Park in Lowell and Lawrence you will see those old steam factories: giant steam engine at one end, rotor belts a kilometre in length, pulleys, machine tools all in a straight line almost as far as the eye can see.

When they first invented electricity, they simply put a big electric motor where that big stream engine used to be. There is an advantage because steam engines have a lot of down time. But it took them about 30 years to figure out that the name of the game was distributed processing. Forget the big motor – put a little motor on each machine tool, then put those in different places on the factory floor and you can get a lot of productivity out of electricity.

Of course, that changed everything. Literally, they made night into day. Before electricity the most expensive apartment was on the ground floor and the cheapest apartment was on the top floor. After electricity and elevators, the penthouse is the most expensive apartment and you put the servants on the ground floor with the noise, the dust and the crime.

We tend to think that the computer is unique in terms of price/performance but it is not. What do you think that the first commercially sold electric light bulb in today's dollars, adjusted for per capita income, sold for? The light bulb that you can by for 33 cents – a 100 watt bulb that burns 1200 hours – sold for $1450 in 1883. Now if light bulbs still sold for $1450 how many light bulbs do you think you would have? The first light bulb was not even thought of as competition for lamp oil, which was the dominant lighting at that time. It was thought of as a safety device. The first light bulb was actually used on wooden ships because if you use a lantern, there is the danger of a storm causing the ship to catch fire – it was worth $1500 to make wooden ships safer from fire. So, if they had had catalogs in that day and age they would not have listed light bulbs as lighting devices. They would have listed them as fire prevention devices because they were too expensive for lighting – you were never going to use them for that purpose.

I think a historian a hundred years from now is going to look back at our period of time, the end of the 20th and the beginning of the 21st century, and say this is the "third industrial revolution." There are a series of six technologies that are not just creating big industries: they are going to change how we do everything. The six technologies are:

- ◆ microelectronics
- ◆ biotechnology
- ◆ the new material sciences – designer-made materials
- ◆ telecommunications
- ◆ machine tools and robotics
- ◆ computers – hardware and software.

I think a historian 100 years from now might very well say that at the end of the 20th and the beginning of the 21st century, 5000 years of local retailing was over. For 5000 years you and I have gone to the local store to buy the things we need. The Egyptians did that in 3000 BC. Now we have electronic retailing. I got a consulting report that claimed that by 2010 half the retail stores in America will be closed. I think that is an exaggeration – a little bit too fast – but it is certainly the right direction. Some very large number of them are going to close. Think of LLBean. A little store in rural Maine selling outdoor clothes now has $350 million in sales in Japan, yet it does not have a single employee in Japan. All of it is done electronically, via the Internet, fax, catalogs, telephones. No employees, $350 million worth of sales on the other side of the world. Or if you bought flowers recently you have contributed to the Dutch economy. The Dutch flower auction controls 90% of the cut flowers in the world. They do not grow them, they do not sell them, but they make all the money. The Easter lily may be grown in Colombia, sold in California but the only people who can get it from Colombia to California so it blooms on Easter are the Dutch. The masters of the logistics system control the industry and nobody has been able to break into the Dutch monopoly on the control of cut flowers.

The shopping mall

Of course, what we see today in terms of electronic shopping is crude as compared to what is coming. I run a program here at MIT called the Lemelson MIT Prize Program, where we give prizes to the inventors of the year. We give a half million dollars to the American inventor of the year and we give some $30,000 prizes to some student inventors. Recently, I gave a $30,000 prize to a group of students in mechanical engineering who have a device that is a little bit like a glove. You put your hand in it, and you can feel what you see on the TV set. It is uncanny. You can squeeze the tomato, and feel the difference between oil and butter, cotton and velvet.

If you are one of the wealthiest women in the world, you can go to one of the great salons of Milan, pick out a dress and they will find a model who has your body type. They will put the dress on the model and they will walk the model around you so you can see what the dress would look like on you. We now have the technology to scan your body type into the computer. We are going to be able to put the dress on the middle class American woman and for the first time in her life she can see what she looks like as others see her. She will receive the same treatment as the wealthiest women in the world.

Technologically, stores can go out of business. I live in a high-rise building. It has been rewired for Internet technology recently and I will never again have to go into the store. I can buy my groceries electronically, my clothes electronically, my liquor electronically, my books electronically, but I do not think that is going to happen because you have to ask yourself, "what are human beings?"

If you take the American mountain lion – the American mountain lion genetically is a hermit. Adult mountain lions have no association with any other adult mountain lions for their entire lifetimes, except briefly to mate. They live alone. And they like it evidently. On the other hand, sea lions pile on top each other on a few rocky islands, when they have the whole Pacific where they could spread out. Now, what do you think human beings are? Mountain lions or sea lions? You go Christmas shopping because you like elbows in the ribs. That is why everyone in retail is talking about entertainment retailing. You are always going to pay 20% more in a real store, but you can have fun. So if you look at the new bookstores that have been built to compete against Internet bookstores, you have a fireplace, lounge, coffee bars, lectures, poetry readings, and it is a great dating bar where you can meet and talk to people comfortably. You know that you are paying 20% more for the book but you are having fun.

If you want to see the future of shopping you go to the Mall of America in Minneapolis-St Paul, which is a clever mixture of Disneyland and shopping. It is now the largest tourist attraction in the state of Minnesota – which may tell you something about Minnesota.

Technically, we could buy everything electronically but sociology is going to dominate. What do you want to buy in a fun environment and what do you want to buy good things cheap? For example, 80% of automobile insurance in Great Britain is already sold electronically. You can think about having fun at the shopping mall, but nobody has fun buying insurance.

We will be surprised, though. The *New York Times* had a competition for the best commercial Web sites. The six finalists were all pornography. Some stripper won because, in the jargon of marketers, people who like pornography are "lead consumers". They jump at new technology, maybe for some obvious reasons. They made the whole movie video business. They made the pay movie business in any hotel you have ever gone to. Half the pay movies are pornographic movies. Not what you imagine, but true nonetheless.

Of course, the other factor that will turn retail upside-down is demography. By 2020 the United States will have a voting majority of people over the age of 65. The USA will be the first human society ever seen on the face of the earth that is numerically dominated by the elderly. That will change sociology, psychology, government and business in ways so profound it is almost impossible to exaggerate them. You and I are in the midst of the biggest shift in purchasing power that the world has ever seen: from the young to the old. I will give you the numbers of the United States. In the last 25 years we have cut in half the share of national income going to people between 18 and 35 years of age and we have doubled the share of national income going to people over age 65. In 1970, the average 30-year-old had 40% more money to spend than the average 70-year-old. Today the average 70-year-old has 20% more cash income to spend than the average 30-year-old. The elderly have money. If you are not taking elderly into account in your company's production, you are brain dead.

Every once in a while *Forbes* produces a list of the world's billionaires. The last list they produced had five people who owned cruise lines. What do you think made cruise lines suddenly successful? This is a very old technology. Cleopatra had a cruise boat. The answer, of course, is the elderly. They have time and money; they don't need to move, we move them; if they don't feel good, they can stay in their state room; the perfect vacation for the elderly. That is exactly who goes. In Boston a few years ago, there was a cruise boat from Canada, headed for New York. It stopped in Boston on an emergency basis because flu broke out. If you have 18 year olds on your boat you do not worry about a flu epidemic. But, on this boat 70% of the people were over 70 years of age and if they were going to be sick they wanted to be sick in the Mass General Hospital and not on the boat.

Here's a brand new opportunity to become a billionaire. Otis Elevator now has a market for two-floor elevators. Elderly people with homes that have more than one floor that want to make it into a one-floor home rather than selling the home and buying a new one. There did not used to be a market for an elevator that only goes up and down one floor. Now there is a market.

And of course some of the things you take for granted are not true. What group of people by age spends more time on the Internet than any other? The elderly. Nursing homes have set this up as baby-sitting. I have a 92-year-old aunt who spends eight hours a day on the Internet. Her "real" friends are dead. All she has are Internet friends. She just cruises the Internet. Of course, who will want to do Internet shopping? A young person may like to be out there lugging the groceries and squeezing the tomatoes, but if you are elderly you just want a tomato.

The global economy

One of the things that is also happening here is that this technology is an extension of what happened 100 years ago. A hundred years ago, the second industrial revolution allowed us to move from local economies to national economies. You should ask yourself a question: there have only been two periods of time in history when we have generated billionaires. The 1890s and the 1990s. There were no billionaires created in the 50s, 60s and 70s. In the 1890s you know the names, the Rockefellers, the Morgans, the Carnegies, the Mellons, and you know the names today.

Why was it that we created billionaires in the 1890s and we are creating them in the 1990s but we did not create them in between? The answer is that if you have a revolution there are tremendous opportunities to do new things. All of those 1890 billionaires were the people who owned the new national companies. What we are doing in the third industrial revolution is that we are moving from national economies to a global economy. If you say who are the billionaires, they are the people who own the new global companies. It creates a threat if you are IBM, Siemens, Philips. It creates a tremendous opportunity if you have the vision and either the good luck or the intelligence to create a new company in a new area.

Now there is a problem here. The problem of course is that when we moved from local to national economies we had national govern-

ments. And it took those national governments about 50 years to figure out how to run these new economies. There was no national bank,
the Federal Reserve in the United States, until 1913. We did not
discover that we needed financial regulations until the Great Depression. We did not discover we needed anti-trust laws until Mr
Rockefeller monopolized lamp oil. As we built this new national
economy, over a 50-year period we built up a whole set of government
rules and regulations designed to get rid of some of the bad things
that came out of the national economy.

This time, however, when we move from national to global
economy there is no global government and there is not about to be a
global government. One of the rules is that you will play a game with
no rules, no sheriffs, no jury, no jail. You can think of it as wild-west
capitalism. You can see it today if you look at global meltdown.

Let us start where the story really starts. Exam question: what is
the fifth biggest banking center in the world? Number one is New
York; number two is Tokyo; number three is London; number four is
Frankfurt; and number five is Grand Cayman islands. Thirty thousand people. Fifth biggest banking center in the world. Why would
anyone go to the Grand Cayman islands? The answer is that it is the
place you want to bank if you do not want government looking over
your shoulder.

There was a firm recently that caused a commotion because it
had borrowed a trillion dollars long-term capital management. It was
not an American firm. It was a Grand Cayman islands firm. American
government has no jurisdiction over that firm whatsoever. It's true
that the people lived in Connecticut, but the firm was in the Grand
Cayman islands. It had the capacity to pull down the entire American economy yet it was not an American firm.

If you look at the global meltdown in Asia, which threatened to
spread around the world, it is very important to understand how
these things interact because globalization did not produce that
meltdown. If you are working with any organization – a country, a
company, a university – you have to understand what you can do
and what you cannot do. There is a whole set of things that every
organization cannot do. Wisdom is understanding what they are. I
have heard Jack Welch, for example, say that at General Electric
they cannot run anything that will not have a half-billion dollars

worth of sales very quickly. If it is going to be a market less than that, they should not be in that business. They are not set up to run small things. They do not have the organization to run small things. They are a failure at running small things and always will be a failure at running small things.

Now if you look at our market capitalistic system, it is important to understand what it does and does not do. What it does is that it is the only system since the industrial revolution that has been able to generate consistent economic growth. We have tried everything else: fascism, socialism, communism, lots of "isms." Nothing else has worked.

The other great positive characteristic is that, if you have money, this is the best system human beings have ever designed for catering to peculiar individual human wants. If you do not believe that, listen to Bill Gates describe his house. This is the most peculiar thing anybody in the world has ever built but I can guarantee you that if you have $66 billion dollars, it will be built.

It is important to know what capitalism cannot do. Two negatives are built into the genetic code of capitalism. First, it has recession and depression cycles, ups and downs. Always has, always will. Paul Samuelson won the first Nobel Prize in economics while at MIT and he partly won that prize for a famous article back in the 1930s proving that that was true. It was called the Multiplier Accelerator Model. The second thing built into the genetic code of capitalism is that is has financial meltdowns. Always has, always will – and you know the great names. Tulipmania, the South Sea Bubble, Louisiana Panic, the Great Crash of 1929 and the Great Depression. And, of course, Tulipmania occurred in the 1620s – nobody was talking about globalization in the 1620s. In the 1930s the Great Depression spread around the world but there was no global economy in the 1930s.

Globalization does not cause financial meltdowns. They have occurred for a long time and frequently before that. If you went back to Holland in 1627, how many tulip bulbs do you think it took to buy one of those nice five-story houses along the canals? The answer was: one black tulip bulb bought a house. You know that that is crazy and the Dutch in 1627 knew that was crazy because in the long run a tulip bulb cannot cost more than the cost of growing a tulip bulb. But there was a time when six tulip bulbs bought a house – that is crazy too, right? Now what happens to you if it is six to one and it goes to one to one and you get out of the market? You lose a chance to multiply your money by a factor of six and that is irresistible. That is why financial meltdowns are in the genetic code of capitalism. Greed, the desire for more, makes capitalism work. And greed, the desire for more, creates financial meltdowns.

Optimism, bubbles and humility

Since everyone reading this book is a smart person I think I need to make you humble here because you will say "that is them, not me." Let me tell you a little story that an MIT colleague by the name of Charles Kindleberger tells in his book *Panics, Manias and Bubbles*. As we go back to the South Sea Bubble, which occurs in the 1740s in Great Britain, I need to tell you some history. The South Sea Company was a royal British company like the East India Company or the Hudson Bay Company. The King of England was Chairman of the Board and it was chartered to slave and fish in the South Seas. The problem was that there are no fish in the South Seas and there are very few people who were made into slaves, so the company never made any money. This was always public knowledge – it was in the papers every day. But like the tulips, for whatever reason, the price of the South Sea shares went up despite the fact that the company was losing money.

Now, in the midst of this I need to give you another exam question. Suppose I said to you, "write down on a piece of paper the name of the person you think is the smartest person who has ever walked on the face of the earth. Then you need to write a two page essay that I will ruthlessly grade on why you think that person is the smartest person whoever walked the face of the earth." Think for a minute. Who would you write down? Some might say Einstein, but I would propose Sir Isaac Newton. I would say in my essay that I can prove to you that Sir Isaac Newton is three times as smart as Einstein. If you are three times as smart as Einstein then you have a definite claim to being the world's smartest human being. Einstein did one great thing in his life: the theory of relativity. Sir Isaac Newton did three things, each one of which in the history of science is more important than relativity. The modern theory of gravity, modern theory of light, and he invented calculus. This was a very smart human being.

Sir Isaac Newton just happened to be alive at the time of the South Sea Bubble. In the middle of this enterprise, he sold some shares, made some money and issued a public statement. He said, "I can predict the motion of heavenly planets, but not the madness of human beings." Suppose the world's most famous physicists last July said the stock market was overvalued, do you think anybody would have paid attention? The answer is no and in the 1740s nobody would have paid attention to Sir Isaac Newton either. And he was a very famous man of his time.

The price of the South Sea Company went up and up and up and about a year later, Sir Isaac Newton could not resist so he bought some more shares. When it all crashed he lost £3000, which was a lot of money for a college professor in that day and age. There is a moral to the story: if Sir Isaac Newton cannot resist, how do you plan to resist?

When they get going, these things are irresistible. Last July, I was at a social function with President Clinton and he said to me, do we have a perfect economy or a bubble economy? And the truthful answer is that we will have to wait and see. Nobody has ever seen a bubble from the inside. From the inside it always looks rational. The real problem between economics and business people is that economics is pretty good on fundamental forces and pressures but it is horrible on timing. It is like geology. Take the San Andreas fault. We know exactly where the fault lies, to the centimeter. We know exactly how it works, thanks to plate tectonics. We know with 1000% certainty that there will be a great earthquake on the San Andreas fault. But we do not know whether it is one second from now or 10,000 years from now, and we never will. Governments used to put a lot of money into trying to figure out how to do earthquake prediction but they do not do that anymore because we discovered that earthquakes are in principle stochastic events and unpredictable. They cannot be predicted. But human beings are optimistic.

At the University of California, La Jolla, you will find a library which is an upside pyramid resting on its point and the point is 137 feet from the San Andreas fault. Californians build houses right on the San Andreas fault. "Yes it will happen, but not in my lifetime." Of course, if you look at the Pacific Rim there were lots of things that were the equivalent of Tulipmania. Here's one. At the peak of the property boom in Japan, take a look at the price that property was selling for around the Emperor's palace – the Emperor's palace is about three square kilometers of land. Then if you calculated how much it was worth being sold, that three kilometers had a market value greater than the entire state of California. That can only be rational if you believe on three kilometers in the middle of Tokyo you can produce all the GNP of California, and of course nobody believes that.

Take any course in international trade that anyone has ever taken or taught in all of human history and everyone will be taught that nobody can run a trade deficit forever. If you run a trade deficit you have to borrow the money from the rest of the world and the second year you have to borrow money to pay interest on the previous year's loan. In year three you are borrowing interest to pay interest on interest. That is called running compound interest and no human being in all history has ever beaten compound interest. It always wins. If you look at the countries that melted down in Asia – Indonesia, Malaysia, Thailand, Philippines, Korea – together they had a trade deficit of $50 billion. You know that cannot go on; it is going to end. This, of course, is where globablization comes in and makes the world different.

The first question you should ask yourself is those countries that melted down had a $50 billion trade surplus ten years previously. What happened? Did they suddenly become dumb? Did they suddenly have bad policies? The answer is none of the above. What happened is mainland China – not quite 25% of humanity, 40% of the developing world – decided to play the capitalist game and when they decided to play the capitalist game they changed the game. They are big enough to produce everything produced everywhere in all the rest of the developing world combined.

If you consider China and Thailand, at the moment everything is better in China. Wages are lower. Education is higher. Bigger internal market. So, China just sucks toy factories, textile factories, export activities out of Thailand into China. If you want to compete with the Chinese there are only two things you can do. You can go down scale and have wages lower than they do, but their wage rates for good high school graduates is 11 cents an hour, so that is pretty hard. They are not very desirable.

The other thing that you can do is go upscale and get above them in terms of technology, but south-east Asia cannot do that because they are more poorly educated than China and do not have the capability to do that. Now the Koreans could have done that but the Koreans had their traditional problem. The Koreans are smart enough to say, "we have to move our low-wage manufacturing activities to China," which they did, "but that means we have to go upscale and sell some high technology stuff" and then they ran into Japan who was expanding its trade surplus at the same time, and they were not good enough to do it vis-à-vis Japan. So a country that had been running trade surplus all of a sudden starts running trade deficits. This time Korea was squeezed economically between its two ancient military enemies as opposed to being squeezed militarily, but it was nonetheless squeezed.

Suppose I use a set of words. Crony capitalism, phony bookkeeping, sweetheart loans to friends and relatives, criminal activities, politicians on the payroll. Am I describing south-east Asia, Japan, Russia or America in the savings and loan crisis? Of course the answer is that I am describing all of the above. There are no moral stones to be thrown. The only question is, are you good at cleaning up the mess? Here comes the problem. The mess is always created locally. But how much money do you think the world's wealthiest country has in foreign exchange reserves? The answer is that Japan has about $200 billion. How much money per day do you think world capital markets move? The answer is about $2000 billion – 10 times as much. In one hour of concerted attack, world capital markets can bankrupt the world's wealthiest country. Governments are now small. That is the fact. The initial bloodletting is done locally but then the world capital markets are like piranha. If they smell blood they charge and they can crush anybody no matter how big you are because they are much bigger than even the world's biggest governments.

Cleaning up the mess

Not long ago the head of Sony accused the Japanese government of being Herbert Hoover and he is right because, as I said, these events are in the bloodlines of capitalism. The question is, are you good at cleaning up the mess? The great crash of 1929 did not cause the great depression, our inability to clean up the mess caused the great depression. In 1979, 50 years after the great crash, I happened to be on leave from MIT working for the *New York Times* writing economics articles, and they asked me to go back and read the newspapers for six months before the crash and six months after the crash. What did people at the time think was happening? For example, you all know the stories of the stockbrokers diving out the windows and the blood on the streets. How many people do you think actually dived out? Zero. It is all mythology. Not a single person died. There was no blood on the streets in Wall Street. They were used to lots of ups and downs and by February of 1930 the market had regained 80% of what it lost. It was like October 1987, 25% in two days, but nothing serious happened, right? And by February 1930 everybody said, "another one of these ups and downs – we have had lots of them in the 19th century, no big deal."

Then, in March of 1930 Herbert Hoover started to let the banks go broke. The first month, four banks, then 20 banks, then 100 banks and between March of 1930 and December of 1932 a little less than three years, every bank in America went broke and of course there was no deposit insurance. Every person loses their bank account, the economy goes down 30%, we produce a 29% unemployment rate, and the rate of inflation is –15%.

When Roosevelt became President in March of 1933 he could not solve the problems. They never were solved. The Great Depression ended when World War II began. The great depression was never solved. In 1939, when the war began, the unemployment rate in the United States was still above 20% and we were having a recession in 1938 inside the great depression. There was no solution after you stopped cleaning up the mess.

The problem in Japan is the same. The Japanese just cannot clean up the mess. They have now had eight years of no growth. We can call it the great stagnation if you like and every year the companies get sicker. Now we have huge Japanese companies, good companies, Hitachi, Toshiba, NEC, all of them losing money. The only companies in Japan making money are a few like Toyota that have huge markets outside of Japan. They cannot clean up the mess.

What you have to do is rather simple on one level but very hard on another level. If you think of our savings and loan disaster, it is almost a model of how you clean up the mess. You basically have to shut people down, auction off assets, close banks. We closed one out of every two banks in America. We started with 30,000 banks we ended with 15,000 banks. When it began, every bank in Texas was owned by a Texan; when it was over no bank in Texas was owned by a Texan. We fired people. We put people in jail. And the taxpayer took a loss which at the peak was estimated to be $900 billion. In the end it was only $550 billion. Only $550 billion. This is on a GNP of about $6000 billion.

How do you do that in a consensus society in Japan? The person you are throwing in jail is your son-in-law. The person that goes into bankruptcy is your classmate at Todei University and if you go broke in Japan you are expected to commit suicide. Your creditors may literally come to your house and sit on your doorstep and wait for you to kill yourself.

In the United States we do not exactly do that. If you have not gone broke once in your life you are not an aggressive businessperson. It is almost a badge of honor in America to have gone broke. The problem is that the Japanese have the capability of making everybody else in the world sick and of course this is one of the morals of the story and why this story is worth telling.

If I were made Czar of America

In 1964 I was working for the counsel of economic advisors and a friend and I were writing the chapter for the 1965 economic report to the president predicting what would happen to the economy that year. For reasons that are not relevant here, not too long ago I had to go back and read that chapter and in that chapter we do not mention the rest of the world once. It was irrelevant. We were 50% of the world GNP, we exported oil, the biggest thing we imported was bananas, and we ran a huge trade surplus. There was no way that anything else in the rest of the world was going to affect the United States.

Today if you are writing that chapter you write a very different chapter. In another meeting I went to, somebody said to me, "if you were made Czar of America how would you make it better?" The answer was: "Forget it. There is nothing I can do for America in America. Make me Czar of Japan and there is a lot I can do for America, because the problem in Japan is its strong companies in a weak economy and in Japan everything is a fixed cost. Capital is a fixed cost. Labor is a fixed cost. You have to take and pay raw material contracts with Australia. As long as you are selling the thing for $1 you are losing less money than if you do not make it.

Car markets in Japan are down 55%. If I am a Japanese car company what do I have to do? I have to march into America and sell cars for less. If I sell them for 33% less, what happens to Ford and Volkswagen? Well, one of two possibilities. They lower their prices 30%, keep their market and lose money, they do not lower their prices 30% lose their market and lose money.

What happens when they are losing money on the stock market? The stock market goes down and we have something very peculiar happening in America that has not happened for 65 years. We have a negative savings rate. People are consuming more than their income, presumably spending stock market wealth. But if the stock market goes down, and stays down, they cannot do that, they will have to make dramatic cutbacks in their own personal consumption because of events that are happening on the other side of the world. In that sense, the United States has joined the world for the first time since World War II.

Think about the merger of Chrysler and Mercedes. This is not an attempt to create an American or a German car company. This I think is the first genuine attempt in the world to create a genuinely global company. When it is over, if it works, it will neither be American or German. It will be global.

If they can make it work, there are incredible synergies. One makes luxury cars, one makes mass cars; one makes big trucks, one makes little trucks; one has a slow development cycle, one has the fastest development cycle; one runs a high-quality operation, the other has quality problems; one is high cost, one is low cost; one is European, one is American; one sells globally and sources locally, one sources globally and sells locally; and if you can do it right you can avoid overlapping research on fuel cells and accident avoidance. Culturally, things are going to be difficult. Basic things too, like the fact that the president of Mercedes is paid $2 million a year and the president of Chrysler is paid $18 million a year. But, if you can make it work, somebody is going to get rich, putting together these global companies.

This third industrial revolution changes everything. Let me give you two or three examples. Suppose I am in the oil business. In the late 1950s and early 1960s when I was going to high school, I lived in eastern Montana and there was an oil strike. We all thought it was going to be a big oil strike, it proved to be a minor oil strike, but I remember a couple summers working as a roustabout on the oil rigs when I was going to college. In the 1950s the oil industry was almost exactly like the James Dean movie *Giant*. Luck and brawn. Punch a hole in the ground and you had 5% probability of hitting oil, and the guys who worked as roustabouts in the oil rigs were literally illiterate. Well paid, but illiterate.

In the last couple of years I have done a lot of consulting for the oil industry. Recently, I was in Saudi Arabia consulting for Saudi Aramco, the world's biggest oil company. You can now see three supercomputers side by side because they are now doing three- and four-dimensional acoustical sounding, horizontal drilling. Similarly, off the coast of Norway firms are drilling in water two miles deep. Norway was supposed to be out of oil by 1998, and it would be except for the fact that we can drill in deep water.

World-wide, the oil industry has laid off two million people and yet it's producing more oil than has ever been produced. The commodity is still oil, but the production technology is so different, this ought to be thought of as a man-made brainpower industry. They do not even talk about drilling on land anymore. Not long ago, I was at the world oil congress in Houston, Texas, now called the off-shore oil congress because no one cares about drilling on land. You have three-quarters of the globe that has never been explored. Meanwhile, people have punched holes everywhere on land, and we know pretty well what is there and what is not there.

OK, now think about a commodity like ready-mix cement. The second biggest cement company in the world is the Mexican company, Cemex. They own most of the Latin American companies; they own the Spanish companies; they own some American companies. They are bit of a technological leader. Cemex in Mexico City had a problem. Ready-mix cement lasts about 90 minutes so the contractor has to tell you 24 hours ahead of time when he wants the cement. What happens if you show up and he is not ready for it? Ninety minutes later it is spoiled and you have to throw it out. In Mexico City about half the time the truck showed up the guy was not ready for the cement. They tried fining the contractors, and bribing the contractors, but they are your customers, so that is pretty hard to do. Finally, they gave up on trying to change the contractors. They went to Federal Express and bought the FedEx logistics system. They went to the Houston police and fire department and got their dispatching system for free. They spent two years training their drivers off the satellite in Mexico City. They bought a transponder with essentially spy capabilities so they can see where every construction project is in Mexico City and now you only have to give them 20 minutes warning. Pick up the phone and they will be there 20 minutes later.

In the United States when a concrete truck shows up they do not want it only about 10% of the time. Cemex owns American companies; they can sell cement for a premium because American companies can do this detail planning but it is much nicer not to – and you save enough money not doing it to pay a little premium for the cement. So they turned a commodity, ready-mix cement, which has been used since the days of the Roman Empire, into something where they can get a premium price by wrapping some brainpower and logistics around it.

Travel, communications and education

Would you buy a city hotel? City hotels make their money on business travelers. Globalization is going to make us travel more and electronic conferencing is going to make us travel less. Which do you think will be bigger? It is already true that about 10% of the events in my life I do not do physically anymore; I do them electronically. I do not need to go to a hotel, I do not need a taxi, I do not need an airline, I do not need an airport. I think the thing is that you and I are going to get our judgments wrong because we did not grow up with this technology. What seems uncomfortable to us will seem very comfortable to our children or grandchildren. If you do not believe that then go to one of these universities that is essentially wired. Look at how people react to each other. I have a son who graduated from MIT several years ago. He had a girlfriend in the same dormitory and the first thing they would do is turn on the interactive TV in the morning and talk to each other as if they were a married couple in the same room. It seemed very strange to me but very normal to them. People my age will say you cannot do a business deal that way. Nonsense. We will sign business deals that way. Our kids will sign business deals that way, which is going to dominate. Well, if you are in the hotel business, this all makes a big difference as to which way your business will go.

What are we going to do with office buildings? People have done studies which say that if we went to some American high-rise office, say, 10 minutes after nine, we will find that 30% of the chairs are empty. That is basically the rule anywhere in America. Who knows whether people are talking to the boss, talking to customers, in the bathroom, but they are not in their chairs. It does not matter where they are.

Why do we do that? It is very expensive real estate. Why don't we have office buildings where, when you come through the door, a sign flashes and says 24/21 and you have just been assigned your office for the day. You go to 24/21, you have your personal telephone number, you call up your computer code, you press a button on the flat screen TV set, your personal picture comes up. It is your office for as long as you are there, but if you leave for any reason, it ceases to be your office. There is a sensor that says when you walk out the door. You will tell me we cannot do that because human beings need a cave. Of course, I am not talking about tomorrow's technology, I am talking about yesterday's technology and there are two office buildings like this in the world now. Somebody is going to make them work. The guy who makes them work suddenly has low cost because most business firms have more white-collar workers than they do blue-collar workers and they are putting them in some very expensive real estate.

Some things we try will not work. Siemens Nixdorf ran the entire company in Sweden without an office, everybody working off their laptops. It did not work – they found they had to hire a hotel every Friday to bring people together to make them feel like they were part of one company. But we will figure out the sociology of how you make it work.

Let me give you a few examples outside the narrowly defined economics area. The basic story I will argue is that these technologies will turn every industry upside down. Not just create big industries themselves, not just create new opportunities, they are going to change the way everybody does everything old. Let us look at a few non-economic things, like military power for instance. The French have recently coined a new word called an ultrapower. A superpower is somebody with missiles and nuclear weapons who can destroy the world. An ultrapower is somebody who can see and hear everything in the world and shut everybody else's eyes and ears off so they are deaf and blind.

The French say there is only one ultrapower in the world, which is the United States. It changes warfare. Tanks now shoot at things over the horizon that the human eye cannot see. The Israeli airforce had to stay on the ground in the Persian Gulf war because we would not give them the friendly codes. Without the friendly codes our airplanes automatically shoot them down before the pilot can see them. They cannot be visually identified. Probably because of the success of *Saving Private Ryan*, if you watch on Boston Public TV they have been replaying a lot of these World War II documentaries. The other night I watched the Battle of Leyte Gulf. Two giant Japanese and American armadas steam at each other. 30,000 sailors are ultimately going to die, but they get within 20 miles of each other and neither side knows the other one is there. Today we know where every ship in the world is to within six centimeters, at every point in time regardless of cloud cover. There is no such thing as hiding a ship.

What it means to be a terrorist is to forget bombs in some markets. You want to be a computer hacker, get into his power system and cause the power plants to short each other out, or destroy his air traffic control system. That is the right way to be a terrorist. But of course change in warfare is in other dimensions for reasons maybe we could explain sociologically, that watching one person die real-time on TV is very different than reading about 30,000 people dying 24 hours later.

Think about this ultrapower and the United States gets kicked out of Somalia because of six deaths – six guys who joined an army because they wanted to fight – by two little war lords. What does it mean to be an ultrapower when you can be kicked out of an entire country by war lords because of six deaths of professionals? Of course, it is not just true in the United States, it is true of everywhere in the world. It is true in Israel, Russia – nobody can take military deaths when you can see them in real time.

Think of Peter Arnett's reports from Baghdad in 1991, using solar cells and satellites. At the time, that system cost half a million dollars. What do you think that system cost today? $4999, and if you do not need the solar cells, $1999. The next time you have war you are going to have 10,000 of your own correspondents in the city you are bombing. You are going to bomb around your own people. How do you fight a war in that context? Where your people are going to sit there and watch their babies die on TV live and watch some of your own correspondents die live on TV. It completely changes the nature of warfare.

Not too long ago I was down in the Persian Gulf. There is a center in the Emirates on strategic studies and there was a conference on how telecommunications technology affects everything – government, religion, business, being a dissident, repressing a dissident. The king of Saudi Arabia has a problem. You can buy a machine that will send a fax to every machine in the country, it does not need to know any numbers, just dials numbers and when it hears a fax tone, it sends a fax. It dials every conceivable number. You cannot have an unlisted number. Somebody in London has one of these machines and they send a fax to Saudi Arabia that says "behead the king of Saudi Arabia" and it comes up on the king's own fax. He wants somebody to stop it. You can shut off the king's fax but there is no way to stop the sender.

Of course, in the Persian Gulf a woman with bare arms is pornography but they cannot get rid of pornography because American companies are going to put women with bare arms on their Web sites. American Congress is equally impotent. We pass laws against pornography but it comes up in Finland where it is not illegal. If you do not want your kids to watch pornography, *you* are going to have to stop your kids because the country is not going to be able to do it for you. That is true in the Emirates and that is true in the United States. In a very fundamental sense, governments have lost control of communication systems.

There is somebody, presumably the Greek government, who buys a satellite television channel for the Kurds in the Middle East, and it broadcasts to Turkey, Syria, Iraq. It says "create Kurdistan, overthrow your governments." Those governments do not like that but they have no capability to stop it whatsoever.

If you think of capitalism, the modern miracle is Coca-Cola – the third most valuable company in the world and all it makes is brown water. There is no secret formula. Any one of the flavor companies within 30 minutes could tell you exactly what is in Coke. You could make Coca-Cola. Think about that – $250 billion worth of market capitalization based on brown water. It is a brand name plus a distribution system. Are brand names going to become more important or less important in the world we are going into? My hunch is more important. How are you going to tell the difference between two students and a real company?

That is why in the Internet commerce game, if you look at Amazon.com, the question economists all get asked is how can it be worth that amount of money when it is not making any money? Of course, the answer is on one level they are making a 30% profit margin and they are putting every dollar's worth of profit into advertising. The minute they quit advertising they make 30%, but the assumption is that there will be only one or two people in this area and you have to create the brand name. So, losing money for a substantial period of time, during which you are creating the brand name and the top lines are growing rapidly, is a good thing to do. We will see in the long run whether that is a winning strategy, but at the moment if you are an e-commerce company and make money you get penalized. You get marked down in the stock market, because the assumption is that you are not putting enough money into advertising, you are not creating the brand name and you are not going to be one of the survivors, because you are not putting your maximum resources into producing the only thing that will give value in the long run: a brand name that the world can recognize.

How about culture? For all of human history culture has been old people telling young people what they should do. That is what culture is. We have a brand new culture that has never been seen on the face of the world before. In the rest of the world it is seen as an invasion of American culture because it is made in America, but this is not traditional American culture, this a brand new culture – Americans feel threatened by this culture too. It jumps right across the generations to the kids. The average teenager in America spends 30 minutes per week having a one-to-one conversation with a mother or father and watches either the television or movies seven hours a week. Which do you think is going to have the biggest impact on the kids? It is a brand new thing. Pavarotti makes more money than all the classical singers in human history. His voice is probably not better than Caruso's but when Caruso sang, the number one tenors went to the big cities – Paris, London, New York – the second-rate tenors went to the middle size cities, and there was room for third-rate tenors in places like Sioux City. Today there is no market for second-rate tenors, there is no market for third-rate tenors; in fact it seems there is a market for precisely three tenors in the entire world.

One of my colleagues in economics has called this the winner-take-all society. If you are not the world's best, forget it. The technology will let the world's best service the entire world. There is no place for second place. There are no bananas for third place. There is only first place in this kind of an operation.

How about education? I live in an industry that has the oldest continuously used technology on the face of the globe. If we took one of the original professors from Oxford, the first university in the world, and we brought him to MIT he would recognize us, professor in front of class, chalk and blackboard behind him. He had that. We now use overheads a little bit but that is just kind of a sophisticated chalk and blackboard. Eleven hundred years of production and not a significant change in technology the entire time.

What happens when you can do cheap electronic video education? At MIT we made a commitment that we have to be masters of this or we are not going to be great university in the 21st century. So, about five years ago we started deliberately, as an experiment, doing a master's program in system design and management to learn how it's done – because it is not so simple as putting a camera in the room and taking a picture of a talking head. It is like the difference between a first-grade teacher and Sesame Street. What works in one place does not work in the other place or cannot be done in the other place. For example, one of the things we discovered was that this technology is now pretty good on student–faculty interaction but it is horrible on student–student interaction. So we actually bring these people into MIT three weeks a year so that they get to know each other, so that they will talk to each other offline and do their homework together.

Who is going to be the leader in education? Maybe it is Otis Elevator. Otis has an interesting education problem: you have these little elevator repair groups all around the world in the middle of Africa, everywhere, some of them are repairing elevators that are 100 years old. How do you train them, get them diagrams, get them the parts? You can bring them into central or regional training headquarters but that is very expensive. The right answer has to be electronic education and electronic diagrams, where you take a picture of the elevator you are trying to repair, then you have it diagnosed as some kind of automatic system. Maybe Otis will be the leader. Once they are the leader, why shouldn't they go into the university business? We are going to do it electronically anyway.

What happens to third-rate universities? Why should I sit in South Dakota listening to a third-rate physicist when I can have a great professor who is a Nobel Prize winner teaching me my class and I will have some grading assistant in the middle of South Dakota. I think it makes tremendous problems for second- and third-rate universities as to what they do in this world. Now I do not think the Harvards and MITs are going to go out of business, because it is a little bit like entertainment shopping. We are social animals. We like crowding together in dormitories having a smaller room than I have at home. If my parents gave me that room at home I would go into rebellion but I like it when it is called a dormitory and I have other young people with me.

Do you think we are going to have congressmen and senators 40 years from now? Why should we? We invented congress and the senators because when it was all set up communication was very bad and so the idea was that we could not all learn the right information. So we had to pick a few people to go down to Washington to live in Washington, where they could get the information, and they would vote on our behalf, expressing our preferences. With today's system why do we do that? Why do I need some congressman to express my preferences? I can press a button and my information is as good as his, maybe better. I think representative government in the long run is in trouble. There is no justification for it and, of course, what we see everywhere in the world is people doing more and more referendums.

The British have never had a referendum but they announced that they will have a referendum on the Euro. Switzerland is run by referendums. And there is no evidence that the places run by referendums are more poorly run than places run by congressmen and senators. The fact is, maybe there's some evidence of the opposite.

Where is the money?

There are three things I need government to do in this new world:

1 I need government to provide an educated workforce. Capitalism cannot do that for itself. It takes about 23 years of investment to create a PhD in science. How many capitalist companies are going to put 23 years' worth of money into training a PhD, when at the end they are not exactly sure what they are going to get? No country has ever become educated based on private spending. That is a fact of life.

2 I need government to make sure I am working in a world with first-class infrastructure. And of course, today's example is the Internet. Why are American companies and the Internet kind of an English language leader? The answer of course was that 30 years ago the Defense Department set up the Internet as a nuclear bomb-proof communication system between military bases. At that time it took an IBM mainframe to use it. Fifteen years later the National Science Foundation paid for a big upgrade so universities were tied in and 25 years later it becomes the most exciting commercial opportunity in the United States. But we lead in it because our government invested in it a long time before anybody else. Of course, it still needs an IBM mainframe – the only difference is that in terms of power the IBM mainframe is inside your laptop.

3 I need government to make sure that we are leaders in research and development. Consider biotechnology, for example. Why are American companies leaders in biotechnology? The answer of course is that in 1960 somebody in the National Institutes of Health who was either very smart or very lucky started to put $2–3 billion per year, in today's dollars, into what was then called biophysics.

Seven or eight years later you had the double helix, then DNA, then recombinant DNA, then 30 years later you have an industry that is going to turn the world upside-down. Ninety-five per cent of all the PhDs in microbiology that have ever graduated in the world have graduated from American universities. That is why it is an American monopoly. What company do you know would have put a hundred billion dollars into biotechnology over a 30-year period of time before you started to get profitable products? The answer is that there is no such company in the world. Nobody else in the world did it and everybody else in the world is practising catch up.

I think the bottom line in terms of economics is very simple. If you are in the middle of a revolution, what other profits are to be made on moving? The winners are the guys lucky enough to be at the right places or smart enough to figure out where they are going to be, because if you think of the value added chain of any commodity the profits to be made are not equal. There is something in the computer business called the "Acer Smile" (so-called because it was first pointed out by Stan Shay of Acer Computer, Taiwan).

If you go back 20 years, the manufacturers were making components and the computer industry made no money. The guy selling computers made no money. But the guys assembling them in the middle like Digital and IBM made a pile of money, so you had a profit curve that looked like a frown, if you went along the value added chain. Today if you look at the computer industry in proportionate terms the profits are exactly the same but the guys making components, the Intels and the Microsofts, are making a lot of money, the guys selling the computers, like Dell, are making money, but now the guys assembling computers make no money. It is a zero profit operation. So the profit curve looks like a smile, the "Acer Smile." The profits are there but seeing where they are is a different matter. IBM at one point owned 20% of Intel, but they sold it – no future, they thought. Intel in market value is now bigger than IBM. They sold their future because they could not recognize where their future was.

In the telephone business, the combination of changes in technology and deregulation are so incredible that nobody knows where the money is. It is virtually impossible to figure it out. Think about

AT&T when it was spinning off Lucent. The head of AT&T at that time, the old AT&T, could have made himself the CEO of the new AT&T or he could have made himself the CEO of the new Lucent. It was his job to choose. He picked the old AT&T. He got it wrong. Lucent has a market capitalization one-third above the new AT&T. He could not even plan his own career because he did not know where the money was going to be made.

What is going to happen in the power business with deregulation? Who is going to make the money? At one point Royal Dutch Shell, the world's biggest private oil company, has a discussion with itself about whether it would go out of the business of owning oil and simply become an oil service company, on the grounds that the profits were all going to be made in the oil service companies. In the end they did not do it, but it is interesting that they seriously thought about it.

What do you think the airlines are trying to do with electronic ticketing? Expand the profits in the airline business or take them all away from the travel agents. We know the answer to that. Take them all away from the travel agents. It was in the newspapers; it was no great secret. A year or so ago I was at Microsoft in Seattle and they were having a meeting with American Express. The idea was to put together a reservation system where you go to big companies and say, "look, we will handle all your travel – airplanes, hotels, limousines, taxis, Broadway plays, everything – and we are guaranteed to cut your costs 30%" and then they would go to the United Airlines and say, "this is what we are going to pay you today for a ticket from Chicago to San Francisco. Don't tell us what you are going to charge. We are your biggest customer. This is what we are going to pay." They were going to take all the profits away from the airlines.

What is going on in HMOs? HMOs are devices for taking the profits away from the doctors. We called it a non-profit industry but the profits just occurred in doctor's incomes in the old days. Any industry can be non-profit if you pay people enough. Where is the money going to be made in anybody's industry? The place where the money is going to be made is different. If you want to make the money you have to figure out where that place is going to be in this new environment.

Let me leave you with one final thought. As you may have guessed by now, I like to play these historical games of "what if?" This time, I want to imagine that I am a historian living in the year 3000, 1000 years from now, I am writing a book about the people who are alive in the year 2000, that is us. What do you think they are going to say about us? What do we say about the people alive in the year 1000? Can anybody tell me anything done between 950 and 1050. Nobody can tell me anything. They were boring. They did not do anything worth remembering. Maybe that is what they will say about us. Boring, did not do anything, not worth remembering. But I think not. I think what that history book 1000 years from now is going to say is that these are the guys who invented biotechnology. For the first time in human history, plants, animals and human beings are partly man-made. Of course it is going to happen, it is happening. In military terms, biotechnology is what you call a dual-use technology. We are first going to deal with genetic defects. But of course, God made genetic defects. Suppose I have a son who is about to be born and he is diagnosed as being a dwarf – genetic defect. He is going to be three feet tall. You are going to let me use that hormone to make him four and a half feet tall. But if you are four and a half feet tall you are not a man's man. So are you going to let me use a little more to make him six feet tall. Once I make him six feet tall, why don't I make him seven and a half feet tall and a basketball player? It is going to happen. It already is happening. You can make your kids 12 inches taller. It is illegal in the United States but we have families going to Mexico to get hormone to make their kids 12 inches taller. It is happening at this moment.

Suppose you can add 30 IQ points to your kids. Wouldn't you want to do that? And if you don't your neighbors will and your kids will be the stupidest kids in the neighborhood. Of course you will. You can like it. You can hate it. But you are going to do it. And for the first time in human history, plants, animals, and human beings will be partly man-made. In five years, the human gene project will be over, and we will know exactly how to tweak everything and change everything. Exactly the levers to pull. It makes it a brand new world – biologically and ethically. What we mean by the natural environment becomes something very different in that kind of a world.

Now I will leave you with a final good wish. Remember at the beginning I said you can understand the forces that are pushing the world around but you cannot predict the world. In that spirit, remembering the movie *Star Wars*, "may the force be with you."

Chapter 14

The Role of Knowledge in the Connected Economy

Stan Davis

and

Chris Meyer,

The Ernst & Young Center for Business Innovation

This is a story about connectivity – about how connectivity is chang-ing everything. When you rub two ideas together and nothing hap-pens, a "yes, but ...," you get a disconnection of ideas, a broken line. If however, there is a concatenation of ideas, a spark, a "yes, and ...," you have a connection, a putting together of ideas, from which new ideas come. We're going to talk about this connectivity in an eco-nomic context, how it's changing the economy and how it works in some specific aspects of business. Then we're going to speculate about what this is going to mean for the financial side of the economy – how knowledge and connectivity are creating wealth.

The four quarters of the economic life cycle

When we started out to write *Blur*[1] we were actually trying to write a book about knowledge, about the idea that, although we may be concerned about the management of knowledge, the point isn't to manage knowledge for its own sake. The real point is about this shift in the economy in which value is created through knowledge and through intangible means rather than tangible ones. As we got into it, we focused on the idea that economies have a life cycle and that the life cycle is in terms of economic value added over time. This cycle can be broken down into the following four quarters:

1 a new scientific or technological development;
2 a vision of a new economic infrastructure;
3 a take-off of change in business; and
4 a period of organizational innovation.

Now imagine you're back in the 19th century. The new science is about electricity, it's about chemistry and metallurgy. This doesn't create a lot of added value because its output is scientific correspondence. But in the second stage, people with vision – the Carnegies, the Mellons, the Rockefellers – see these developments and say, "I can take this new understanding and create new things with it, a new economic infrastructure." What you get is the birth of a steel industry, a petroleum industry, an electrical equipment industry. Once that happens all business can change the way it works. In that third quarter marked "business," you get a take-off of change, you get every business figuring out how to use that new infrastructure to do business differently. For example, to keep your food cold in Texas you would have needed to ship ice that you sawed out of a lake in Maine to Galveston, Texas, and put it in an icebox. Now you can get sheet steel and an electric motor and chemical refrigerants and create a refrigerator that gets delivered in a truck and plugged into an electrical network. So you've met the same economic need in a brand new way. And in the fourth quarter you get organizational innovation. Big national organizations are born because the scale of the industrial economy requires national markets to support efficient manufacture. For instance, in the 1920s, Alfred Sloan developed the divisionalized model of General Motors with functions underneath it, and that's the organizational model we've lived with for the last 75 years.

So where are we today? We are at a point in this third quarter where every business is changing the way it operates. We've built an infrastructure of operating systems, of networks, of silicon foundries, and everybody's trying to figure out how to use information technology as the new infrastructure in transforming the way they do business. We've reached a moment where we're going from the first infrastructure, analogous to the railroad and telegraph infrastructure in the industrial era, to the second, the cars and telephone and broadcasting infrastructure, which is about connection. The first information infrastructure was about "crunching," whether in mainframes or isolated desktops – it's all data processing. Now we're moving to "connecting" and that is changing how value is created because it makes room for very rapid concatenation of ideas to add value, those "yes, ands" we started talking about.

Now, as we thought about that kind of economy, we realized that there are three factors that feed on each other, and they are speed, connectivity and intangibles. In *Future Perfect*[2] Stan wrote a very simple syllogism: time, space, and mass are what the universe is made of. Your business is part of the universe, so time, space and mass affect you. How the relationships among them are changing in the economy, is something you need to be consciously acting on. So speed is the way time gets reflected in business, connectivity is the way space gets reflected, and mass and intangibles are reciprocals of one another. What do we mean when we talk about intangibles? We mean, first, the service component of products, so-called "after sale service," although a better phrase for that would be "during use service." It also refers to the service sector itself, information businesses, selling information or analyzing information; these are all sources of value added in the economy.

So just to give you an example of how fundamental this can be (because it's not necessarily about electronic connectivity), in the mid-1800s there was a lot of pressure against the corn laws in England, and there was an anti-corn law league that was trying to overcome the corn laws. They were pamphleteering and sending out literature, but they weren't having much effect. At the same time, somebody was investigating the corruption of the use of franking privileges by people in government, and finding that nobody was using the mail system because only the privileged could use it. They had a contest and got 8500 suggestions for what to do about this, and the stamp was invented. When the stamp was invented the head of the anti-corn law league said, "There go the corn laws" because he was able, in the next three months, to deliver a massive amount of literature about the corn laws to people in England. So he achieved a different kind of connectivity, with the technology of the day, that changed the way politics works.

Today we're seeing fundamental changes in the way speed, connectivity and intangibles work. When we look at speed, the big idea is that things are changing at such a pace that you cannot assume they will reach equilibrium. The industrial assumption of the past was that you design your machine, you get it up and running and you leave it alone because you've got a stable system. Over time the machine wears out or the environment changes or the design changes and you need to fix it or change it, and then you assume you're in equilibrium again. It's static and it's not going to change. We've reached the point where you need to assume that things are changing all the time and develop a system that assumes no equilibrium. Reduced intervals between sending and receiving, producing and selling, purchasing and delivering, are shortening not only product life cycles but business model life cycles and, maybe most relevant here, a rapidly shortening half-life of knowledge, so that you can expect the knowledge that you have in your organization to obsolesce extremely rapidly.

Connectivity is the key

Communications

Communications overcome one barrier after another. The first barrier that telecommunications overcame was distance. Originally you had to be in the same place to talk to somebody. Then you get telecommunications and you are connected over space. It used to be that you had to be talking or sending and listening at the same time. Then you got technologies that enabled you to be asynchronous – you can send an e-mail or a voice mail or a page – but you had to be tethered to a device. Now we have mobility. But communications still aren't available everywhere. There wasn't a cell site everywhere. Soon, we'll have low-earth orbital satellites that will give you connection to the network everywhere on the planet. There's another barrier however, which is that you don't necessarily want to talk to everybody. You want some authenticity guaranteed. Now, we know your identity, who's calling. You know that you can establish authenticity across a network. And sometimes, as you'll see, you want to know where the person you're communicating with is.

Let me give you an example that pulls these three variables together: the General Motors car with an OnStar system. This is a new system, offered in the last year, where if you're driving and your air bag goes off, your car calls the OnStar service bureau, and the service bureau calls you back on the cell phone in your car, which is part of the OnStar offer. If either you or your car are too cracked up to answer the phone, they send an ambulance. Where do they send it, you might ask? Well, you have a GPS terminal on the car and your location gets sent to the service bureau at the same time. So what do you have here? The real change is speed. An ambulance gets to a sick person faster. That's the core change. It happens through connectivity, through the GPS and the cell phone, and the value that you pay $1800 to General Motors for is an intangible value of assurance that in the event of a mishap you'll be taken care of. And that makes a point about these three drivers of the economy: that they potentiate one another; that because intangible value is easily delivered over networks in many cases, it creates a demand for connectivity. Electronic connectivity is very fast, and the faster things go the higher customer expectations get for speed and responsiveness, and therefore the more intangible value derived from speed and responsiveness: this goes around in a virtuous circle.

We put these ideas together and we said, "How does this affect every aspect of your business plan?" – which is why our book, *Blur*, is really organized around the chapters of the business plan. The normal chapters would be product, market, strategy, structure and people, and capital, and so what we did was to look at how these factors are changing each of those dimensions of your business.

Think about a planet with 92 chemical elements on it, you know, the original planet. How do you get to everything you see around you?

Did anybody design it? How did it come to pass that we have all of these compounds and all of these shapes? Imagine that for the first time hydrogen meets oxygen and we get water, and then it washes over some sodium and you get sodium dissolved in the water and some chlorine wafts by and dissolves as well. Now you have salt water. And now that you have salt water, all kinds of other reactions are made possible. Each time one new piece gets added to a compound it creates a whole new set of adjacent possibilities. Through this process of one addition after another, you get to more and more complicated compounds, and you get these things called organic molecules, and then an organic molecule develops with self replication, and you get life. The same story, scaled up, happens in business. Capabilities get put together to offer the economy new value. A while back Hewlett Packard, EDS and Cisco got together and said, "you know what, there's nobody who offers e-commerce infrastructure as a package, and we have these three capabilities. Let's mate them and create this new offer." And that's how the economy continues to roll forward.

Imagine that you take a couple of hundred buttons, and you throw them out on a table. You take a piece of thread and you choose two buttons at random and tie the buttons together with the thread, and then you plot the longest connected set of buttons. Then you take another string and you tie two more buttons together and you plot it again, and you just keep doing that. Now what you might expect is a linear growth in the connectivity of the system, but that's not what you get. You keep tying and tying and tying and not much happens, and then all of a sudden you reach a saturation point where the system changes its phase from unconnected to connected. People play that game with their kids where you make a lattice of dots and you draw a line between two of them, and when you make a box you get to put your initial in it. Is this a familiar game? So, how does it work? You draw and you draw and you draw and nothing happens, and then all of a sudden the system changes its phase.

It's not just about communication networks. It's about any kind of connection. Some of you may remember the Northeast power blackout in 1967. That happened because one circuit breaker in Canada tripped. Because it was connected to the electrical network, there was a cascade of effects that affected 50 million or so households in the Northeast. Similarly, in 1987 the New York Stock Exchange lost

20% of its value because there were program trading instructions that were logically connected by their prices. When you create these connections, you create non-linear systems. You create the possibility for big jumps, some of them great, some of them catastrophic, but the systems behave in a much less predictable fashion, appear to go much faster, and create different ways of creating value.

Connectivity in the marketplace

The basic notion is a simple one that everything that has a beginning has an ending. We are in an information economy whose cycle is shorter that any previous economy in history. It began in the early 1950s, and will probably be only about a 75- or 80-year economy. It was preceded by industrial, agrarian, and hunting and gathering economies, which lasted for eons. Bets have already been placed on biotechnology as the successor. We're living in a rare time. In my lifetime, I'll probably see three economies, the industrial one when I was young, the information economy for most of life, and the bio-economy toward the end of my life. We are more than halfway through this economy. We're in the third quarter, the beginning of the third quarter. The first half was dominated by the computer as a crunching tool – mainly spreadsheets and word processing. The second half is dominated by the computer as a communicating or networking tool. It is that shift in the economic foundation, which is shifting all sectors of the economy. We've mentioned speed, connectivity, and intangibles as the major drivers, which are simply the application of time, space, and mass to the business world. Let's give you some examples and then bring it down to all levels of the economy to show you how it's playing itself out.

Let's take one, for example, with regard to time. How often do you close your books in your business? How often do you do a performance review? How often do you change prices? All of these sorts of things tend to occur periodically and what is happening is, as things speed up, the periodicity gets shorter, shorter, shorter until it looks as though it's continual. How does this play out in regard to specifics? Take pricing. We make a distinction in the business world between real markets and financial markets. Truthfully, financial markets are more real than the real markets in the sense that the financial markets, with the volatility, the tremendous swings, the unpredictability, they're not going to be confined to the financial marketplace. They're going to migrate into the real marketplace. The way we price in the real market today is, we get a lot of data, analyze it, and make an executive decision, internally, after endless meetings. Then it's out there in the marketplace for a while, we gather information about how well it's selling or not, analyze it again, and the whole cycle repeats itself. I don't know how often you change prices in your business on your products or your services, but the probability is it's periodic. In many of your businesses it might be very viscous or near glacial, so that you might change your prices every couple of months at best, more usually every six months or every twelve months. In health care for example, it might be every 18 months at best. Contrast that with the financial world where, if you don't get to your broker in time on the telephone, the price of the stock might have changed. Well the point of the matter is that all pricing is moving toward real-time pricing. That is already in the financial world, and remember the financial world was the first sector to embrace the connected infrastructure. They were the first ones to adapt to the crunching period and now to the connecting period.

It's spreading. We go to fill up our gas tank. We're used to the price of gasoline having changed overnight. We get on an airplane seat, and we know the person on the left of us and the person on the right of us has paid a different price than we have for our seat on the airplane. Yield management systems on airplanes allow them to change the price of every seat on every flight up to seven times a day. That's heading toward real-time pricing. In the supermarket business they've got a lot of SKUs, you know all those boxes of cereals and cans of peas and tens of thousands of SKUs. Every one of them has got a little piece of paper on the top that says this is 79 cents. Well that's very labor-intensive, very expensive, and you can't change the price on that until you get rid of the inventory. So they went to bar coding, except for one decade they used bar coding only to shorten the lines at the check-out counter, because they were focused on controlling their labor cost. Then after using it for 10–15 years, just a few years ago they started using bar coding for inventory control. We still don't use bar coding and the like for real-time pricing. Imagine on the edge of the counter, instead of a piece of paper that tells you how much that box of cereal is worth, a simple little LED screen which is connected electronically to the commodity futures on the wheat and barley that's in the cereal box. That's real-time pricing. That's where it's headed.

Let me shift and give you an example with regard to connectivity from a very different industry. Coca-Cola has a number of distribution channels, one of which is vending machines. They've got a lot of vending machines in the world. In Japan alone Coca-Cola has almost one million vending machines. That's a saturation of about one for every 140 people in the population. Every vending machine's got a chip in it. That's the crunching power. And every one of those chips is connected up into a system. That's the connectivity. Now the operative question is, what does your vending machine want to know? You don't have to be in the soft drink business to begin to answer that question. The first thing it probably wants to know is, am I full or am I empty? As soon as it knows that, then it affects the delivery system, therefore distribution, manufacturing, and purchasing. So it affects the whole operating side of the business. The second thing a vending machine might want to know is, what am I selling? Caffeine-free diet Fanta – how's it selling? Well now you're down to market segmentation to each vending machine. So it's affected the operating side, it's affected the marketing side. What Coca-Cola is playing with now is the pricing side. You go up to a vending machine, Coke is 75 cents. If it's 110 degrees outside would you pay a buck? Or if it's 50 degrees outside and they lower the price to 50 cents would that increase the overall revenue stream? So what you're getting is not just real-time pricing in terms of speed, but you see how the connectivity is affecting the operating, marketing and financial side of that business.

Let me give you a totally different example with regard to intangibles, getting more concrete. My sister and brother-in-law have retired and they bought an RV and they go tooling around all of North America for tens of thousands of miles, and then they decide that they want to upgrade the engine and the transmission. Well back in the 1920s General Motors established the annual model change. The technology improves, and if you want the better, newer stuff, what you have to do is trade in to trade up. That idea of trading in your old vehicle, to trade up to the next year's model has persisted to this day, so that if you want Microsoft Office Suite 7.0 instead of 6.0 you have to trade in to trade up. That's yesterday's model. I mean that's really using an industrial model. Now here's what happened with my brother-in-law. He calls up the manufacturer, says I want to upgrade my engine and transmission. They send over a software engineer, a nice young man dressed in a jacket and tie. He plugs his PC into the steering column and he downloads the upgrade in about a half an hour. Now you know that within two years he's going to be disintermediated and you'll download it directly off the Internet yourself, so where's the value added? It's migrating away from the steel and the metal and the rubber and the trading in to trade up model, and it's migrating into a software model which we could call "download the upgrade." Download the upgrade could change the entire economics of Detroit. Imagine all of our cars, that we're not focused on trading in to trade up, but where we're focused on, as the technology improves we simply download it into our continually owned and existing automobile. In fact we may not own it, because we may lease it and therefore it's a financial play rather than a material play, and once again we're into intangibles.

Health care

Speed, connectivity and intangibles are playing themselves out in terms of making all businesses a hell of a lot smarter and fundamentally changing the economic model involved. Now this is not limited to the more traditional sectors of manufacturing and services that I just described. This is true of every sector in the economy. So let me give you a quick tour, starting with the largest sector in the economy, which is health care. Again, in order to do this what I want to do is reiterate the basic point. Because most of you are not in health care I'm not talking about health care *per se* or for health care's sake, any more than for vending machines' sakes or recreational vehicles or what have you. The point is that when the foundation of the economy shifts – and we're talking about a shift here from crunching to connecting – when the foundation of the economy shifts, everything changes, specifically the economic model for how you do business. We are at such a period. It doesn't occur that often. It occurred in the early 1950s when we left the industrial model and entered into the early information period. Now we're at the midpoint with the shift from the early crunching period to the late connecting period, and the economic model is changing once again. The economic model will probably change once more in your lifetime after this, and that's when we shift, really two plus decades from now we'll shift into a bio-economy. But right now it is shifting in a fundamental sense, so let me show you how it's playing itself out.

The largest sector of the economy is health care. The old economic model of health care was medical treatment. It was really sick care. How did you make money in that kind of a world? You filled the hospital beds. Well today, the economic model is managed care, and the way you make money is empty the hospital beds. Turned on its head, okay? The current model, managed care, is really only a transitional phase that will last one to two decades. We're in the midst of it right now, and on the far side we will have health care. So we're going from, in a sense, longitudinal care, lying down, filling the hospital beds, to vertical care, get them up and out of the hospital as fast as possible. With all of the minuses as well as pluses, we know that, when these things change, when these economic models change, when the foundation shifts and the economic models change, it's so fundamental it's never all for the better or all for the worse. You're going to have good things and bad things, and on the far side of it, where you have health care, it's shifting where it's from horizontal care to vertical care to longitudinal care. In the earlier model it's episodic, which is like the periodic pricing. In other words, when to engage the health care system. Oh, only when you're sick. It's episodic. When you get onto the far side, in the future, as we emerge into a health care model, it's going to be longitudinal care, constant monitoring.

I was on a speaker's platform a while back with the CEO of a company called Medtronic. Medtronic makes implantable medical devices. It's a $3 billion company with a $27 billion market cap. A nice ratio. It represents the future. They make these implantable electronic medical devices, and what they are doing is they are connecting them all. If you had a pacemaker a number of years ago and you didn't think it was working properly, and you called up and made an appointment. How about instead, you take that telephone and you put it up to the pacemaker and it reads it in real time. Well if you could read it in real time there's no reason that it couldn't adjust it in real time, and that is now coming on-stream. Then you have to stay close to the monitor, you know, close to the box, but with the connectivity they've got it up to 40 feet. Within a year or two it will attached to your cell phone, and in other words, we're going to be walking around and we'll be electronically connected with all of this stuff and it will be monitoring us in a longitudinal way.

So you begin to see how the system in health care is shifting in a fundamental sense. It shifts the locus of power. In the medical treatment paradigm, it's the providers who have the power, that is to say the hospitals and the doctors. In managed care, the locus of power shifts to the payers. In the health care model, it's going to migrate to the periphery. Power migrates to the periphery just like it does from a mainframe to a handheld. Who's on the periphery? Well inside the circle called the health care delivery system, it's the nurses at the front line, and basically power is migrating to the consumer, to the customer, to the patient. So what you get is an increased number of home health care testing kits. You know, do I have AIDS, am I pregnant, do I have diabetes and all that, stuff you had to go to the doctor for in the old paradigm, now you can buy over the counter. On the Internet, you see all kinds of patient self-help groups in terms of chronic care, and end of life, and things of this sort. Power is migrating again. In other words, every time the economic model shifts, how you make money shifts. How value is created, how you make money from that newly defined value, how you organize to deliver it, where the locus of power is, it all shifts.

Education

Take the next largest sector of the economy, which is education, the same thing is happening. Now here, it's happening more glacially. When we were an agrarian nation, the church and the family were the major educating institutions. Then as we became industrialized, we began to realize, slowly, over decades, that we had an educational system for an economy and society that didn't exist any more. Over a period of 100 years, from the Civil War to the end of this economy, over a period of almost a century, you got the migration of the mantle of responsibility for our educational system. It migrated from church to state, and government emerged as the major educating institution. We tend to think about our educational system as if it's always been that way, but it hasn't. So when the economic foundation shifted historically from an agrarian to an industrial society, the responsibility for our educational sector shifted from church to state, that is to say local governments mainly, religion to government. Same thing is happening again. Now we're no longer an industrial nation, we're well into the information economy. We still have an educational system developed in, by, and for an industrial era. No wonder our educational system is in crisis. It's a fourth-quarter educational system, to speak euphemistically. It's hanging on to the edge of the life cycle. And you know what happens to institutions that are in the fourth quarter of their life cycle. They have enough power to hang on but not enough power to really make themselves healthy. And so what they try to do is improve the efficiency and prop up the declining productivity curves. They look at things like cost cutting as a solution. All that does is prop up the declining cycle. It does not reinvent a new cycle to get into. You've got to predict that the mantle of responsibility for our educational system will shift once again. Who's going to inherit the mantle this time? Business is going to emerge as the major educating system in our economy. Now this does not mean it's going to take over the school systems. That's not what's going to happen. Business doesn't feel it's in the business of education, doesn't want the mantle of responsibility, doesn't have a choice any more than government had a choice.

Here's how it's going to play out. In the early era, in the agrarian era, you were educated from seven to fourteen years of age. In the industrial era, the bandwidth, if you will, expanded and we evolved a system of kindergarten through college. Well now the pace of technology change is greater still. The half-life of an engineering degree today for example is slightly less than four years. That means that what your daughter learned as a freshman in engineering school, half of it is useless by the time she graduates. That means you have to upgrade your education and your knowledge throughout your life cycle. We can no longer, the way our grandparents did, get educated in the first two decades, and then work for the next four on the basis of that education. You must upgrade your education throughout your life cycle. Now the simple notion therefore is, you're going to get educated by the institutions where you're spending the most time, namely as an employee in the workplace and as a consumer in the marketplace. What's going on right now is employee education in effect.

In life-cycle terms students are up in the fourth quarter. They are the very mature and declining segment of the educational marketplace. The enormous growth segment of the marketplace is employee education, and the one that's still in gestation and hasn't even taken off but will ultimately by the end of this economy be the largest segment, is consumer learning. Because in an era of smart products and knowledge-based business and intellectual capital and the like, what you will find is that it's repositioning the customer as learner and the provider or business as educator. So we've got a phenomenal shift going on in health care and education, and we'll give you one last example, and that's from the third largest sector, the defense sector, where the same thing is happening.

Defense

With regard to defense, the purpose of the military is to defend the nation and be prepared to do battle with its enemy. How do you do battle with your enemy? The idea is to destroy the enemy's productive capacity, and depending upon the economic foundation, that productive capacity is different in each case. So in an agrarian era, if you need to destroy the enemy's productive capacity, what you want to do is burn his fields, or if you're really vicious, salt them. And in an agrarian era that leads to the downside, the raping and pillaging in the villages. But in an industrial era destroying the enemy's productive capacity means bombing the factories which are located in the cities, which bring in a large urban population for the first time. Different kind of warfare. Now in the information era, destroying the enemy's productive capacity means destroying their information infrastructure. That's a totally different kind of warfare again. Electronic terrorism can engage the heart of the defense system without ever engaging the troops directly. We're already worried about warfare in the biological era, which will be a different kind of warfare again.

Now let's link this to speed, connectivity and intangibles. In World War II, for example, a tank would sight a target, it would shoot some volleys, it would finally hit the target. The average was twenty shots. Now with information technology in the Gulf War the average was 1.4 shots. You get it down to 1.4 shots and you've shifted the nature of warfare. In the agrarian era, you had the Hundred Years' War. In the industrial era, wars lasted for a decade, and in the information era, you have the six day war, which means fewer casualties, less personnel, different logistics systems and the like. Again, every time the foundation of the economy shifts, the way in which you conduct your business gets fundamentally redefined. You may still be in agriculture, you may still be in soft drinks, you may still be in baseball, you may still be in whatever the business is that you're in but the economic model for it and the way in which you conduct it fundamentally shifts. It's fundamentally shifting today. We've got a connected model, connected infrastructure and the rules of how you create value, how you create wealth, how you deliver the goods, how you manage and organize, it's all changing.

Software

Let's stick with this change, the change to intangible value, and relate it to some specific characteristics of offers that we have derived from the software business. We looked at how the nature of wealth creation and value creation is changing and we said, software is the least tangible industry so maybe there are characteristics of software that determine how people are going to be adding value through offers. The notion we came up with that's at the heart of this is that there will be no product without service and no service without product, that every offer will be a blend of the two. The way it works is that the product has to be smart enough to offer service, so the car can't just get you from A to B, the car has to know where you are, has to navigate, has to call the ambulance, has to control the climate, has to control the entertainment and on and on. And also the service has to be productized. We've seen that in relation to health care, the home health care tests are really productized knowledge of how to construct and read a test, to tell you what your blood sugar is or whatever. If you push that further, you'll have this home health care appliance that does non-invasive testing that will constantly get data on you as a well person and will be smart enough, will have productized the service of diagnosis enough, to look at your data and tell you when there's an issue. Of course, the next step is to download it to either smarter software or to a live doctor or whatever the next step in the system is.

So how do you create these connected offers? We came up with ten characteristics that are manageable for any business. You can look at this as a checklist and say, "Is my offer productizing its service, because that's the only cost-effective way to deliver service, and has my product got sufficient intangible value adding capability to deliver enough service?" I saw a bumper sticker recently that said "Objects in the future are closer than they appear." We went through these characteristics of software and we found that the automobile industry is already doing these things. Your vehicle is already a real-time device. It controls its traction, its brakes, its engine in real time. It's available to you anytime. It's just getting connected. Mercedes Benz is working on a maintenance system that does onboard analysis, the home health appliance for your car. It's on the car. It's reading the data. It's searching for faults. If it finds one, it connects to the dealer's software – this is like downloading your health data to your doctor – and it gets diagnosed, and you may get a call on your cell phone that says you have an appointment with your car dealer to fix this problem before you know you have a problem. And since, with the advent of the mobile phone, you can receive this message anyplace, it's giving you any time, any place service.

Attributes of BLURRED offers

Speed	Connection	Intangible
Anytime customer access and response	Online	They learn
Real-time operation	Interactive	They anticipate
	Anyplace customer access and response	They filter
		They customize
		They upgrade

What about the intangibles in a car? The intangibles of a product or a service, an offer that learns, that anticipates, that filters information for you. In Europe, the auto radio will monitor the traffic broadcasts even if it's off, and you're not listening to anything. Because you have an onboard navigation system, your car knows where you're going, the radio listens for traffic updates about your destination and your route, and turns itself on to tell you when it's appropriate. So it's filtered on a customized basis, it anticipates the problem you're going to have, and it's learned from you where you're going. Transmissions learn from you how you drive and change their shift points. So the reason to go through this set of variables, if you will, is that you can take your own offer and say, how is it doing those things? Is it customized? Is it learning from the person who's using it? Is it filtering information as a part of how it offers value to that customer?

We know someone who works for a large company that produces diapers, and he said, "come on, we make diapers. What's the connected diaper? What does a diaper want to know? " Well the obvious one is its state, is it wet or dry? But go beyond that. If it's got something that's telling you wet or dry what about pH of wet or dry? What about temperature of the child? For those of you who think that this is weird and wild and ridiculous, just remember that microprocessors that used to cost a fortune now cost fractions of a penny. They are as tiny as a postage stamp and a hell of a lot cheaper. They therefore are going to be embedded everywhere, in everything. For every one that's in a box, called a PC or something, there are ten out there that are in toaster ovens and tennis sneakers and doorknobs, so it's not outrageous that they will, in very short order, be woven into the fabrics of our clothing, which includes for kids, diapers.

The connected offer

Learning is an important part of your design. Products used to be designed to be fixed and uniform so they were easy to manufacture. The point of service came to be to make it customizable, because it was the luxury that people were paying for. Now the offer is designed to do both of those, to be a standard piece of software that learns so it can offer the advantages of both.

Now another point about where we are in the life cycle: we're at that moment where everybody is learning how to do business differently. If you went to business school sometime in the last 20 or 30 years you might be told something like this: you're primary duty is to protect your existing product and existing market. Your job is to lower the cost, which has led to decades of reengineering to lower cost, to downsizing, to protecting the existing market. If that's not sufficient for your growth, you might take your existing product to new markets. One of the things that people like about globalization is we can take our existing knowledge and know-how, or so goes the theory, take it to a new place and it'll work. Third choice would be go to the old market with a new product but above all no new products for new markets. That's very consistent with a fourth-quarter economy. We've talked about the fourth-quarter education system. In a fourth-quarter economy you have these stable oligopolies in every industry and it's all sewn up and you fight like hell for a tenth of a market share point, but there's not a lot of innovation going on. So you better worry about your cost curve as the fundamental driver of your room to maneuver strategically.

In the third-quarter economy, where everybody is discovering new ways to do business, hanging on to your existing product and your existing market is like hanging on to the ice market while this guy Westinghouse is making electric motors. Not a good idea. You may be able to take your old products and find a new market for them for a while. Certainly your existing market is going to look for new offers, but the real opportunity is to create a portfolio of options in the new offer, new market space, the things that don't exist yet. What we've talked about here is a change in the way you manage the existing notion of product or service to managing offers. At a strategic level it's important to have a portfolio of offers because, while there is an enormous proliferation of new things, it doesn't mean all of them are going to succeed. So it is not sufficient to take one chance on the future. It's necessary to find this new way of doing business and make a series of bets on it so that you participate in the growth of this new economic cycle. There's a difference at the management level, and a difference at the strategy level.

What does that mean for you as an enterprise? We've been talking about what you do in the market place with your offer. What kind of a company acts this way? We touched on it with the notion of continuous pricing. One of the things that is true about this enterprise is that your offer is connected to the customer. Your offer is in the customer's car, or in the customer's pocket, or in the customer's refrigerator. We also talked about the real and the financial markets, that the financial markets have embraced this connected infrastructure – you're going to run your market or be part of your market as if it were a financial market, which means letting the market manage your offer. Give up the idea that you are managing your offer any more than you manage the stock price of the stock that you hold. So we talk about letting the market price your offer, and whether that's the head of lettuce changing prices continuously or the Coca-Cola machine saying "Well what's it worth to you, buddy?" on the seventeenth hole. Of course if there's a Pepsi machine next to the Coke machine it may say "Hey wait a minute, I've got a better offer for you." You run an auction right out there on the golf course. Why not? You run auction for every stock transaction. American Airlines is auctioning off seats on airplanes. Now, you can auction your trip to the airlines. There's a Web site where you say, "I want to go to New Delhi and I'm willing to pay $800," and you wait and see if somebody comes along and takes that offer. NECX, New England Chip Exchange has created a secondary market in electronic components. So you're seeing these auctions – there's *auction.com* or *auction online* – where all kinds of things are being auctioned off. So increasingly every market is going to benefit from symmetric information between the parties as in the financial markets.

What else does a product manager do? Well, product managers decide what the offer's going to be. They develop it. They decide what features it will and won't have. But increasingly companies are letting the market develop their offer. Look at the Netscape "bugs for bounty" program, where they release beta version software to the market and they pay you to find bugs in it. That's outsourcing product development of a certain kind. I saw a catalog the other day for grommets and wire guides. This is a guy who keeps the wires on your desk from flying all over the place because he makes the holes in your desk and he makes the legs that guide the wires and stuff. The first six pages of his catalog show pictures of his customers who have designed the products that he makes. Every year there's a product of the year, so the market is designing his product. The Dilbert comic strip is written by the readers who write in with examples of bizarre management behavior for Scott Adams to draw. So, you can give up your product designers if you're willing to let the market design the offer. And similarly the market will market your offer if you are willing to listen.

The idea is that you can take this business model that says, let the market manage your offer. You can look at the infrastructure and how it's changing customer microeconomics. We said the tradeoffs between tangibles, intangibles, speed and connectivity change all the time. What's changing here is the cost of acquiring data about your customers. For Henry Ford, "any color you want as long as it's black" made sense. That was the way to create value by lowering cost in an undifferentiated market. Move up to the 1970s. For Proctor & Gamble, a highly segmented market made sense. Maybe there are 50 kinds of shampoo you can buy in a supermarket because the shampoo market was large enough to support that level of differentiation. It's now so cheap on the one hand to get information about the individual customer, to know your customer, and on the other hand, so cheap to customize your offer on the production side, that you take this mass customization to its extreme. You have each individual design and set the price for the offer that he or she wants, and each enterprise connected enough with the customer to say, "yes I'll give you your trip to Delhi for $800," or "I won't, it's not worth my while." The implication for knowledge is that you need knowledge of your production process in real time. If you're an electric utility, it's not good enough to know your average cost for the year. If you're going to participate in power auctions, you need to know your marginal cost right now so you know what to bid on power. You have to be aware of your production capabilities in real time, and on the other side, you have to be aware of the customer tradeoffs.

Another component of this is the ability to simulate another piece of information infrastructure. If you can capture knowledge about your customer by doing these live experiments, it is now possible through a technique called agent-based modeling to start simulating your market. You can take that knowledge and, if you will, productize it, embed it in software just the way the medical test was embedded in software for your home diabetes or blood sugar counter. But now we can take what you learn about your customers in the marketplace, embed it in models of customers and start simulating your market so that you can learn how the market will respond to your offer. We're building toward an individual working in these connected enterprises who is equally connected.

One image that goes some way to illustrating the point here is the film, *The Truman Show*. Truman is this guy who's the star of a 24-hour live soap opera. But he doesn't know it. He's living in a thousand acre bubble in the Hollywood Hills surrounded by 2200 paid actors, each with an embedded chip. The chip enables the director to tell them what to do as Truman's coming along. Truman is, therefore, unaware that he's being watched by cameras in people's buttonholes, in his sink, or wherever. There are cameras all over the place. Now that's the industrial model of service. You want complete service, your life catered for, then it takes 2200 people and somebody controlling the whole thing – a great infrastructure. So that's not likely to be the path of economic growth. Now, here's what's happening.

Think of this. When you make a phone call, the world knows you're coming. Your number is signaled to the recipient who decides to route it to voice mail or pick it up or forget it entirely, whatever. When you go to a Mobil station now you can call up Mobil or do it on the web and you tell them what credit card you want your gas charged to. Then they send you a little radio, which was originally designed, by the way, to be implanted in cows, to track where cows were going in and out of gates, and when you drive into the Mobil station the pump lights up. When the pump is lit you just pick up the handle and put the gas in your car and leave and you feel like you never paid. It's an open to buy. It changes your behavior, trust me. And tomorrow there'll be a whole cybersystem. It'll say, "Hi, Stan. We know you like your coffee black," or "We know you sprained your ankle. There'll be somebody right out with a cup of coffee."

We've got Amazon.com where you log on and it says "Hi. Here's what people like you are reading. Maybe you want this set of books," or now it says "this set of CDs" and pretty soon it'll be "this set of furniture" and everything else for your lifestyle. So Amazon.com sees you coming. What we want you to think about is not that it's one big bubble for one person. We're each living in an information bubble that is getting us connected to the commercial system. So the commercial world is the set of individual bubbles traveling around, getting what they want from a system that configures itself around them, and that's what is happening one Mobil, one Amazon.com at a time.

Notes

1   Davis, Stan and Meyer, Christopher (1998) *Blur: The Speed of Change in the Connected Economy*, Addison-Wesley.
2   Davis, Stan (1987) *Future Perfect*, Perseus.

Afterword

Whither Knowledge

Management?

Given all that has come before, what lies ahead for knowledge management? As is apparent in the spread of opinion as to where the practice lies along Gartner's acceptance curve, there are many responses to this question. In our opinion, there are two possible outcomes that knowledge management could take: continuing as a distinct trend or becoming a ubiquitous part of all business practices.

Distinctive trend

The knowledge management movement, as a distinct trend, continues to rise in attention and importance within organizations. Knowledge management departments would be represented in organizational charts (and meetings) just like finance, human resources, and operations. Of course, this route may not be a smooth one. For instance, Gartner Group itself thinks that "knowledge management" will fall out of favor by 2003 because of disillusionment, then it will pick up again through 2010 (or in the words of Sam Marshall of Unilever Research, "Hold on tight!"). They base this idea on the fact that the tools are still under development, and that organizational development issues will get in the way. This can also be seen as a by-product of expectations of immediate results. Organizations looking for a quick fix, calling themselves a knowledge-based business and expecting that the rest of the pieces will fall into place on their own are in for a big surprise. Still, as more and more organizations are able to show positive results, others will learn as well. Not every organization need go through the full rollercoaster ride depicted by the Gartner curve. In fact, the more companies that reside in the plateau of productivity, the easier it will be for others to jump right in without having to suffer the earlier stages.

Ubiquity

Ubiquity means that it is quite possible that "knowledge management" will fade away as a stand-alone trend or organizational function, but that its practices, tools, and techniques will live on within organizations, incorporated into what are considered everyday good business practices. Because knowledge management may become more like a discipline than a project, we believe that its lifecycle would copy that of quality rather than, say, business process reengineering. In this way, although the "quality movement" has left the center of many management discussions, quality itself hasn't. In fact, it became a part of *everything*, in a way far more powerful than if it were just one person's job. Perhaps the same will happen with "knowledge." Maybe, like total quality management, knowledge management is primarily a learning breakthrough about how to run organizations. Also like TQM, the impacts may migrate from industry to industry. If you were a manufacturing organization, TQM was like manna from heaven, and it still holds a very significant place in the management conversation. It may very well be that knowledge management is to consulting companies as TQM is to manufacturing. Other types of organizations can incorporate the elements of KM that make sense for them into their current practices, without having any identifiable "knowledge management" process, function, or responsibilities.

How knowledge management will evolve, no one knows for sure, but we believe that the ideas and activities which have come to light in the context of this discussion have already had a significant impact. Some may argue that knowledge management as a term may lose some people's attention due to overhype, but we agree in principle with Temple-Inland's Director of Information Systems, Gregory Sieg, that "when you couple the complexity of the business environment with the speed of change, knowledge management has, and will continue to have, a positive and critical role." We have been witness to individuals and organizations grappling with the large-scale organizational implications, such as how to structure firms, and more local-level aspects, including even interpersonal communications, of gaining the "knowledge advantage." In the midst of all of this, the term "knowledge management" may evolve to different meanings, but it seems inevitable that the nature of the work we are all engaged in – more effectively leveraging knowledge to create value – will continue to grow as the primary concern and occupation of management.

Appendix

Participants in

The Knowledge Advantage

Academics, researchers and journalists

W. Brian Arthur, Santa Fe Institute

Bernard Avishai, Adelphi University

Christopher Bartlett, Harvard Business School

Tom Davenport, Andersen Consulting's Institute for Strategic Change

Stan Davis, author

Peter Drucker, The Claremont Graduate School of Business

Nancy Dixon, George Washington University

Liam Fahey, Babson College and Cranfield University

Murray Gell-Mann, Santa Fe Institute

Michael Hawley, MIT Media Lab

John Kao, Harvard Business School

David Klein, Boston University

Chris Meyer, The Ernst & Young Center for Business Innovation
Ikujiro Nonaka, University of California at Berkeley
James Brian Quinn, Amos Tuck School of Business, Dartmouth College
Aleda Roth, University of North Carolina
John Seely Brown, Xerox PARC
Tom Stewart, *Fortune*
Bob Sutton, Stanford University
Karl-Erik Sveiby, author
Lester Thurow, Massachusetts Institute of Technology
Alan Webber, *Fast Company*
Edward O. Wilson, Harvard University

Organizations

Bechtel
British Petroleum
Canadian Imperial Bank of Commerce
Capital One
Chrysler Corporation
Cisco Systems, Inc.
CRL
Digital Equipment Corporation
Eli Lilly and Company
Ernst & Young
Ford Motor Company
General Motors
Haags Montessori Lyceum
Hewlett-Packard Company
Hughes Space & Communications Company
IBM
Intel
Invention Machine Corporation
Kyocera International
Manpower
Microsoft Corporation
McDonnell Douglas Aircraft
McKinsey & Company

Mobil
Monsanto Corporation
Motorola
Nortel
Philip Morris USA
Pioneer Hi-Bred
Polaroid Corporation
Senco Products, Inc.
Skandia
UPS
US West
Wachovia Corporation
The World Bank
Xerox Corporation
Yoyodyne

Index

Akers, John 213
Allaire, Paul 93
Amazon.com 202, 203, 265–6
amoeba organization 130
Armstrong, Richard 12, 60
Arthur, Brian 185
Asea Brown Boveri (ABB)
    birth of global competitor 113
    emerging perspective 116–17
    global matrix 113–15
    management process 115–16
AT&T 242

Ba 81–2
    characteristics 82–5
    dialoging 83

exercising 84
multiple 84–6
originating 82–3
systemizing 83–4
Barabba, Vince 11–12
Barnevik, Percy 113, 116
Bechtel 12, 126
biophilia 33–5
Black and Decker 125
Boeing 198
Brown, John Seely 100, 101, 208
Brown, Lynn 12
Buckman, Bob 46–7
Buckman Labs 46–7
business, difference to an organization
    164–72

business process reengineering (BPR) 3

calligraphy 33
capitalism
    and cleaning up the mess 228–30
    failure to adjust 214–16
    future of 213–43
    and global economy 222–5
    and the government 240–43
    making things better 230–33
    and need for money 240–43
    and need for optimism, bubbles and
        humility 225–8
    and the shopping mall 219–22
    and third industrial revolution 216–19
    travel, communication, education
        233–40
change, implementing 97–8
Coca-Cola 167, 253, 263
cognitive neurosciences 28
communications 69–70, 233–40, 248–51
communities 95–7
    multi-functional 95–6
    sense of mission 96
    time to develop 96
    unique intellectual property 96
competitive advantage 109–10
conferences 6
connectivity 246–66
    and communications 248–51
    and connected offer 261–6
    and defense 258–9
    and education 256–8
    and health care 254–6
    in the marketplace 251–4
    and software 259–61
consilience 25–39
    gene–culture co-evolution 35–9
    human nature/epigenetic rules 29–35
    knowledge bridges/borderlands 25–9
Cook, Scott Nolan 100
core competencies 93–5, 131, 138–9
Cox, James 8
Cusumano, Michael 76

Danforth, Douglas 107
Darwin, Charles 34
DataQuest report 6–7
Davenport, Tom 69
Davis, Stan 5
defense 258–9
dialog 69–70, 152
Digital 199
Dorsey, David 42
downsizing 3
Drucker, Peter 1, 12, 16

ecology 92–5
economic life cycles 163–4, 246–8
economies of scale 132–4
economy 18–19, 191–3
education 233–40, 256–8
Edvinsson, Leif 3
Encyclopedia Britannica 209
environmental sciences 28
erotic aesthetics 35
evolutionary biology 28
Exxon 214

Flour 126
Fortier, Charles 34
Fuji Xerox 79–80

Gartner Curve 10–11, 14
Gartner Group 268
Gates, Bill 76, 207, 209
Gaukel, Dennis 12
General Electric 214, 215
General Motors 12, 249
Ghoshal, Sumantra 103
Gilder, George 5
global economy 222–5
Gore, W.L. 139
Goulds Pumps 186–7, 189
Greenspan, Alan 129
Grove, Andy 200

Hamel, Gary 94
Hammer, Michael 45

Hewlett Packard (HP) 69, 250
high-tech economy 197–9
  casino 205–8
  culture of 200–202
  hierarchies in 201–2
  seeing through the techno-fog 208–10
  see also technology
Hillis, Danny 166
hollow corporations 109
Home Depot 125
human genetics 28
hypertext organization 78–80

IBM 109, 209, 214, 241
increasing returns
  law 202–5
  model 173–5, 185–6, 191
individual 15–16, 21–3
information 86–7, 170–72
  qualities 91–2
information-focused strategy 185–90
information technology (IT) 185–7
innovation 89–90
  champions for 135–7
  economies of scale 132–4
  institutionalizing 118–19
  intellect and organization 137–40
  maximizing 123–40
  outsourcing everything not world class
    127–31
  shift to intellect economy 124–7
  strategies to compete 131–2
Institute for Research on Learning 93
intangible assets 179–90
  goodwill 179
  McKinsey example 184–9
  managing external structure 183–4
  managing internal structure 181–3
Intel 178–80, 200
Internet 202–3, 205, 237

Jordan, Michael 108

Kirby, Robert 107

knowing 90–92
  learning/supporting 99–101
  supporting 99–101
knowledge
  and communities 95–7
  definition 91
  and ecologies 92–5
  and information 86–7, 170–72
  and knowing 90–92
  as power 41–9
  tacit/explicit 65–6, 69–70
  unity 27–9
knowledge advantage, colloquia 11–14
knowledge creation 63–5
  activity 68–81
  Ba 81–6
  combination 66, 70
  externalization 66, 69–70
  hypertext organization 78–80
  intellectualizing systems/organization
    74–8
  internalization 67, 70
  middle-up-down management 80–81
  SECI model 65–8
  socialization 66, 69
  strategy 72–4
  vision 71–2
knowledge management 1–2, 143
  assembling large knowledge base 152
  benefits 150–57
  case study *see* World Bank
  development of data 152
  dialog space 152
  directory of expertise 152
  distinctive trend 267–8
  engagement information 152
  external access 152
  external application 9–10
  global 150
  help desk 152
  history 2–5
  internal application 9
  recent developments 5–6
  rise 6–11

knowledge management (*continued*)
   ubiquity 268–9
knowledge revolution 41–2
   as alternative to reengineering 46–8
   participation in 48–9
knowledge workers
   in context 51–2
   as dismally unproductive 52–4
   results, manners, responsibility 55–6
   as volunteers not employees 54–7
knowledge-based business approach 12–13
Kyocera 130

leadership 3, 47–8, 56, 76
Lego, Paul 108
Lemelson MIT Prize Program 219
Leonard-Barton, Dorothy 7
lifestyle creative systems 75–7, 78
Lumsden, Charles 37

3M 71, 74
   institutionalizing innovation in 118–19
McKinsey 184–5
McNealey, Scott 211
management
   by walking around 69
   changing role 112
   elements 112
   middle-up-down 80–81
   new philosophy 112
market size 7
Marous, John 108
Matsushita 71–2, 104
Mazzie, Mark 142
MCI 134
Medtronic 255
Meyer, Chris 5
Microsoft 76–7, 136, 197, 254
Mooder, Scott 90
Moore's Law 174

NEC 74
new economy
   dark side 42–5

existence of 195–6
and high-tech economy 197–210
law of increasing returns 202–5
and old economy 196–7
strategies 172–5
strategy 210–12
Nonaka, Ikujiro 2, 7
Norton Company 118
Not In My Back Yard (NIMBY) operations 135

old economy 196–7
organizations 16–17, 59–61, 103
   bureaucracy, fragmentation, stagnation 106–7
   case histories 113–19
   constraining doctrine to liberating philosophy 120
   control to empowerment 119–20
   core competency 138–9
   difference to a business 164–72
   doctrine 104–11
   example 107–8
   flat 137
   and intellect 137–40
   inverted 138
   mergers/acquisitions 108, 109
   moving to knowledge-based 111–20
   network 137–8
   new competitive practices 109–10
   new forms 110–11
   as processes/roles 116–17
   quick fixes 108–9
   strategy 104–5
   structure suited to its time 105

PARC 92–3
Peters, Vicki 60
Polanyi, Michael 4
Porter, Michael 110, 205
Prahalad, C.K. 94
Proctor & Gamble 264
Product Portfolio Management 72

products
    electronic connection 166–8, 170
    smart car 168–70
    TV Guide 170–72
Reed, John 208

reengineering 43–4
    knowledge revolution as alternative
        46–8
    in practice 44–5
Rockman, Alex 34

sales 74–5
SECI model 65–8, 71
Senge, Peter 3
Service Master 126
Sharp 75–8
Shay, Stan 241
shopping mall 219–22
Sieg, Gregory 269
Simon, Herbert 4
Skandia 12
software 259–61
Sony 132, 228
South Sea Bubble 225–6
Special Interest Groups (SIGs) 95
spider's web networks 137–8
Stewart, Tom 2–3
strategic business units (SBUs) 105, 108
strategic technology domain (STD) 73
strategy 17–18, 141–3
    designing 177–90
    development 131–2
    for a new economy 172–5
    new economy 210–12
Sun Microsystems 174, 180–81, 211

Takeuchi, Hirotaka 2, 7
Tanii, Akio 104
Taylor, Frederick 45, 52
team working 4, 77–8, 138
technology 4–5, 101, 140
    core 72–3

STDs 73
    see also high-tech economy
Toolkit Working Group (TWG) 90
Total Quality Control (TQC) 3
Total Quality Management (TQM) 53,
    268
Toyota 49
Toys "R" Us 125
travel 233–40
Trist, Eric 47
TV Guide 170–72

urgent project system 77–8

Wal-Mart 132, 216
Welch, Jack 99, 106
Westermarck, Edward 32
Westinghouse 107–8
Wheatley, Margaret 3
Whewell, William 26
Wolfensohn, James D. 10, 145
World Bank 10, 18, 142
    benefits of managing knowledge 150–57
    brainpower/information technology 149
    described 144–5
    external access 160
    five most unexpected lessons 156–7
    four bad breaks 153–4
    four toughest issues 157–60
    getting best practice 159
    global knowledge management 160
    making communities of practice work
        157–8
    making organizational culture shift
        158–9
    persuasion 146–8
    and promise of change 145–6
    seven (slightly) smart things 151–3
    six pieces of dumb luck 154–5
    three biggest blunders 155–6
    three-part success 150–51

Xerox 91, 93, 96–7, 132, 208